AF820424

Pictorial Research by Elizabeth Jochimsen
"Partners in Progress" by Baxter J. Williams
Introduction by Gerald A. Smith

Produced in Association with the
San Bernardino County Museum Association

Windsor Publications, Inc.
Woodland Hills, California

Late afternoon sun lengthens the shadows of the jumping cholla in Joshua Tree National Monument. Courtesy, John Elk

SAN BERNARDINO

County: Land Of Contrasts

Walter C. Schuiling

Windsor Publications, Inc.
History Books Division
Publisher: John M. Phillips
Design Director: Alexander D'Anca
Production Supervisor: Katherine Cooper
Senior Picture Editor: Teri Davis Greenberg
Senior Corporate History Editor: Karen Story
Marketing Director: Ellen Kettenbeil
Production Manager: Dee Cooper
Typesetting Manager: E. Beryl Myers
Proofreading Manager: Doris R. Malkin

Staff for *San Bernardino County*
Editor: Pamela Taylor
Text Editor: Hedy Oliver
Picture Editors: Kevin Cavanaugh, Julie Jaskol
Corporate History Editor: Phyllis Gray
Assistant Corporate History Editor: Judith Hunter
Editorial Assistants: Patricia Buzard, Patricia Pittman, Lonnie Pham
Typographers: Barbara Neiman, Cynthia Pinter
Layout Artist: Ellen Ifrah
Production Artists: Beth Bowman, Ellen Ifrah

Library of Congress Cataloging in Publication Data

Schuiling, Walter C., 1919-
San Bernardino County, land of contrasts.

"Produced in association with the San Bernardino County Museum Association."
Bibliography: p. 202
Includes index.
1. San Bernardino County (Calif.)—History. 2. San Bernardino County (Calif.)—Description and travel. 3. San Bernardino County (Calif.)—Industries. I. San Bernardino County Museum Association. II. Title.
F868.S14S33 1984 979.4'95 84-10423
ISBN: 0-89781-116-X

©1984 by Windsor Publications
Published 1984
Printed in the United States of America
First Edition
ISBN: 0-89781-116-X

CONTENTS

Following page, left: *Graceful pampas grass grows in the less arid landscapes of San Bernardino County.*

Following page, right: *From the mountain views of Mountain San Gorgonio to the desert, San Bernardino County offers sweeping vistas of wide variety. Courtesy, John Elk*

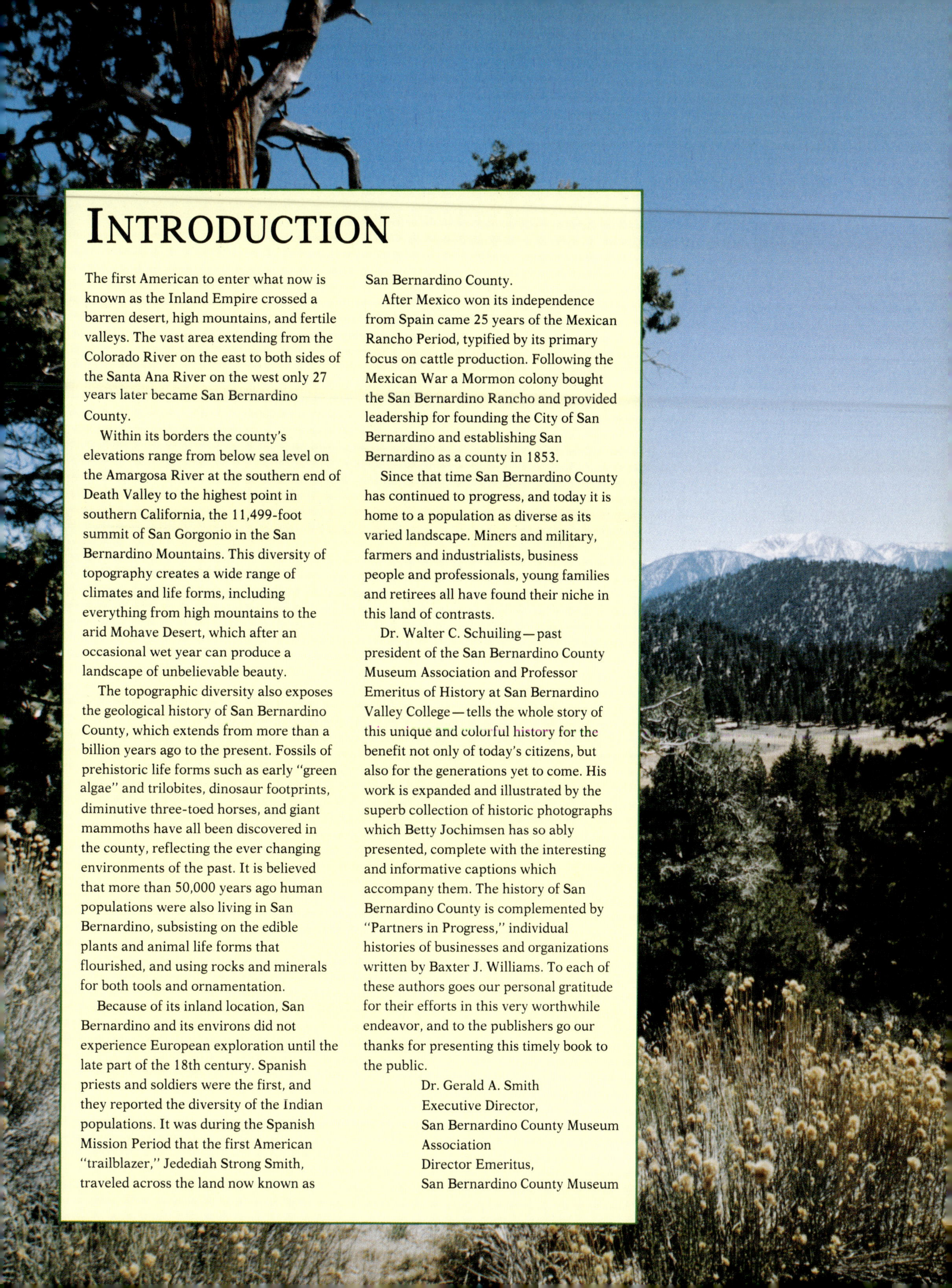

INTRODUCTION

The first American to enter what now is known as the Inland Empire crossed a barren desert, high mountains, and fertile valleys. The vast area extending from the Colorado River on the east to both sides of the Santa Ana River on the west only 27 years later became San Bernardino County.

Within its borders the county's elevations range from below sea level on the Amargosa River at the southern end of Death Valley to the highest point in southern California, the 11,499-foot summit of San Gorgonio in the San Bernardino Mountains. This diversity of topography creates a wide range of climates and life forms, including everything from high mountains to the arid Mohave Desert, which after an occasional wet year can produce a landscape of unbelievable beauty.

The topographic diversity also exposes the geological history of San Bernardino County, which extends from more than a billion years ago to the present. Fossils of prehistoric life forms such as early "green algae" and trilobites, dinosaur footprints, diminutive three-toed horses, and giant mammoths have all been discovered in the county, reflecting the ever changing environments of the past. It is believed that more than 50,000 years ago human populations were also living in San Bernardino, subsisting on the edible plants and animal life forms that flourished, and using rocks and minerals for both tools and ornamentation.

Because of its inland location, San Bernardino and its environs did not experience European exploration until the late part of the 18th century. Spanish priests and soldiers were the first, and they reported the diversity of the Indian populations. It was during the Spanish Mission Period that the first American "trailblazer," Jedediah Strong Smith, traveled across the land now known as San Bernardino County.

After Mexico won its independence from Spain came 25 years of the Mexican Rancho Period, typified by its primary focus on cattle production. Following the Mexican War a Mormon colony bought the San Bernardino Rancho and provided leadership for founding the City of San Bernardino and establishing San Bernardino as a county in 1853.

Since that time San Bernardino County has continued to progress, and today it is home to a population as diverse as its varied landscape. Miners and military, farmers and industrialists, business people and professionals, young families and retirees all have found their niche in this land of contrasts.

Dr. Walter C. Schuiling—past president of the San Bernardino County Museum Association and Professor Emeritus of History at San Bernardino Valley College—tells the whole story of this unique and colorful history for the benefit not only of today's citizens, but also for the generations yet to come. His work is expanded and illustrated by the superb collection of historic photographs which Betty Jochimsen has so ably presented, complete with the interesting and informative captions which accompany them. The history of San Bernardino County is complemented by "Partners in Progress," individual histories of businesses and organizations written by Baxter J. Williams. To each of these authors goes our personal gratitude for their efforts in this very worthwhile endeavor, and to the publishers go our thanks for presenting this timely book to the public.

Dr. Gerald A. Smith
Executive Director,
San Bernardino County Museum Association
Director Emeritus,
San Bernardino County Museum

NAVAL ORDNANCE TEST STATION MOJAVE RANGE B
MOJAVE ANTI-AIRCRAFT RANGE
NEVADA
ARIZONA
MOJAVE
BARSTOW
YERMO
BAKER
VICTORVILLE
HESPERIA
APPLE VALLEY
LUCERNE VALLEY
LAKE ARROWHEAD
BIG BEAR LAKE
LUDLOW
AMBOY
BRISTOL DRY LAKE
CLAREMONT
UPLAND
ETIWANDA
ALTA LOMA
CUCAMONGA
RIALTO
HIGHLAND
SAN BERNARDINO
EAST HIGHLANDS
FONTANA
COLTON
ONTARIO
BLOOMINGTON
REDLANDS
LOMA LINDA
BRYN MAWR
POMONA
CHINO
RIVERSIDE
YUCAIPA
BEAUMONT
BANNING
PIONEERTOWN
JOSHUA TREE
YUCCA VALLEY
TWENTYNINE PALMS
PARKER DAM

I.
THE NATURAL SETTING

San Bernardino is a county of unusual size and extraordinary contrasts. With over 20,000 square miles in area, it is the largest county in the contiguous 48 states—bigger than any of the nine smallest states. Its population of over a million exceeds that of 12 states. Contained within its borders are three major natural areas: a valley basin, a series of high mountains, and a vast expanse of desert. Such diversity of topography and climate results in great variations in vegetation and wildlife.

The San Bernardino Valley is the eastern arm of a basin extending from the Pacific Ocean into the interior. Most of the county's population is concentrated in the valley, with several cities merging into one another to form one metropolitan area.

In its natural state the San Bernardino Valley was a grassland, with native trees growing in the foothills and along the banks of the streams which flowed out of the mountains and meandered across the valley floor. Most of these trees were removed for timber or firewood as settlements in the valley grew, or they died as the water table lowered because of the increased demands for water.

Water and climate have been two keys to the valley's development and growth. The climate has a Mediterranean character with hot, dry summers and cool, moist winters. High daytime summer temperatures, frequently in excess of 100 degrees F., are moderated by the low humidity and cooler nights. Winter temperatures infrequently fall to freezing or below.

Most rainfall comes to the valley during the winter as part of Pacific storm systems moving into the area from the northwest. Although yearly rainfall will usually be no more than 15-20 inches, the valley is amply watered. The mountains to the north and east receive much greater precipitation, providing the moisture which finds its way down to the valley in numerous creeks and streams. Upon reaching the valley much of this water percolates downward into the alluvial material of the valley floor and is stored below the surface.

The Santa Ana River is the major stream of the valley. Originating high in the San Bernardino Mountains, it descends as a rushing mountain stream to the valley, where much of the flow disappears into the Santa Ana Wash, a vast expanse of boulders, gravel, sand, and silt. During periods of heavy precipitation or rapid snowmelt, however, the river can reach torrential proportions. Its intermittent flow is a characteristic of modern times, since before 1860 the Santa Ana was described as an all-year stream, flowing through the valley in a confined, tree-lined channel.

Because of its climate and topography, the valley developed into the principal agricultural area of the county—first as rangeland and grain fields, then as vineyards, citrus groves, and dairies, replaced in

Facing page: *This map of San Bernardino County shows clearly the mountains that divide the desert and San Bernardino valley, with Cajon Pass as a pathway between them. Courtesy, San Bernardino County Museum Association (SBCMA)*

These rocks have weathered into this fantastic formation in Joshua Tree National Monument. Courtesy, John Elk

The Yucca whipplei is a spectacular plant native to the Southern California mountains and Baja California. The long stem topped with a cluster of creamy white blossoms has prompted its nickname of "Our Lord's Candle." Courtesy, Paul Curty

Top and Bottom: *Lupine, poppies, and hedgehog cactus bring color to the desert. Courtesy, Helen Bybee*

Right: *Mormons called the Yucca brevifolia Joshua Tree, from the Book of Joshua: "Thou shalt follow the way pointed for thee by the trees." Courtesy, John Elk*

recent years by commercial and residential urbanization.

Two impressive mountain ranges—the San Bernardino and the San Gabriel Mountains—separate the valley from the desert. Both ranges are great uplifted blocks, bordered and bisected by earthquake faults. The San Andreas, the largest fault system in California, passes diagonally between the two ranges, north of the main body of the San Gabriels and forming the southern boundary of the San Bernardinos.

The San Gabriel range, the westernmost of the two, attains its greatest height at Mount San Antonio (10,080 feet) on the San Bernardino-Los Angeles County line. This peak is more commonly known as *Baldy,* because of the lack of vegetation on its summit. The San Gabriels are older than the San Bernardino Mountains; their deep gorges, steep-walled canyons, and knife-edged ridges indicate a longer period of erosion.

The San Bernardino Mountains cover a larger area and reach greater heights. They extend eastward about 60 miles from Cajon Pass, with a greatest width of approximately 30 miles. Mount San Gorgonio, or *Grayback,* the highest mountain in Southern California, rises two miles above the San Bernardino Valley to a height of 11,502 feet. More scenically impressive for most valley residents is Mount San Bernardino (10,624 feet). The western part of the San Bernardino Mountains has a less rugged topography than the San Gabriels, with more mountain meadows and broader valleys. Several small lakes fill natural basins. Other basins have been made into man-made lakes for purposes of recreation or water supply—Big Bear, Arrowhead, and Silverwood are the best known.

Differing elevations and rainfall patterns result in great variations in the mountain vegetation. The lower southern slopes of both ranges are thickly covered with chapparal, a combination of brush and scrub trees, including chamise, buckbrush, and manzanita. Above 4,000 feet the chapparal gives way to forests of pine and fir. On the drier northern slopes piñon pine and juniper are common, replaced by Joshua trees on the lower elevations of the desert. Sycamore, oak, alder, and willow grow in the canyon bottoms and flood plains.

Deer and black bear still inhabit the mountains, but in ever decreasing numbers. Bighorn sheep and mountain lions may still be found in some of the more isolated areas. Coyotes, skunks, raccoons, and squirrels have adapted to living in proximity to man.

All land routes into the San Bernardino Valley and the Los Angeles Basin from the north and east must skirt or cross the mountains. Two natural openings provide access between the desert and the valley. Cajon Pass lies between the San Gabriel and San Bernardino ranges, while San Gorgonio Pass separates the San Bernardinos from the San Jacinto Mountains to the south in Riverside County. Both passes carry major interstate highways and transcontinental railroad lines.

The mountains, once a source of lumber for the early development in the San Bernardino Valley, have become a playground, not only for San Bernardino County residents but also for the millions of people in the greater Los Angeles area who live within a few hours' driving distance of the mountains.

Lying north of the San Gabriel and San Bernardino mountains is the vast desert portion of San Bernardino County. This desert, the Mojave, lies mostly within the county, but it extends into adjoining Los Angeles, Kern, and Inyo counties, and the neighboring states of Nevada and Arizona.

The Mojave Desert is a region of great diversity, displaying many different land forms—mountains, alluvial deposits, great fans, dry lakes, ephemeral rivers, lava flows, cinder cones, and sand dunes, along with a great variation of plant and animal life. Only in places with extreme alkaline conditions will one find no indication of life. Desert elevations within the county vary greatly, from sea level at the extreme southern end of Death Valley, to a height of nearly 8,000 feet on Clark Mountain near the Nevada border.

The topography of this desert is typical of the arid lands of the West, consisting of a series of small mountain ranges and isolated knobs or buttes separated by broad basins of varying sizes. Playas—dry lake beds—are located in the center of many of these basins. After sudden summer rains or winter

storms, they may be covered with shallow water. Searles Lake in the northwestern corner of the county, and Soda Lake, northwest of Baker, are two of the largest playas of the desert.

The principal desert river of the county is the Mojave, nearly 100 miles long. Rising in the San Bernardino Mountains, it flows as a perennial mountain stream until it reaches the porous alluvium of the desert. Then it flows above ground only at those points where geological barriers force it to the surface or in times of heavy flooding.

The county's largest river, of course, is the Colorado. This great river of the Southwest, whose watershed includes portions of seven states, forms the eastern boundary of San Bernardino County. Once subject to great seasonal fluctuation, its flow is now controlled by several dams.

The vast desert landscape of San Bernardino County supports a variety of life. Courtesy, John Elk

Hot summers and mild winters with little rainfall and much sunshine characterize the climate of the Mojave Desert. Daytime temperatures of over 100 degrees F. are common in the summer. Daytime winter maximums are usually in the 50 to 70 degree range, with temperatures often falling below freezing at night. Precipitation varies from less than 5 inches annually to as much as 15 inches, dependent upon location and elevation. Winds are a constant feature of the desert environment, especially in winter and spring. Most days are sunny. Even in the winter months the desert receives 60 to 80 percent of its sunshine potential.

The desert supports many varieties of plants. The creosote bush, 2 to 7 feet high, is the dominant vegetation over much of the desert. Joshua trees, or tree yucca, 10 to 20 feet high, grow on the alluvial fans nearer to the mountains. Cottonwood and mesquite thickets may grow on the flood plains or along river bottoms. In the spring after a rainy winter, the desert changes from brown to green, with splashes of yellow, orange, white, and purple from the blossoms of many varieties of annual and perennial plants.

The desert also supports an abundant animal life. Most burrowing mammals are nocturnal and are not usually seen by the casual traveler. A few bighorn sheep still frequent the higher desert mountains. Many species of migratory and resident birds are found near the desert rivers and springs. Numerous lizards, a few snake species, and the desert tortoise make up the reptile population.

To the 19th-century settlers, the Mojave Desert was a barren wasteland, a barrier to be crossed. Later it was seen as a potential El Dorado, furnishing much of the county's mineral wealth. It is still the primary access route into Southern California for railroads, highways, and utility lines. Transportation, mining, grazing, and agriculture, where water is available, continue to provide a livelihood for desert residents, but military bases, retirement living, recreation, and tourism now account for an increasing share of the region's economy.

Top: *Camp Cady, the largest fort on the Mojave Road, lies east of Barstow near an oasis of the Mojave River. Courtesy, Arda M. Haenszel*

Bottom: *Mountain San Gorgonio rises above the San Bernardino valley. The highest mountain in Southern California, its peak reaches two miles above the valley. Courtesy, John Elk*

Right: *The Rim-of-the-World Highway snakes along the fog-shrouded mountains. Courtesy, John Elk*

effigies of bighorn sheep. Radiocarbon dating of the split-twig figurines and dart shaft fragments indicated they are from 3,000 to 3,700 years old.

Such discoveries led Southern California archaeologists to undertake a coordinated archaeological survey of the dry lakes of the Mojave Desert. This study, conducted between 1955 and 1965 under the direction of Ruth D. Simpson, disclosed three distinct cultural horizons. Evidence of a late prehistoric people using the bow and arrow, more refined stone tools, pottery, and basketry was found near existing water courses and desert springs. Remains of an earlier, pre-bow and arrow culture, such as was originally described by the Campbells, were associated with the shorelines of some of the Ice Age lakes. And on terraces well above these shorelines were found implements of an obviously older culture, comparable to those of the Lower Paleolithic in the Old World—scrapers and choppers and hand-axe type tools, but no projectile points.

The finding of these older surface artifacts attracted the attention of Dr. Louis S.B. Leakey, famous African prehistorian, and led to further investigations in the area. Archaeological excavations in the eastern Calico Mountains begun in 1964 under the sponsorship of the San Bernardino County Museum and the National Geographic Society, have resulted in the recovery of a large assemblage of chopping and cutting tools and other artifacts. Calcium carbonate deposit encrusted on some of the artifact surfaces has been dated at an age of approximately 200,000 years. This date, far older than any other dated evidence of man in the western hemisphere, is forcing the rethinking of the whole story of man's entry into the New World.

The relationship between Early Man and the Indians living in the San Bernardino County area in historic time is by no means clear. The later inhabitants may have been more recent immigrants into the region rather than direct descendents of those who were here many thousands of years ago.

The native population of San Bernardino County at the time of European entry included two major linguistic Indian groups, the Yuman and the Shoshonean. The Yuman people were the Mojaves, living in small villages along the Colorado River in the general area of present-day Needles. They were the only Indians of the county who practiced agriculture, growing corn, beans, and squash in the rich bottomlands of the Colorado, depending upon seasonal flooding to provide the necessary moisture. In addition to the cultivated crops, the beans of the wild mesquite were a staple food, ground into meal and then eaten raw or made into a dough by adding water and baking on hot stones. Hunting was of less importance than fishing, most of which was done with seines or nets in the lagoons and sloughs of the river.

Mojave dwellings were of better construction than those of other Southern California Indians. Framed by cottonwood logs, thatched with arrow weed, and plastered with river mud, the rectangular buildings were quite substantial.

The men wore breechcloths, the women a front and back skirt or apron, usually made from willow bark. Both men and women painted their bodies and

The Black Canyon petroglyph is among the most dramatic. Mountain sheep are being pursued by Indians pictured on the lower rocks. Petroglyphs were made by pecking through the natural dark patina on the desert rocks. (SBCMA)

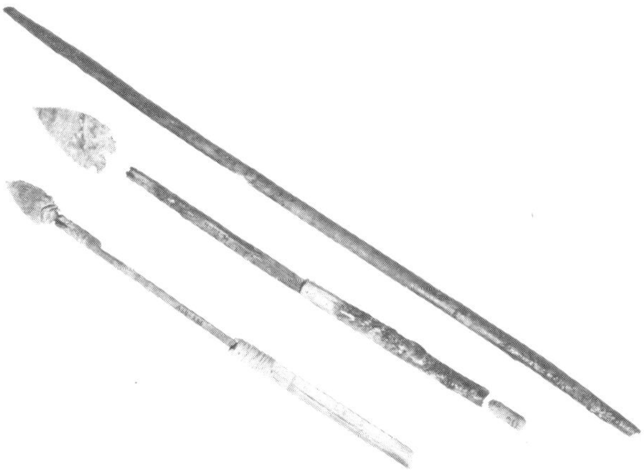

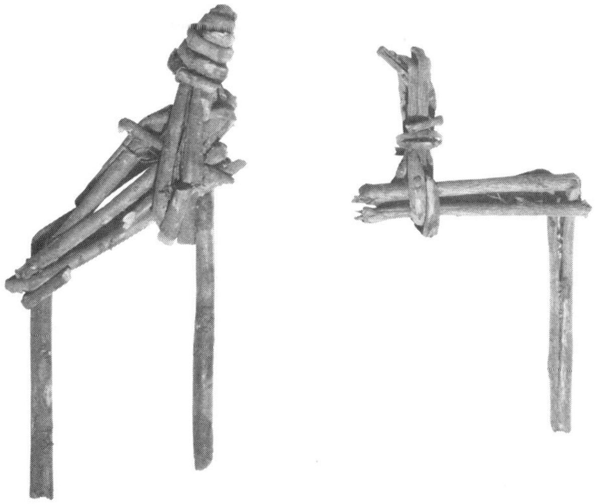

faces, and tattooing was common, especially among the women. Rows of lines or dots on the chin, or a circle, a stripe, or a few dots on the forehead were the usual designs.

The Mojaves were less skilled in basketmaking than some of their neighbors, but they excelled in making pottery. Bowls, pots, and storage jars were painted with intricate designs. Other items such as pipes, dolls, toys, and effigy figures were made of the fired clay. After contact with Europeans, the Mojaves became skilled in beadwork, creating neck and arm bands and colorful shoulder capes of great beauty.

Although quite peaceful among themselves, the Mojaves had the reputation of being the most warlike of the desert tribes; they frequently raided and looted other Indian settlements east of the Colorado River. They also were the desert's greatest traders and travelers, going down the Colorado River to visit and exchange goods with their kin, the Yuma, and westward across the Mojave Desert and over the San Bernardino Mountains to trade with the coastal Indians. The path they blazed, the *Mojave Trail,* was the road followed by the first white explorers and traders.

Excavations in Newberry Cave in the early 1950s uncovered some atlatls which were used with the spear-thrower, enabling hunters to throw spears farther and more accurately. Some of the atlatl shafts at this site were decorated with black, red, and green paint. (SBCMA)

Top: *Split twigs of willow were twisted into animal shapes by early hunters. These found in Newberry Cave were the first split-twig figures found in California. (SBCMA)*

Bottom: *Students and volunteers in 1981 dig at the Calico Mountains Archaeological Site. Courtesy, Daniel J. Griffin*

Top: *Dr. Leakey and Ruth Simpson, San Bernardino archaeologist, examine findings at the Calico site in 1965. Courtesy, Daniel J. Griffin*

Top, right: *Chopping tools, gravers, scrapers, blades, and cores were found at Calico. Courtesy, Daniel J. Griffin*

Bottom: *The Calico Mountains Archaeological Site is shown here in 1980, against the Calico Mountains. On the right is a stockpile of material from the pits. A path in the foreground leads down to the visitor's center. Courtesy, Daniel J. Griffin*

Six Shoshonean tribal groups made their homes in or frequently traveled into the San Bernardino County area. The Chemehuevi or Southern Paiutes, neighbors to the Mojaves, lived in small groups throughout the eastern Mojave Desert. They lived at a subsistence level on small game, seeds, roots, lizards, and insects. They excelled at basketmaking, using native fibers to make tightly woven baskets with beautiful artistic designs. A few hundred years ago, with the permission of the Mojaves, some Chemehuevi came to live along the Colorado River.

Another small Shoshonean group found in the northern part of the county was the Koso or Panamint Indians, residents of some of the most inhospitable and arid sections of eastern California and southwestern Nevada. Concentrated around the few waterholes in the Death Valley area, they wandered the desert in search of food and made seasonal migrations into the Panamint Mountains to gather piñon nuts. In answer to the needs of a gathering culture, they, too, made fine baskets, including utilitarian winnowing trays, burden baskets, and seed beaters. Tightly-woven, narrow-neck containers waterproofed with pine pitch were used as water bottles or canteens.

The Shoshonean people of the San Bernardino Mountains and valley have been divided somewhat arbitrarily by anthropologists into smaller groups according to geography and outside cultural influence, although their basketry, pottery, dress, food, customs, and general living patterns were quite similar. Those who had direct contact with the San Gabriel and San Luis Rey Missions farther west and south were identified by the Spanish as Gabrielenos and Luisenos, respectively. The Serranos had somewhat less contact with the missions and were therefore less influenced by them. Although named by the Spanish, the Serranos *people of the mountains* lived permanently in the eastern San Bernardino Valley or in the high desert to the north, traveling into the mountains in the summer and fall to hunt and to gather acorns and piñon nuts. Another closely related group, the Cahuilla, made their home in the Coachella Valley, with some living in San Gorgonio Pass and San Timoteo Canyon.

At the time of the white man's coming about 1,500 Indians inhabited the San Bernardino Valley and the adjacent mountain area. They lived in small settlements, called *rancherias* by the Spanish, each quite independent of the others. Such present-day place names as Cucamonga, Muscupiabe, and Yucaipa are derived from the names of Serrano settlements. Other rancherias were located on the desert side of the mountains and in Cajon Pass. Each rancheria, located near a stream or spring, contained from 10 to 30 dwellings. Their circular huts were constructed by covering a framework of poles with

Irataba, chief of the Mojave Indians, visited San Francisco and Washington in 1864. Fort Mojave was built in 1859 about 12 miles north of Needles to "pacify" the Mojaves and make travel safer across the Old Government Road from Barstow to Fort Mojave. Courtesy, Smithsonian Institution National Anthropological Archives

brush or tules. They were used mostly for sleeping and during inclement weather, as the Indians lived and cooked outside as much as possible.

Acorns provided one of the most important foods of the Serranos. Each fall during the months of October and November, the Indians traveled into the mountains to gather acorns. These would be pounded into a meal in stone mortars, the bitterness leached out with water, and the meal then served as an acorn mush. Pine nuts or piñones were also a favorite food, and they are still gathered each fall by both whites and Indians. Grass seeds, wild berries, mesquite beans, small game, lizards, and certain insects were all used as food by the Indians of the valley. Although bows and arrows were used in hunting some larger game animals, a throwing stick was a more common hunting tool. Nets and snares were also used.

Serrano pottery, made by the women, was more functional than artistic, designed for cooking and storage. The Serranos were extremely skilled as basketmakers, with artistic designs woven into the baskets in colors of red, black, brown, or white.

The Serranos were a friendly, gentle people. Such fighting or disputes as took place usually arose from personal differences rather than territorial agression.

The coming of the white man brought great changes in the lives of these native residents. Many died of diseases to which they had no natural

The Mojave Indians built houses of cottonwood logs, plastered with river mud. The only opening besides a smoke hole was a door. The men wore breechcloths. The women wore skirts usually made from willow bark. This drawing by Baldwin Mollhausen is dated 1854. Courtesy, Smithsonian Institution National Anthropological Archives

immunity. As the white culture became dominant, some Indians adapted to it, while others tried to adhere to the old values and way of life. A few of their descendents still remain, often unrecognized as Indians by more recent residents.

San Bernardino County's first European visitors were Spanish soldiers and padres traveling to and from the Southern California missions. The establishment of a chain of missions by Franciscan friars under the leadership of Junipero Serra was a key factor in the Spanish plan of occupying and holding California. In theory the missions were to "Christianize" and "civilize" the Indians, and after a sufficient period of training in agriculture and the crafts, the Indians were to be given land and livestock, and were to be allowed to operate the workshops as private owners. Although this goal was never realized, the missions did become the first major Spanish settlements of the state.

The most economically successful of all the California missions was the Mission San Gabriel Archangel, founded in 1771. Its outlying ranch lands constituted a vast pastoral empire, eventually extending many miles inland into the San Bernardino Valley. Its grain fields, orchards, and vineyards were the most productive of the missions. The mission compound was like a small frontier city, with dormitories, apartments, barracks, storehouses, and many shop buildings, including a gristmill, sawmill, tannery, olive press, soap factory, blacksmith and carpentry shops. The labor was supplied by Indians, who were enticed to the mission by guarantees of food and security. Once the Indians had been baptized at the mission, however, they were no longer free agents. A few trusted converts might be given permission to visit tribal relatives or friends, but for most Indians, to leave the jurisdiction of the mission was to desert, and soldiers could be sent to find them and bring them back. Corporal punishment, usually flogging by the soldiers, was used to maintain discipline.

In 1769 a Spanish expedition led by Captain Gaspar de Portolá blazed a trail from San Diego to Monterey. Although it passed to the west of what is now San Bernardino County, its members saw the high peaks of the San Gabriel and San Bernardino mountains. To the former range they gave the name, Sierra Madre.

The first Spaniard to explore a portion of San Bernardino County was Pedro Fages, military commander in California. While at San Diego in 1772 he led a small party in pursuit of some deserters who had fled eastward across the mountains. After losing their trail in the Imperial Valley, he decided to return directly to his headquarters in Monterey. Guided by Indians from a Cahuilla rancheria, Fages traveled west of the San Jacinto Mountains and into the San Bernardino Valley. Deciding to bypass San Gabriel, he crossed the mountains in the Cajon Pass area, swung westward through the Antelope Valley portion of the Mojave Desert, and crossed the Tehachapis to enter the San Joaquin Valley. In his journal Fages made reference to the abundance of "palm trees." He was obviously referring to the forests of Joshua trees in the high desert.

The next Spanish entry into the county was made

The Chemehuevi, or Southern Paiutes, from the eastern Mojave Desert made beautiful baskets. (SBCMA)

in 1774 when Juan Bautista de Anza blazed an overland trail from the mainland of Mexico to San Gabriel. His 34-man expedition traveled from the Spanish settlements in Sonora and Arizona to the Yuma Indian villages at the confluence of the Gila and Colorado rivers, then across the Imperial Valley and northwestward to the Santa Ana River. After crossing the river in the Riverside area, he camped along San Antonio Creek near present-day Ontario, naming the place *Arroyo de los Osos,* or "Bear Gulch." Less than two years later he led a much larger expedition of settlers to California over much the same route. On both expeditions de Anza was accompanied for part of the journey by the Franciscan padre, Francisco Garcés.

Father Garcés occupies a special place in the history of the explorations of San Bernardino County and the Southwest. Accompanied only by Indian companions he wandered from one southwestern tribe to another. He was the first European to visit and develop friendly relations with the Yuma Indians, a contact which made the de Anza expeditions possible. He was the first white man to visit the Mojave Indians and the first to travel across the Mojave Desert from the Colorado River to the San Bernardino Valley. No white man at the time was more respected by the Indians. His colleague, Father Font, provided an insight into the personality of this remarkable man with the following description:

Padre Garcés is so fit to get along with the Indians, and to go about among them, that he seems like an Indian himself. . . . He shows in everything the coolness of an Indian; he squats cross-legged in a circle with them, or at night around a fire, for two or three hours together or even longer, all absorbing, forgetting aught else, discoursing to them with great serenity and deliberation. . . .

Father Garcés left the second de Anza expedition to remain with the Yumas, and then traveled up and down the lower Colorado River to visit other Indian villages. In February 1776, while with the Mojaves in the vicinity of present-day Needles, he learned of their trading with coastal tribes, and considered the use of the Mojave Trail as an alternate route from Sonora to San Gabriel. Securing Mojave guides, he took off on a 20-day journey across the desert to San Gabriel. On March 9 he arrived at the sink of the Mojave River, and noted in his journal: "I . . . arrived at a gap in the sierra that I named Pinta for the veins that run in it of various colors. Here I encountered an arroyo of saltish water that I named [Rio] de los Martires. There is good grass."

Following the Mojave upstream to the San Bernardino Mountains, he ascended the Indian trail up Sawpit Canyon to the summit and descended into the San Bernardino Valley on the ridge between Devil and Cable Canyon. His journal entry of March 22 records this part of his journey: "I went three leagues and passed over the sierra by the south-southwest. The woods . . . reach to the summit of the sierra, whence I saw clearly the sea, the Rio de Santa Ana, and the Valle de San Jose. Its descent is little wooded."

After a brief rest at the Mission San Gabriel, Garcés journeyed northward into the San Joaquin Valley, crossed Tehachapi Pass to the Mojave Desert, and returned to the Colorado River. Later explorations took him through northern Arizona, to the Grand Canyon, and to the Hopi settlement of Oraibi.

Father Garcés suffered a martyr's death in 1781 during a Yuma Indian uprising. That event and the continuing hostility of the Yumas led to a permanent disruption of communication over the inland route between Sonora and California. For a quarter of a century the interior regions were largely unvisited by the Spanish except for a few attempts to recapture deserting mission Indians. This was to change when Father José Maria Zalvidea was placed in charge of the San Gabriel Mission.

In 1806 Zalvidea journeyed into the interior while traveling from Santa Barbara to San Gabriel. He traveled northeastward into the San Joaquin and Antelope valleys, came to the Mojave River and followed it upstream, crossing the mountains in the Cajon Pass area and descending into the San Bernardino Valley. En route he visited a number of Indian rancherias and baptized several elderly inhabitants.

The influence of the San Gabriel Mission on the inhabitants of the interior valleys increased greatly under Zalvidea's leadership. Grazing lands were extended as the mission's herds of cattle and flocks of sheep grew larger. Pastoral outposts, each often associated with an Indian rancheria, were established inland from the mission. It was to one of these that Father Francisco Dumetz came in 1810 and gave the

The San Manuel Reservation is located in the foothills of the San Bernardino Mountains. It was established by presidential order in 1876, and was named for the leader of the few surviving Serranos settled here by force after an 1866 campaign to eliminate the mountain Indians. (SBCMA)

name that today identifies a valley, a city, a county, a mountain, and a mountain range—San Bernardino.

At that time Father Dumetz was living at the San Gabriel Mission in semiretirement following a distinguished 40-year mission career. On May 20, 1810 he visited one of the San Bernardino Valley rancherias and erected a capilla (a small temporary chapel), celebrated a mass, and gave the location the name of San Bernardino. May 20 is designated on the Catholic calendar as the feast day of San Bernardino de Siena, a great Italian churchman of the late 14th century.

The exact location of that religious service has been the subject of controversy. Father Juan Caballeria, writing a history of the San Bernardino Valley in 1902 and using San Gabriel Mission records, since lost, placed the location at De Siena Springs in the Bunker Hill area of San Bernardino-Colton. The historian George Beattie later located the site a few miles east at the rancheria of Guachama in what was to become known as Old San Bernardino along Cottonwood Row. Other local historians have suggested that a likely location would have been the Indian rancheria on the Rialto Bench overlooking Lytle Creek.

Mission records told of frequent visits to the valley by the San Gabriel padres during the years 1810-1812. Although the valley Indians were friendly to the Spanish, the same could not be said of those living in the mountains and the desert. In November 1810 a band of Mojave Indians, probably led or instigated by mission deserters, came into the valley and threatened

the San Gabriel Mission itself, advancing to within six miles of it before returning to the desert with their stolen livestock.

Mission influence suffered another setback in 1812 as a result of a series of severe earthquakes in the valley. New hot springs appeared and old ones became more active. The terrified Indians blamed the phenomenon on the anger of the spirits over the presence of the Spanish padres and the new religion. Several Christianized Indians or "neophytes" were killed or forced to flee, and mission activity in the valley ceased for several years.

The continuing pressure for more pasturage and cultivated land, however, resulted in a revival of activity in 1819, with the establishment of the San Bernardino Rancho headquarters near the Indian rancheria of Guachama, west of present Redlands. It was an ideal location, with fertile soil and a good growth of native grasses for pasture. Two adobe structures were built to house the mayordomo in charge and to serve as a granary and storehouse.

To obtain a plentiful supply of water for the fields and orchards of the rancho, a *zanja,* or irrigation ditch, was dug in 1819-1820 to tap the flow of Mill Creek 12 miles away. This ditch, dug by local Indians using sticks and shoulder blades of cattle as tools, was the most extensive irrigation project constructed in California during the mission period.

Olive trees, fruit trees, grapevines, and vegetables were brought for planting from San Gabriel. Some fields were planted to grain. Indians from surrounding rancherias came for agricultural instruction at the invitation of Father Zalvidea. The water not needed for the trees and crops was turned on the pastures, which then became capable of supporting larger herds of cattle. It was the cattle industry that provided the basis for San Gabriel's wealth. By 1830 the mission had over 25,000 head of cattle, and in that year no less than 4,000 cattle were slaughtered in the San Bernardino Valley, with the hides and tallow brought to San Gabriel for trading purposes.

Although the San Bernardino Rancho was the most developed mission operation in the valley, other ranchos were established nearby. The Jumuba Rancho was located south of the Santa Ana River in the vicinity of the present freeway interchange. The Agua Caliente Rancho was north of the river, probably centered in the Harlem Springs area. Another rancho was started in the Yucaipa region.

In 1826 one of the Southwest's greatest adventurers and explorers arrived in the valley, becoming the first American to travel to California overland. Twenty-seven-year-old Jedediah Strong Smith led a party of 15 trappers from the Salt Lake

A second group of buildings for the Asistencia of the San Gabriel Mission was built in 1829 on Barton Road and was used until 1834, when Indian raids damaged the buildings. After the Mormons bought the property Bishop Nathan Tenney moved in and his wife kept school there. Courtesy, Steele's Photo Service (SPS)

Valley to Southern California. He followed the Sevier and Virgin rivers southward to the Colorado River and the Mojave settlements, where he was well received and provided with two guides to take him across the desert. Following much the same route as did Father Garcés 50 years earlier, he came to the Mojave River, which he named the Inconstant, and followed it upstream into the mountains. He entered the San Bernardino Valley late in November and proceeded on to the San Gabriel Mission, where he was welcomed by the padres. The Mexican governmental authorities were considerably less cordial, however, and after a period of detention and some lengthy negotiations, the Smith party was ordered to leave over the same route by which it had come. The group returned to the San Bernardino Valley and camped for some time at the Jumuba Rancho, where they collected food and acquired horses for their return journey. Instead of directly returning to Salt Lake, they traveled into the San Joaquin Valley, where most of the men remained to trap. Smith and two companions then crossed the Sierras and traveled to the Salt Lake Valley.

Smith returned to California in late summer 1827, leading a party of 18. Their initial reception by the Mojaves seemed as friendly as before, but the group was ambushed while making the river crossing. Ten men were killed. The remainder escaped under cover of darkness and crossed the desert to the San Bernardino Valley, where they stayed for five days. There Smith replenished the supplies, killed some mission cattle for dried beef, and dispatched a letter to Father Sanchez at San Gabriel explaining his predicament and justifying his actions. Leaving one of the wounded in the care of the mayordomo of the San Bernardino Rancho, Smith and the other survivors recrossed the mountains and traveled on to the San Joaquin Valley to join members of the first party left there earlier in the year. Smith explored farther into northern California and Oregon before returning to his rendezvous in the Rocky Mountains. Later explorations took him to the southern Great Plains, where he was killed by Indians on the Cimarron River in 1831.

In 1829 the San Gabriel Mission authorities determined to build larger and more permanent structures on their San Bernardino Rancho. This was in line with a long-range plan of developing a chain of *asistencias,* auxiliary missions, inland from the parent missions. The site chosen for the new buildings was on higher ground, about a mile and a half east of the old rancho headquarters. The construction plan provided for residences, warehouse space, a chapel, and a corral. Altogether, 14 rooms were built. The adobe walls were made from the materials at hand. The wooden beams to support the tule thatch roofs were cut from timber in Mill Creek Canyon.

Although built on the original foundations, the San Bernardino Asistencia as presently reconstructed on Barton Road is considerably more attractive and permanent than the original. Spanish tile has replaced the tule thatch, the corral area has become an attractive courtyard, and a bell tower has been added.

Secularization and Indian unrest spelled a short life for the San Bernardino Asistencia. A series of Indian attacks occurred almost as soon as the new buildings were finished. The abundance of cattle in the valley was a constant temptation to the Indians of the mountains and desert. In 1831 a band of desert Indians raided the rancho, damaged some of the asistencia buildings, and drove off livestock. The most serious raids occurred in 1834. In October Cahuilla Indians from the San Gorgonio Pass area raided the rancho granaries, seized ornaments and sacred vessels from the asistencia chapel, and moved on toward San Gabriel. En route they were met by Father Estenaga from the mission, who tried to convince them to return home. Estenaga was taken prisoner and carried off, but he was released a few hours later when the Indians withdrew, taking their loot with them.

A raid on December 30, 1834 had more serious consequences. A war party of about 200 Indians under the leadership of two ex-neophytes from San Gabriel attacked and laid siege to the asistencia compound at dawn. After repeated attacks the Indians gained entrance to the corral. The defenders surrendered and the buildings were sacked and set afire. Fourteen neophyte defenders were killed. Others were wounded or taken captive. The

plundered and burned buildings were abandoned.

It was not the intention of either the Spanish or Mexican governments that the missions would become permanent economic empires. As early as 1813 the government in Spain had adapted a decree of secularization, freeing the priests from the missions and ordering the lands parceled out among the Indian converts. This decree had no appreciable effect since Mexico was then undergoing the first phases of its struggle for independence. After that independence was finally achieved in 1821, however, the process of secularization began.

Secularization of the mission lands was finalized by the Mexican government in 1833, and was implemented in California the following year. Mission buildings and lands were confiscated and placed under the jurisdiction of administrators appointed by the government. The missions were to become no more than parish churches, and although many padres stayed on and tried to continue their missionary work, they found it to be a hopeless struggle with the economic base of the missions removed. Fields and orchards fell into disrepair, irrigation systems broke down, and thousands of cattle were slaughtered for their hides and tallow. Within two years the vast herds of cattle and flocks of sheep were gone.

Secularization not only brought ruin to the missions but to the neophyte Indians as well. Those who for years had been treated like children were forced out on their own, and most found it difficult to survive in either the new economy or the old. Some returned to their tribes to live again with their non-Christian kinsmen. Others became "hangers-on" in a white society that treated them as outcasts.

The mission period had come to an inglorious end.

The reconstruction of the Asistencia by the W.P.A. does not resemble the original building. A gabled roof covered with tile replaces the flat thatched roof. The reconstructed Asistencia has been open to the public since October 10, 1937, and is now under the jurisdiction of the San Bernardino County Museum. (SPS)

III.
THE DAYS OF THE DONS

The years between the secularization of the California missions (1834) and the American occupation of California during the Mexican War (1846) are often referred to in California history as the Rancho Period. During this time the Mexican government gave large land grants to many influential citizens. Several such grants were made in what became San Bernardino County: the ranchos Cañon de Santa Ana, Jurupa and El Rincon, Cucamonga, Santa Ana del Chino, San Bernardino, and Muscupiabe. Recipients of the land grants included Spanish gentlemen (dons) from many of the first families of California, such as the Lugos, Sepulvedas, Yorbas, Bandinis, Tapias, Palomares, and Picos.

To obtain a land grant from the Mexican government a petition to the governor had to be made, describing the land desired and stating the name, age, nativity, and occupation of the petitioner. Since no definitive surveys had been made by either the Spanish or Mexican governments, the land description was often vague, referring to such boundary landmarks as trees, streams, or mountains, and with distances or areas being measured in leagues, more or less.

The first Mexican grant that included land in San Bernardino County was made in 1834 to Bernardo Yorba, the son of Antonio Yorba, an early settler who had been granted a rancho in Orange County. The younger Yorba's grant of about 13,000 acres, the

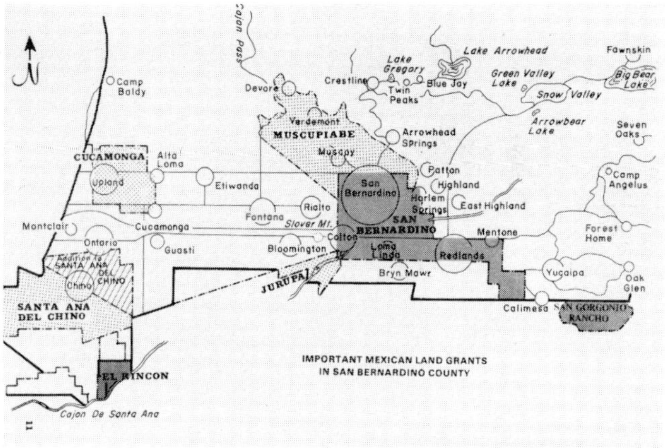

Rancho Cañon de Santa Ana, included land in the southwestern part of the county. It was this portion at the head of Santa Ana Canyon that Bernardo Yorba gave to his son Raimundo as a wedding present. Raimundo constructed an adobe on the land between 1851 and 1853. He sold the adobe and a thousand adjacent acres to Fenton Slaughter, a Los Angeles businessman, in 1868. The adobe, known today as the Yorba-Slaughter Adobe, has been preserved as part of the county museum system.

A 25,000-acre grant along the Santa Ana River—the Jurupa Rancho—was made in 1838 to Juan Bandini, a prominent political and social figure in Southern California and the civil administrator of the secularized San Gabriel Mission. Bandini received an additional 4,000-acre grant—Rancho El Rincon, lying adjacent to the west. There, on a bluff

Facing page: *Juan Bandini came to California about 1820 with his father, a Spanish sea captain. Bandini was well-educated and a U.S. supporter, and held a number of minor political posts. He sold portions of his Jurupa Rancho to Benjamin Wilson, Bernardo Yorba, and his son-in-law, Abel Stearns. From* History of California, *edited by Zoeth Skinner Eldredge*

This map shows the important Mexican land grants in San Bernardino in the 1830s and 1840s. (SBCMA)

overlooking the river, Bandini built a home, using lumber from the San Bernardino Mountains.

The first migration of non-Hispanics into Southern California also took place during this period, and some of these also became landowners, including the Americans Isaac Williams, Benjamin Wilson, Louis Rubidoux, and Isaac Slover, as well as the Englishman Michael White and the Frenchman Victor Prudhomme.

In 1843 a portion of the Jurupa Rancho was sold to Benjamin D. Wilson, who had come to Southern California in 1841 with a party of colonists from New Mexico. A popular figure with the Mexican people, Don Benito, as he was known, married a daughter of Bernardo Yorba but retained his American citizenship. Wilson kept his part of the Jurupa Rancho only a few years, selling it to Louis Rubidoux in 1847.

Rancho Cucamonga was granted to Tiburcio Tapia, a prominent Los Angeles merchant and public official, in 1839. He built an adobe on top of Red Hill, overlooking the valley. Upon Tapia's death the property passed to his daughter and her husband, Victor Prudhomme. Although Rancho Cucamonga in the 1840s remained a livestock range as it had been in mission days, a small vineyard was planted there—the beginning of a grape culture that would make the Cucamonga area famous.

It was rumored after Tapia's death that he had hidden gold some place on Red Hill. Tapia's "buried treasure" was never found, although generations of treasure seekers pockmarked Red Hill in their search for it.

Rancho Cucamonga was sold by the Prudhommes in 1858 to John Rains, a Southerner who had come to California in about 1849. Rains built a new home of fired brick on the property. Today the Rains House is maintained as another facility of the San Bernardino County Museum.

In 1841 Governor Alvarado granted the 22,000-acre Rancho Santa Ana del Chino to his uncle, Antonio Maria Lugo. Lugo, born at the San Antonio Mission in 1775, was the son of a soldier. Although uneducated, he became one of the wealthiest and most influential men in Mexican California.

Lugo deeded half the ownership of the ranch to his son-in-law, Isaac Williams. Williams, a friendly,

Fenton M. Slaughter, shown here in 1894, was a member of the State Legislature in the early 1870s, and a San Bernardino County Supervisor in the 1880s. Courtesy, Chino Valley Historical Society

Raimundo Yorba, son of the owner of Rancho Cañon de Santa Ana, built this house between 1850 and 1853, just south of Chino. Fenton Slaughter purchased the house and 3,000 acres in 1868 and lived in it until his death in 1897. In 1928 Slaughter's daughter, Julia Fuqua, obtained the property and restored the house. It is now under the care of the San Bernardino County Museum. Courtesy, Robert P. Jochimsen

extroverted American frontiersman, had come to California in 1832. He became a merchant in Los Angeles, was naturalized as a Mexican citizen, converted to Catholicism, and married Lugo's daughter, Maria de Jesús.

Williams not only built the Chino Ranch into a huge pastoral empire, but he planted many field crops as well. He grew wheat and constructed a mill to produce flour. He planted a vineyard and fruit trees and established a soap factory. Visitors described his home, a large quadrangle enclosing an interior courtyard, 250 feet on a side, as the "largest and best arranged private home in California." The roof was of tule thatch, waterproofed with asphalt brought from the La Brea Tar Pits in Los Angeles.

Several prominent Southern Californians competed for the land that had been the San Gabriel Mission's Rancho San Bernardino. In 1937 the Pico brothers, Antonia and Andres, asked for the land but their application was rejected. Ygnacio Palomares, owner of the Rancho San Jose in the present Pomona area, applied for grazing rights for his cattle in the eastern San Bernardino Valley and followed it up with a formal application for title. Although his application was approved by the prefect in Los Angeles, it was denied by Governor Juan Bautista Alvarado, who instead approved a plan for settlement advanced by Antonio Maria Lugo.

Land grants to individuals were limited to no more than 11 leagues (about 48,000 acres), but the size could be greater if other families could be induced to settle on the property. Lugo proposed to colonize the San Bernardino area, listing the names of 27 prospective settlers. A permit for the colonization of 18 leagues of land was issued in 1839.

The settlement plan was not successful, so in 1841 Lugo prepared another petition requesting a land grant in the name of three of his sons, José del Carmen, José Maria, and Vicente—and Diego Sepulveda, a lifelong friend of José del Carmen. In a letter to Governor Alvarado, Lugo stressed the plight of the more than 200 baptized Indian residents of the valley who had been without spiritual guidance since 1834, and he indicated a willingness to maintain a priest in the area if the grant would be favorably considered. The grant was approved in 1842. Although the prefect had recommended that the grant include only the three mission ranchos of San Bernardino—Guachama, Jumuba, and Agua Caliente—Alvarado also added Yucaipa.

All four of the grantees established homes in the area, but only one of the Lugo brothers, Jose del Carmen, made it a permanent home until 1851 when the rancho was sold. He repaired the abandoned San Bernardino Asistencia and made his home there. The other two brothers spent much time looking after other family interests in Southern California, and

Abel Stearns was born in Massachusetts in 1799, and became a naturalized Mexican citizen in 1828. He came to California a year later, and married Arcadia, Juan Bandini's daughter. A trader and large landowner, Stearns was a member of the Constitutional Convention in 1849. From History of California, *edited by Zoeth Skinner Eldredge*

their residence in the valley was sporadic. Diego Sepulveda built his home, a two-story adobe, in the Yucaipa Valley in 1841-1842. Now part of the county museum system, this adobe is the oldest standing residential building in San Bernardino County.

The Lugos' San Bernardino Rancho was primarily a livestock range. Four thousand cattle were brought from the elder Lugo's ranch in the present Lynwood-Compton area of Los Angeles County. Diego Sepulveda ran cattle in the Yucaipa Valley, but also raised a number of swine. The latter especially prospered on the acorns of the live oaks growing in what came to be known as Cañon de Puerco (Hog Canyon), the present Wildwood Canyon.

The last of the major land grants in the San Bernardino Valley was the Rancho Muscupiabe, acquired in 1843 by Michael White, known to the Mexicans as Miguel Blanco. White was an English sailor who came to California in 1817 and became involved in the coastal trade. He became a Mexican citizen and married the daughter of the housekeeper of the Mission San Gabriel.

Hoping to reduce the depredations being suffered by the valley ranches from Indian raids, the Lugos persuaded White to apply for land below the mouth of Cajon Pass. White built a fortress home of logs and

John Rains married Maria Merced Williams September 16, 1856, the day after her father, Isaac Williams, was buried. With his wife's money Rains bought Rancho Cucamonga in 1858. In 1862 he was murdered on his way to Los Angeles on business. Courtesy, Casa de Rancho Cucamonga Historical Society (CRCHS)

Maria Merced Williams married John Rains when she was only 17 years old. Her life was shattered when her husband was murdered. She lost her property eventually and moved to Los Angeles. Her daughter married Henry Gage, who became governor of California in 1899, and Maria Merced made her home with them. (CRCHS)

earth on the bench west of Cable Canyon, overlooking both lower Cajon Pass and the old Mojave Trail. White's tenure on the Muscupiabe Rancho was a brief one. Not only did he fail to stop raids into the valley, but he lost his own livestock to the raiders. After nine months he abandoned the place.

Rancho living in the 1840s was a pastoral, almost feudal way of life. Indians from the various rancherias in the valley furnished much of the labor. Although raising cattle and horses was the primary activity, crops were cultivated to provide much of the food needed. Corn, wheat, barley, potatoes, peas, beans, onions, and peppers were grown. Some fruit trees were planted, and grapes were grown and processed into wine.

Rodeos or roundups were regularly scheduled after the calving season to brand, mark, and geld the livestock. Cattle within a designated area would be driven to one ranch location. Livestock not belonging to that ranch would be separated and driven to the ranches of their owners. The whole operation was supervised by a Juez del Campo (Judge of the Plains), who acted as a referee in cases of dispute, and whose decisions were final.

Recreational diversions were few and simple. Guests were welcomed and enthusiastically entertained. To suggest paying for overnight accommodations or meals was considered an insult.

John Rains started building a brick house in 1860, making his the oldest fired-brick house in the county. In 1971, teacher Maxine Strane brought her class to see the house, and to her dismay a bulldozer was knocking a gaping hole in the patio wall. She succeeded in saving the house, and the restoration has been financed by the Casa de Rancho Cucamonga Historical Society. In 1982 the verandah was rebuilt around the house. (CRCHS)

Several religious holidays were regularly observed by Mexican Catholic families. Such holidays were a time for fiesta—a time for visiting, singing, dancing, and feasting.

Horse racing was the most popular sport of the day, and this, along with cock fighting, often involved spirited betting. Bull and bear fights were also common. Grizzly bears were usually captured in the Patton-Highland area where they were especially numerous. A bull and a bear would be turned loose in an enclosed area. Invariably the bull was killed by the bear, but often not before the bear had been almost gored to death. José del Carmen Lugo constructed his own *Plaza de Toros* for bull-bear fights. This cruel sporting event continued in the valley well into the American era, with the last bull-bear fight being held in 1864.

Economic contacts with the outside world were events of special significance. Trade between New Mexico and Southern California began in the early 1830s and continued on a somewhat regular basis for nearly 15 years. The first New Mexican trading expedition arrived in California during the winter of 1830-1831, following a circuitous route of about 1,200 miles from Santa Fe to Los Angeles. This route, which became known as the Spanish Trail, traversed such rugged desert and mountain country that the trade goods had to be carried by pack horses and mules rather than in carts or wagons. The journey usually took about two months, with the party leaving New Mexico in October.

The New Mexican traders brought woolen goods to California, and in turn purchased or traded for mules and horses, as well as for silks and other Chinese goods that had been brought to the West Coast. In some years as many as 2,000 horses and mules left the San Bernardino Valley for New Mexico. The San Bernardino Valley provided excellent pasturage for the livestock of the trading expeditions, and the bottomland along the Santa Ana River near present Colton was the principal rendezvous for the returning traders. This site became known as Politana, probably named for Hipolito Espinosa who occupied land nearby.

Horse stealing from the valley ranches was rampant, and suspicions that all the horses and mules leaving the valley with the traders might not have been legally obtained led the Mexican government in 1839 to require that livestock be inspected and marked and their purchase certified before leaving California.

The Spanish Trail also provided a route for American and New Mexican immigration into Southern California. An 1841 New Mexican caravan included a group of over 20 American colonists, among them Benjamin Wilson. Another member

Don Antonio Maria Lugo was alcalde, or mayor of Los Angeles, from 1816 to 1819 and juez del campo, or judge of the plains, from 1833 to 1834. With his three sons and Diego Sepulveda he was granted Rancho San Bernardino in 1842 by his grandnephew, Governor Alvarado. Courtesy, Security Pacific National Bank Photograph Collection, Los Angeles Public Library

of the party, Lorenzo Trujillo, after learning of the desire of the Lugos for settlers to provide protection from Indian raids, returned to New Mexico and recruited several families to return as colonists the following year.

Raids on livestock by the desert and mountain Indians, which had been a constant threat to the ranches of the San Bernardino Valley during the Mission Period, became an even greater problem during the Rancho Period. California horses and mules were especially valued for their size and stamina. They became an important trade item throughout the Southwest, so horse stealing was no longer restricted to local tribes. The scourge of the valley in the 1840s was the Ute chief, Walkara. With 200 well-armed horsemen, he ranged the Southwest

Top: *Benjamin Wilson bought part of the Jurupa Rancho from Don Juan Bandini in 1843. When he sold the Jurupa Rancho, he bought Rancho San Pasqual, which he later helped develop into Pasadena. He's shown here with his daughters and his first wife Ramona, Bernardo Yorba's daughter. Courtesy, Security Pacific National Bank Photograph Collection, Los Angeles Public Library*

Bottom: *The Yucaipa adobe house built by Diego Sepulveda in 1842 is the oldest house in the county. The house is shown here in 1955, before Yucaipa residents and the San Bernardino County Museum Association purchased and restored it. Courtesy, Arda Haenszel*

from central Utah to the present Mexican border, exacting tribute from caravans along the Spanish Trail, supplying Indian slaves to the Navajos and the Mexicans, and trading in California horseflesh. Also involved in the horse rustling were a number of American adventurers, former trappers, and mountain men known to the Mexicans as *chaguanosos.*

The most sensational raid into the valley, a well-coordinated effort by Walkara and mountain men Pegleg Smith and Jim Beckwourth, took place in early 1840. Beckwourth came into the valley first, claiming plans to hunt sea otter along the coast. For a time he was a guest of Isaac Williams at the Chino Ranch from where he scouted the territory and located the various herds of horses. Beckwourth met with Smith and Walkara in Cajon Pass to make final plans. The raiders were divided into small groups, each with a specific ranch objective, and each to strike at the same time. Ranches were raided all the way from San Luis Obispo to the Santa Ana River. At least 5,000 horses and mules were said to have been driven through Cajon Pass. Three separate parties of Californians were organized to pursue the thieves into the desert, and they were successful in recovering about 2,000 of the animals. In their haste to escape, the thieves lost many animals who perished from exhaustion, thirst, and hunger. The cause was finally abandoned by the Californians because of the exhausted condition of their own horses.

It was to protect the region from such raids that colonists were encouraged to settle in the San Bernardino Valley. A group of New Mexican settlers arrived in 1842 under the leadership of Lorenzo Trujillo, a friend of Benjamin Wilson. They first settled at Politana at the urging of Vicente Lugo, whose home was nearby. There they built homes, dug irrigation ditches, and planted crops.

Problems soon developed between the New Mexicans and Vicente Lugo. Lugo had built a rodeo center north of the Politana settlement, and his cattle frequently damaged the irrigation ditches, cutting off the water supply. Another problem was that the settlers were never given individual land allotments as they had hoped. After about two years, Trujillo and a few other families moved to land downstream, given them by Bandini. This "Bandini Donation," which had been insisted upon by Benjamin Wilson as a condition of his purchasing part of the Jurupa Rancho in 1843, became the location of two small New Mexican settlements: Agua Mansa north of the Santa Ana River, and La Placita to the south. Other settlers gradually moved from Politana to the new area, with each family receiving an allotment of land, and additional families came from New Mexico.

One of the first settlers was Isaac Slover, the only one of the original group who was not a New Mexican, although he had a New Mexican wife. Slover eventually made his home by the mountain in Colton which bears his name, now a quarry of the California Portland Cement Company. Slover Mountain, a prominent valley landmark, was originally known to the Indians as Tahualtapa (Raven Hill) because it was the nesting place for large flocks of ravens. Isaac Slover spent much time hunting in the mountains, a pastime which eventually led to his death by being mauled by a grizzly bear in Lone Pine Canyon.

After some years the New Mexicans began constructing a larger church to replace the small temporary chapel they had been using. In 1852, after many months of volunteer labor, the adobe walls of the new structure crumbled and the entire building collapsed because of inadequate foundations in the water-saturated soil. The construction site was abandoned and a new church built north of the river on firmer, higher ground. This structure at Agua Mansa was dedicated in 1853.

After the New Mexicans left Politana for Agua Mansa and La Placita, the Lugos brought in a number of Cahuilla Indians from the Santa Rosa Mountains, under the leadership of their chief Juan Antonio, to provide protection for the valley. Both Juan Antonio's Indians and Trujillo's New Mexicans took their protective responsibilities seriously, and both had many opportunities to demonstrate their loyalty to the rancheros.

Raids into the San Bernardino Valley through Cajon Pass and over the Mojave Trail continued through the 1840s. As Justice of the Peace for the

Jurupa District, Benjamin Wilson was commissioned by Governor Pio Pico in 1845 to lead a punitive expedition against a band of Indians on the Mojave River. Wilson led his group over the mountains, stopping for a day of bear hunting in a high mountain valley. The men paired off in couples and lassoed 11 bears. We know this area today as Big Bear Valley.

Wilson and Trujillo, riding ahead of the main group in the desert, suddenly came upon four of the Indians, one of whom shot Wilson in the shoulder with a poisoned arrow. The Indians were killed by the remainder of the party. Trujillo, by sucking the poison from the wound, is credited with saving Wilson's life.

Wilson led two other expeditions into the desert in 1845, one through San Gorgonio Pass into Cahuilla country, the other into the Mojave Desert, where an Indian village was destroyed. All the men of the village were killed and the women and children were captured and brought to San Gabriel.

During another battle in 1845, known as the Battle of Pigeon Pass, three of Trujillo's sons were wounded while pursuing Indians who had run off livestock. In spite of being wounded, the Trujillos captured the thieves and recovered the stolen animals.

Such protective activities generally ended the troubles caused by the local Indians, but the incursions of Walkara and the Utes continued. In late 1845 Walkara, accompanied by some of his men and their families, came into the San Bernardino Valley, supposedly on a peaceful trading mission. They were welcomed and treated as guests at the Chino Rancho by Antonio Maria Lugo. When they left, however, they stole and drove off whole herds of horses. Vicente Lugo led a group in pursuit of the Indians, but withdrew when it became evident that his group was outmanned and outgunned by the raiders.

After California came under American occupation in 1846, raids instigated by such renegade Americans as Pegleg Smith came to a halt, but the Utes continued to harass ranches in the valley until Walkara's death in 1855. The American military governor authorized the formation of a company of volunteers to protect the eastern valley. The group was first stationed in Cajon Pass, but because of inclement weather soon moved to the Politana area.

The Mexican War created difficulties for those Americans living in the San Bernardino Valley. Although most were sympathetic to the American cause, they also had strong Mexican ties. Their self-interest dictated that they appear to be neutral, but neutrality proved impossible, and a chain of circumstances unfolded which led to the so-called Battle of Chino, the one instance of conflict in San Bernardino County during the Mexican War.

In September 1846 Los Angeles was occupied by a contingent of American troops under Captain Archibald Gillespie. Benjamin Wilson, who had not renounced his American citizenship, was requested by the American Commodore Robert F. Stockton to scout the movements of the retreating Mexican general, José Castro, who had abandoned the town. Wilson, accompanied by a small group of horsemen, did so until satisfied that Castro was withdrawing from California. At about the same time, however, Captain Gillespie lost control of the situation in Los Angeles and sent a message to Wilson for help. Although reluctant to get too deeply involved, Wilson and a party of men from Jurupa started for Los Angeles, but stopped off at Chino Ranch at the invitation of Isaac Williams, hoping to get more ammunition and gunpowder there.

A number of native Californians, including Diego Sepulveda and José del Carmen Lugo, aware of the Americans' movements, determined to prevent aid from reaching Gillespie, and they placed the Chino ranch house under siege. At first only taunts were shouted back and forth, but a mounted attack by the Californians was made the morning of September 27th. The attackers were temporarily held off and one was killed. They finally succeeded in gaining a secure position under the shelter of the ranch house walls and set fire to the roof, forcing the defenders to surrender. After the flames were extinguished with the help of the Californians, the prisoners were marched to Los Angeles. Although a few Californians, incensed by the death of their colleague, wanted to kill the prisoners, and others advocated their shipment to Mexico as prisoners of war, cooler and older heads prevailed. Palomares and the elder Lugo urged greater caution and restraint,

probably considering the possibility of American retaliation should Mexico lose the war. The prisoners were paroled to Lugo, who took the responsibility of caring for them and tending the wounded. The group was freed when other American forces reoccupied Los Angeles.

The Treaty of Guadalupe-Hidalgo in 1848, ending the Mexican War and ceding to the United States much of our Southwest, recognized the land-ownerships legally established by the Mexican government. After California was admitted as a state in 1850, Congress created a Board of Land Commissioners to determine those lands which would remain in private ownership and those in the public domain. Each private land claim was individually examined, and following approval of title and a definition of boundaries, a patent was issued to the ranch owner. Since Mexican grants had been made in the valley area only, the greater part of what was to be San Bernardino County remained in the public domain.

The end of the Mexican War signaled the demise of the Rancho Period. Although many old land titles were confirmed by the new American government, large grants of land for new ranches came to an end. Livestock raising gave way to agriculture. A new population of a different cultural background began moving into the area, and the predominant Hispanic or Mexican culture was displaced, but not eliminated, by growing numbers of Americans.

Lugo gave some New Mexicans land in exchange for their help in defending his livestock from Indians. The Lugo's rodeos and horse racing ruined the settlers' gardens. Juan Bandini offered the disgruntled settlers land, and in 1845 Agua Mansa was started on the banks of the Santa Ana River just west of Colton. On January 22, 1862, a flood wiped out the settlement. Only the church and cemetery remained. A replica of the little church was dedicated in June 1978. (SPS)

IV.
THE PIONEER AMERICAN YEARS

The first decades under American rule were a time of tremendous change in Southern California. The Mormons who settled in the San Bernardino Valley in 1851 played a dominant role in establishing the county and city of San Bernardino. Many other Americans also migrated to the area, especially after the discovery of gold in the San Bernardino Mountains, so that by the middle 1860s San Bernardino County had lost much of the Hispanic character of 20 years before.

The San Bernardino Valley had first become known to the Mormons through the Mormon Battalion, a contingent of young men recruited in Iowa from Mormon emigrants on the way to the Salt Lake Valley. Reaching Southern California too late for the fighting, the Mormons were assigned to occupation duties, during which time they became well acquainted with the San Bernardino Valley. Beginning in June 1847 some on detached service lived at the Chino Ranch and aided in the harvest and in building a gristmill. While there they learned from Isaac Williams of his willingness to dispose of the ranch. Apparently disillusioned by his recent Battle of Chino experiences and ostracized by many of his former friends, he indicated that he would sell out for as little as $500 down and with very generous terms for paying the balance.

In the winter of 1847 Jefferson Hunt, a Mormon Battalion captain who was discharged early and traveled to Salt Lake in September 1847, led a party from Salt Lake back to California to obtain supplies, seed grain, and livestock for the Utah settlements. Returning to Utah the following spring, he was followed by a large party of the Mormon Battalion who had just mustered out of the service. This group arrived in Salt Lake City in early June with a pack train of 135 mules and one wagon, the first wheeled vehicle to make the journey over Cajon Pass and across the Mojave Desert. The western part of the old Spanish Trail had now become the Salt Lake Trail.

Amasa Lyman was one of the leaders of the Mormon march to colonize San Bernardino in 1851. He was elected the first mayor when the city was incorporated in June 1854. Courtesy, Church Archives, The Church of Jesus Christ of Latter-Day Saints

Facing page: *From left to right: William Holcomb, John Brown, Jr., John Brown, Sr., George Miller, and B.B. Harris were all members of the San Bernardino Society of Pioneers. (SPS)*

Late in 1849 Jefferson Hunt led another expedition from Salt Lake to Southern California. They were gold-seekers traveling too late in the season to use the more direct route across the Sierras to the goldfields, so they engaged Hunt to guide them to California over the Salt Lake Trail. The emigrant train, made up of more than 100 wagons, traveled without incident as far as the Mountain Meadows area in southwestern Utah. There most of the group, against Hunt's advice, left the Salt Lake Trail and turned westward, seeking a shortcut to the goldfields. Hunt and those remaining with him continued on their journey and came into the San Bernardino Valley in time to celebrate Christmas at the Chino Ranch, after which they went on to Los Angeles before going north to the Mother Lode country. Those who had left the Hunt wagon train encountered great difficulties. Breaking up into a number of smaller groups, most eventually made their way into the great desert basin now known as Death Valley. A few died; all suffered extreme hardships.

Other immigrants to California continued to use the southern route, following the Salt Lake or old Spanish Trail through Cajon Pass to Los Angeles. Many of these travelers lingered at San Bernardino Valley ranches. Isaac Williams was an especially generous host, often having 10 to 20 guests at his dinner table, and frequently loaning supplies or money to the transients. To the gold-seekers the Chino Ranch in the south became a counterpart to Sutter's Fort in the north—a stopover for rest and supplies. Rancho Cucamonga was another way station for emigrants from the East coming through Southern California in 1849.

After 1849 the valley experienced increased lawlessness as embittered and unsuccessful miners and criminals drifted into the area. One gang of outlaws, renegade Americans led by John *Red* Irving, terrorized the valley in 1851. They were finally cornered and all but one killed by Juan Antonio's Cahuilla tribesmen in San Timoteo Canyon.

By 1851, the leader of the Mormons in Salt Lake, Brigham Young, was favorably inclined to purchase the Chino Ranch and to establish a small colony in the San Bernardino Valley. Not only would it provide such agricultural products as grapes, sugar cane, and cotton, but it could also serve as a rendezvous and outfitting point for Mormon converts who arrived by ship in Southern California on their way to Utah. Although Young approved of a small Southern California settlement, he was distressed at the number of people who volunteered to go. Over 400 people gathered at Payson, Utah, to organize for the trip.

Charles Rich, along with Amasa Lyman, led the Mormons who came to San Bernardino in 1851. He and Lyman arranged for the purchase of the San Bernardino Rancho and secured the loan from San Francisco to buy out Don Antonio Lugo and his family. (SPS)

Young wrote, "I was sick at the sight of so many of the Saints running to California, chiefly after the god of this world." The party left the Salt Lake Valley in March 1851.

Two of the church's Apostles, Amasa Lyman and Charles Rich, were designated as leaders of the new colony. The migration route followed the route traveled by Jefferson Hunt and the returning Mormon Battalion. The 437 people who made up the party included 26 blacks, slaves of Mormons from the southern states. The group traveled in 150 wagons, and drove with them more than a thousand head of livestock—588 oxen, 336 cows, 21 calves, 107 horses, and 52 mules.

A small advance group arrived in the San Bernardino Valley on June 9, 1851, and promptly went to Chino to negotiate the purchase of the ranch from Isaac Williams. The first wagon company arrived in the valley on June 11 and established a camp at Sycamore Grove at the mouth of Cajon Pass. The Mormons remained at Sycamore Grove throughout the summer, setting up a well-regulated tent and wagonbox city. One large wagon served as a day school for the children. A central area was cleared of chapparal as a place for meetings, religious services, and social events.

The Mormon leaders were disappointed to learn that Isaac Williams had changed his mind and that the Chino Ranch was no longer for sale. However, they were able to negotiate the purchase of the Rancho San Bernardino from the Lugos. The purchase agreement was finalized on September 22, 1851, with ownership in the name of Lyman, Rich, and Company.

At the time of the purchase Lyman and Rich were not aware that they were buying less than half of what they assumed was the San Bernardino Ranch. The final determination of the purchased acreage was not made for several years, creating many individual land title problems. Lyman and Rich were first inclined to select the higher elevations near the foothills, thinking it to be the best agricultural land. The dry years of the middle 1850s, however, convinced them that access to a dependable water supply was essential. They finally selected land closer to the Santa Ana River, as well as in the Yucaipa Valley.

A townsite in the present Highland area was first considered, from which time City Creek got its name. However, a site farther to the west was finally selected and named San Bernardino, after the ranch. Even before the purchase negotiations were completed, the Mormons had planted a field of grain to provide a cash crop. By October the Lugos had removed their livestock and Mormon families began moving from Sycamore Grove into the new settlement.

Only a few cabins had been constructed before news came that Indians under the leadership of Antonio Garra were organizing to drive the whites out of Southern California. The Mormons responded to this threat by hastily erecting a stockade. Cabins already built were skidded to a location near the present courthouse site (Arrowhead Avenue, between 3rd and 4th streets), and placed side by side to make a solid wall. This wall was continued by using split cottonwood and sycamore logs to make a rectangular enclosure about 700 by 300 feet. Lean-to shelters were built inside. Town Creek was diverted through the stockade to provide a water supply. Working day and night, the Mormons completed the project in 20 days, occupying the stockade by mid-December. A type of martial law prevailed with a 24-hour watch being maintained. An alarm system was agreed upon—a blast of the six-foot bishop's horn by Grief Embers, one of the black settlers. The horn also summoned the group for other meetings.

The Indian threat soon subsided. Garra was unsuccessful in enlisting the Mountain and Pass Cahuilla to his cause, and he was captured and turned over to military authorities by Juan Antonio, the Cahuilla chief who for several years had served the Lugos with such loyalty. Most of the colonists continued to live within the stockade, however, staying there for a year or more. A large tent was set up in one corner of the enclosure to serve as an assembly hall, a church, and a school.

To become as self-sufficient as possible, and to produce goods for sale, the Mormons wasted no time in developing agriculture and lumbering. By mid-

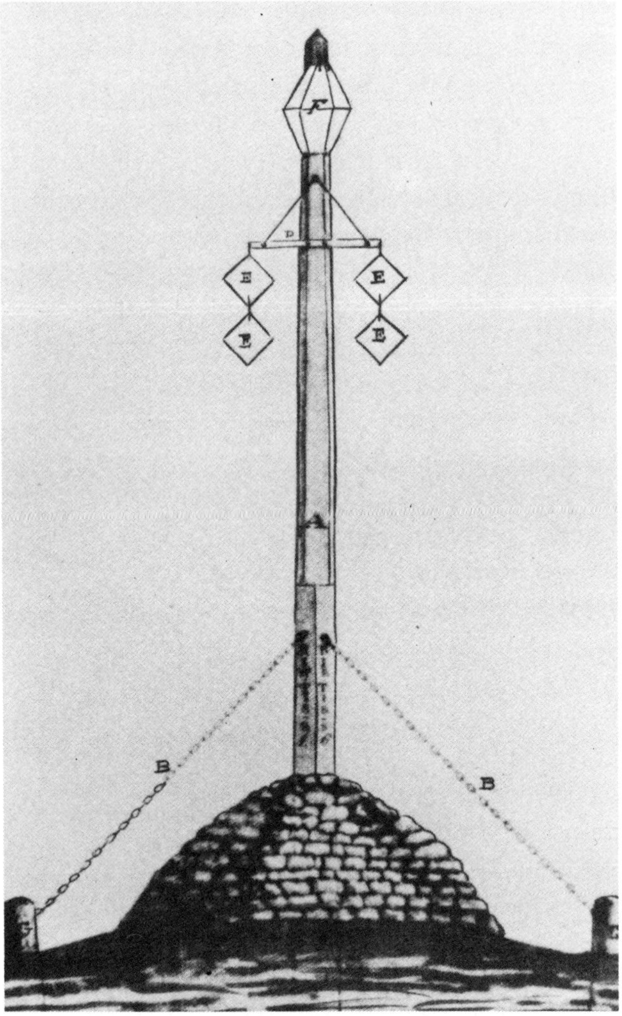

December 1851 plowing began on a 1,500-acre grain field between Little Mountain and the base of the San Bernardino Mountains. Another 300 acres were planted to summer crops in 1852. A vineyard was laid out and fruit trees were planted. Near the present intersection of Mill and Allen streets a flour mill was built. Water diverted from Warm Creek to the mill site furnished the power to turn an undershot water wheel.

Although the first sawmills were in Mill Creek Canyon, the Mormons soon directed their attention to the better timber over the crest of the mountains to the north. A logging road built up Hot Springs (Waterman) Canyon in the spring of 1852 provided access to some of the finest timber stands in Southern California. A sawmill began operating in Seely Flats in the summer of 1853, and by late 1854 six sawmills were running in the mountains. Lumber was in great demand throughout the southland and it provided a valuable source of income for the San Bernardino colonists. In Los Angeles the lumber was often referred to as "Mormon currency."

Agricultural efforts were equally rewarding. A bumper crop was harvested in 1852. A harvest festival held in September displayed a cornstalk 16 feet tall, and four onions weighing 9.6 pounds. Prices were good. Wheat sold in Los Angeles for $4 a bushel, and flour at $32 a barrel.

Col. Henry Washington, U.S. deputy surveyor, set a flag on Mount San Bernardino in November 1852 to serve as the initial point for a base line for official surveys in Southern California. Base Line Street follows the line of the survey. (SBCMA)

Jefferson Hunt, an officer in the Mormon battalion, first saw the San Bernardino Valley in 1847. He has been called the Father of San Bernardino County because as assemblyman from Los Angeles County, he introduced legislation to separate San Bernardino County from Los Angeles County. Courtesy, San Bernardino Redevelopment Agency (SBRA)

Each year more land was brought under cultivation. By 1858 6,000 acres were planted to wheat and barley, 2,000 acres were in corn, and 2,000 pounds of butter along with 100 dozen eggs were shipped to Los Angeles weekly. Vines and fruit trees were beginning to produce. In 1857 the first orange trees in the county were planted by Anson Van Leuven in the old San Bernardino Mission district.

After California came under American jurisdiction, the area was more accurately mapped and laid out in a grid of townships and sections. For this purpose, Colonel Henry Washington, a U.S. Deputy Surveyor, came into the valley in the latter part of 1852. Building a monument on the west peak of Mount San Bernardino to use as a reference point, Washington's crew mapped an east-west base line and a north-south meridian. Working from these survey lines, the rest of Southern California was eventually mapped. The San Bernardino Base Line gave its name to one of the principal east-west thoroughfares in the San Bernardino Valley.

Henry G. Sherwood, the engineer who laid out Salt Lake City, surveyed the townsite of San Bernardino in 1853. The city was one mile square, with a grid of wide streets forming the boundaries of eight-acre blocks. One block in the center of the city was designated as a Temple Block. This block became the Mormon Plaza, now known as Pioneer Park. The east-west streets were numbered one to ten from south to north, and except for Rialto Avenue, which was then known as lst Street, they bear the same designations today. The north-south streets, however, received names, all of which have been subsequently changed.

Agricultural land was offered by Lyman and Rich to the colonists for $11 to $16 an acre. Bishop Nathan Tenney established his residence at the Asistencia and was named Manager of Agriculture for the area south of the Santa Ana River. Transported water was

Top: *Dr. Ben Barton bought the Asistencia Mission property from Lyman and Rich in 1857. Barton lived in the Asistencia until his home was built ten years later. He was the first practicing physician in the area, the second postmaster, and the first druggist. Courtesy, San Bernardino Public Library (SBPL)*

Bottom: *The first public building in San Bernardino was built by the Mormons in 1852. It was a two-story adobe with a shingle roof. It was used as the post office, council office, school, and church, and when the county was created in 1853, the building became the first courthouse. (SBCMA)*

essential for many crops and the Mill Creek Zanja continued in use as an irrigation ditch. In the late 1850s additional canals were built diverting water from the Santa Ana River.

Juan Antonio and his Cahuilla band were displaced from the land they had occupied under the Lugos and moved some distance up San Timoteo Canyon. Even here they suffered constant encroachment from white settlers.

As the Mormons left the security of the stockade to build their own homes or places of business, San

Bernardino began to take on the appearance of a city. The two most imposing buildings in the new town were both built near the present courthouse site. A two-story Mormon Council House served as a church office and became the county's first courthouse. Amasa Lyman's two-story house was in the same area. Both Lyman and Rich, being polygamists, needed large homes to provide separate apartments for the wives who had accompanied them to San Bernardino. An adobe assembly hall known as the Bowery was constructed on the south side of 4th Street, between present Arrowhead Avenue and D Street. During the week the hall was used as a day school, and on Sunday church services and Bible classes were held there. In 1854 six lots were selected and deeded for school sites. Two adobe buildings were erected as schools, one on the site of the present Warm Springs School. A third school was established at the Asistencia for the children of families in that area. San Bernardino's first hotel, the Bella Union, was built in 1857 at the southwest corner of 4th and D streets. So much construction was taking place in the middle 1850s that there was a lumber shortage.

Both the Mormon and non-Mormon population grew rapidly. Large numbers of immigrants continued to come from Salt Lake. Charles Rich noted that nearly all states and several foreign countries were represented among the Mormon colonists. In late 1854 the population of San Bernardino was estimated to be about 1,200, of which 900 were Mormons. Among the non-Mormons who came to the San Bernardino area in the 1850s and who later attained positions of prominence were John Brown, Sr., James Waters, the Cram brothers, and Lewis Jacobs. The latter, along with the Meyerstein brothers, was an early merchant, and he established the first bank in the county, the Bank of San Bernardino.

San Bernardino experienced a number of political changes as a result of the sudden influx of population. Originally part of a gigantic San Diego County, the San Bernardino area was transferred to Los Angeles County in 1851. Los Angeles was entitled to two assemblymen in the legislature, and when the Mormons were still encamped at Sycamore Grove in the summer of 1851, a Los Angeles delegation came to offer the new settlers the choice of one assemblyman. Jefferson Hunt was chosen, and he served in the legislature until 1857.

Within two years, on April 26, 1853, a separate county of San Bernardino was created. Jefferson Hunt introduced the legislation establishing the new county, which included all of the present area of the county, the northern portion of what is now Riverside County, and some of southern Inyo County. (A separate Inyo County was formed in 1872, and

With the help of an experienced miller, George Sirrene, Lyman and Rich chose the site of a mill, at the present-day intersection of Mill and Allen streets. The mill was erected by William Davies in 1852. It had two sets of burr stones driven by water brought from Warm Creek, a mile away. It also featured a water-powered thresher and a 30 by 70 foot adobe storehouse. The mill was destroyed in the flood of 1862. (SPS)

Riverside County came into being in 1893.) The county was divided into three townships: San Bernardino, San Salvador, and Chino. All county officials chosen in the first election were Mormons, with Jefferson Hunt continuing to represent the area in the legislature. San Bernardino was designated as the county seat, with the Mormon Council House serving as the first courthouse. A three-member County Board of Supervisors was elected in 1855, made up of two Mormons and Louis Rubidoux, who was elected chairman.

The city of San Bernardino was incorporated on April 13, 1854. Amasa Lyman was elected its first mayor. Ordinances were quickly passed prohibiting gambling and liquor within the city. Courts were set up to settle minor issues. Cases on the court calender usually involved one or more non-Mormon litigants since personal disputes among the Mormons were traditionally handled within the church structure.

The Mormons submitted to church leadership in political matters as well. In the presidential election of 1852 they voted unanimously for the Whig candidate, Winfield Scott. Four years later they solidly backed the Democrat, James Buchanan.

The first evidence of political dissension within the Mormon ranks occurred in the 1855 election for county supervisors. The church leadership selected two candidates to run for two of the three positions. Two other Mormons, Frederick Van Leuven and Benjamin Grouard, filed to run against the official church candidates. They were soundly defeated. Following the election the church authorities asked the two to apologize for their divisive action. They refused to do so and were "disfellowshipped," or

In 1867 Dr. J.R. Riley leased the Arizona Hotel on the southeast corner of 4th and D streets in San Bernardino. The hotel was a two-story adobe, built in 1857. Riley changed its name to the Bella Union. (SPS)

suspended, from the church. These apostate Mormons were joined by others who were dissatisfied with church policies, and together with a growing non-Mormon population, formed an anti-Mormon faction usually referred to as the Independents.

Even more serious dissension resulted from land disputes. The specific boundaries of the land purchased from the Lugos were not finally defined until August 1857. This uncertainty as to what was private or public land led to many squatter problems. Frederick Van Leuven settled on land near present-day Loma Linda believing it to be public domain, but was notified that he was on land which must be purchased from Lyman and Rich. He moved to the Yucaipa Valley only to learn that here, too, he was trespassing on private property. He finally made a permanent home in the East Highlands district. The Cram brothers, who came to the valley in 1854, also became East Highland residents after two earlier attempts to settle elsewhere in the area. John Brown, Sr. moved into the Sepulveda Adobe in Yucaipa, but in 1856 was notified that he was occupying Mormon property and must vacate the premises. He agreed to do so, but a number of his friends and neighbors met and drafted a "remonstrance" pledging their support. Although he refused to leave at that time, he soon moved to San Bernardino and the Yucaipa property was sold by the Mormons to James Waters.

Perhaps the best-known altercation over land ownership involved the Mormon apostate, Jerome Benson. He took up land immediately south of the Santa Ana River thinking it outside the San Bernardino Rancho boundaries. Lyman and Rich, however, insisted that the property must be purchased from them. A court decided against Benson, but encouraged by other Independents, he defied the court order and fortified the property by building ramparts and installing an old Mexican War cannon. Fort Benson, as the place was known, was maintained for about a year. He finally abandoned the property when the official survey determined that it was a part of the San Bernardino Rancho.

The dominance of the Mormons in the San Bernardino area came to a sudden halt with the recall of the colonists to Utah in late 1857, due to the imminent threat of hostilities between the Mormons of the Salt Lake Valley and the U.S. government. After the election of Buchanan as president, Brigham Young was replaced as territorial governor by a non-Mormon, who was accompanied on his journey to Utah by a large army contingent. Young, convinced that this was to be the beginning of another period of harassment and persecution, elected to concentrate his people in the Salt Lake Valley and, if necessary, fight the federal government to protect the Mormon heartland.

Young's decision to recall the San Bernardino colonists was probably not based entirely upon the threat of the U.S. army, however. He was never reconciled to the size and independence of the San Bernardino settlement. Lyman and Rich had already been called back to Salt Lake in April 1857, leaving the business affairs in the hands of a third partner, Ebenezer Hanks. In a sermon delivered in the summer of 1857, Young indicated his unhappiness with the growing dissension and apostasy in San Bernardino: "Were [Brother Lyman] to tell you of the true situation of that place, he would tell you that Hell reigns there, and that it is just about time for . . . every true Saint to leave that land."

In late October the colonists received word from Salt Lake to return to Utah. Something over half of the San Bernardino Mormons responded to the recall. The rest elected to remain. The hasty exodus of the returning Mormons required immediate sale of their land and the disposal of much of their personal property, providing the opportunity for those remaining in the valley to purchase at bargain prices. In February 1858 Hanks deeded the remaining unsold ranch property to William Conn, George Tucker, and Richard Allen for $18,000, enough to retire the outstanding debt.

The threatened hostilities between the Salt Lake Mormons and the U.S. army did not develop. After an amicable settlement had been reached, several Mormon families returned to California, but after the recall the San Bernardino Mormons had neither the numbers nor the discipline to again dominate the political affairs of the county. No Mormon church existed in the valley after the recall until 1864, when a

branch of the Reorganized Church of Jesus Christ of Latter Day Saints was started. This group, sometimes known as Josephites, were followers of Joseph Smith and did not recognize the Salt Lake leadership.

During San Bernardino's Mormon period, the federal government had studied a number of transportation routes into the southland. Possible railroad routes examined were a route approximating the 35th parallel, one through Cajon Pass, and another through San Gorgonio Pass. In 1857 Lt. Edgar Beale was commissioned to survey a wagon road to California, an extension of the already existing route to New Mexico. Beale's survey was unique in that he made use of camels as pack animals. They were obtained for the purpose by the War Department from Arabia and Asia Minor. A couple of camels and their riders left the main party in the desert and descended Cajon Pass to travel to San Bernardino and Los Angeles, arousing great interest among the citizens. Beale was astonished at the strength and the stamina of the camels, noting that each could carry an average load of 600 pounds for distances up to 30 miles a day. In correspondence to his superiors he praised their performance: "There was never anything so patient or enduring and so little troublesome as this noble animal. . . . They are the salt of the party and the noblest brute alive." In spite of Beale's enthusiasm, camel transport never caught on in America.

Of course the most traveled route into Southern California during the Mormon period was the road between San Bernardino and Salt Lake. Not only was it the route of new immigrants but in 1855 the company of Hopkins and Rollins began commercial freighting between the two Mormon centers. They were soon joined by the Los Angeles firm of Alexander and Banning. T.B. Sanford of the Los Angeles firm opened an easier wagon road over West Cajon through what became known as Sanford's Pass. By 1860 freight traffic had grown so that as many as 2,000 wagons crossed the Mojave Desert annually.

Another route into California was pioneered by the

Freighting wagons with their teams stand on D Street just north of 3rd Street in the 1890s. Freighting was an important occupation and San Bernardino became a transportation center because of Cajon Pass. From the Steele Collection. Courtesy, San Bernardino Redevelopment Agency, (SC, SBRA)

JOHANNESBURG

famous Butterfield Stages in 1858. Beginning in St. Louis, the line was originally projected to go through the San Bernardino Valley and over Cajon Pass, into the western Mojave Desert, and through the Central Valley to San Francisco. The route actually followed, however, was farther to the southwest—through Warner's Ranch and Temecula to Los Angeles. The city of San Bernardino was bypassed, with the stages going through San Bernardino County only in the Chino area. The announced reason for the change was the greater availability of water, but many San Bernardino citizens ascribed the change to the greater political influence of Los Angeles.

After 1851 there was constantly increasing wagon travel between San Bernardino and Los Angeles, carrying lumber and agricultural produce, mail, and passengers. Early travelers to Los Angeles had a choice of two routes. A southern route followed the Santa Ana River through Agua Mansa, then veered westward. A northern route went toward the mouth of Cajon Pass where it joined the road which followed the old Mojave Trail below the base of the mountains toward the coast. Jefferson Hunt, one of several Mormons in the freighting business, saw the desirability of a more direct route and initiated the construction of a road from San Bernardino straight west to Cucamonga, where it merged with the existing northern route. By 1858 a regular stage service had started, traveling by way of Cucamonga and El Monte. One-way fare between San Bernardino and Los Angeles was $8.

The best known and most traveled road from the Colorado River into Southern California in the 1860s was the Government Road from Fort Mojave into the San Bernardino Valley. Travel across the Mojave Desert had become increasingly hazardous in the late 1850s because of raids and ambushes by Mojaves and wandering Paiutes. Indian hostility frequently delayed the mail. In September 1858 Mojaves attacked a

Freighting has always been pictured as a hot and dusty business, but it could be cold, too. This borax wagon driven by Harry N. Carrow stands beside the Johannesburg Hotel and Teagle's General Store, around 1890. Courtesy, Fred E. Davis

wagon train from Santa Fe at the Colorado River crossing and killed several people. As a pacification move, in the spring of 1859 the army established Fort Mojave on the Arizona side of the river, about 12 miles upstream from present Needles. When provisions for the new fort could not be regularly supplied by river boat, a road was built across the desert to San Bernardino and supply wagons traveled to Fort Mojave monthly with a mounted escort for protection.

The establishment of Fort Mojave resulted in the successful pacification of the Mojave Indians, but small raiding Paiute bands continued to create problems for desert travelers. To provide greater protection the army constructed a number of small forts or redoubts along the Government Road. The principal western desert base was Camp Cady, situated near the forks where the Salt Lake Trail and the Government Road diverged. Other outposts were built at Soda Lake (Fort Soda or Hancock Redoubt), Marl Spring, Rock Spring, and in the Piute Range (Fort Piute). Redoubts were also built on the Salt Lake Trail at Bitter Spring and Resting Spring.

The desert forts were occupied for approximately a decade. Although originally established to protect the desert traveler, the forts served an additional military function during the Civil War, keeping the road to Southern California open for the Union, but denying the road to parties being recruited for the Confederate armies. By 1870 the army outposts had been abandoned but the Government Road continued in use until a rail line was built across the desert in the 1880s.

The desert Indians were not the only threat to public safety in the post-Mormon years. San Bernardino County experienced a period of increasing lawlessness following the Mormon recall. Law enforcement had been a minor problem before 1858. Not only were most residents law-abiding

Freighting wagons stand ready in front of the newspaper office. The San Bernardino Argus *was published from 1873 to 1878. (SPS)*

SAN BERNARDINO ARGUS

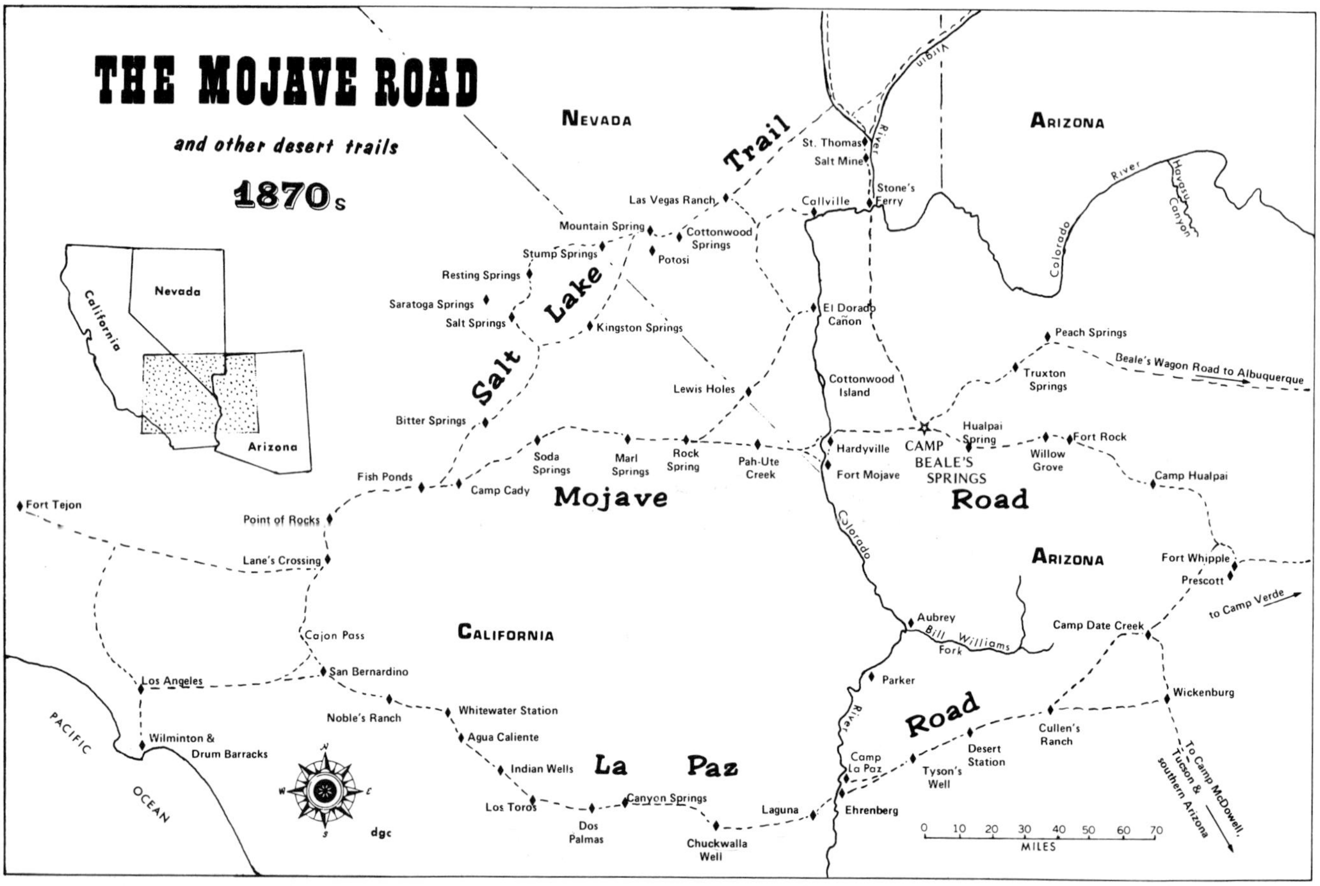

This map of desert trails of the 1870s shows the important shipping routes between San Bernardino and Los Angeles. From Reopening the Mojave Road, *by Dennis Casebier*

citizens but many disputes which might have ended up in the courts were resolved by counseling or arbitration by the church leaders. The departure of the Mormons resulted in a temporary weakening of civil authority, a weakening taken advantage of by lawless elements. Justice could not even be expected from the courts. Both judges and juries were sometimes intimidated to the degree that they acquitted obviously guilty parties, lest a guilty verdict bring about greater violence.

Lawlessness and vigilante justice became more prevalent after the discovery of gold in the San Bernardino Mountains. Following the initial rush to the northern California goldfields in 1849, many prospectors fanned out to other parts of the state seeking the precious metal. Some gold was found and recovered on the Amargosa River south of Death Valley in 1850. Later finds were made in the Leach Lake district north of Barstow and in Lytle Creek Canyon and Big Bear Valley. Southern California's biggest gold rush occurred, however, after the discovery of gold in Holcomb Valley.

When tracking a wounded grizzly in the spring of 1860, prospector-adventurer William F. Holcomb discovered placer gold in a valley north of Big Bear. By midsummer Holcomb Valley was full of prospectors. By fall some miners were making as much as $50 a day, and by 1861 the Holcomb Valley population had reached 2,000. Towns developed, the most important being Belleville, named for Belle Van

Dusen, whose mother had hurriedly made an American flag for a Fourth of July celebration. Stores and markets, restaurants and hotels, saloons and gambling dens sprang up, and Belleville soon outstripped San Bernardino in population. San Bernardino barely won an election to retain the county seat, but the story persisted in the mountains that the victory for San Bernardino was only won because a ballot box from Belleville was "accidently" kicked into a bonfire on election night.

The first route into Holcomb and Big Bear valleys was by a wagon road up the Santa Ana River and then by pack train over the mountains. Seeking an easier route, Holcomb Valley miners raised $1,500 and hired Jed Van Dusen, a local blacksmith, to build a wagon road down the north side of the mountains into the desert. There it met a toll road through Cajon Pass which had been recently completed by John Brown, Sr.

The Holcomb Valley gold rush was short-lived. The diggings were shallow and were worked out in a few years. However, the impact on San Bernardino County was great. An estimated $350,000 in gold was recovered from the area in 1861-1862. It brought a great influx of people into the county, many of whom were transients, ruffians, and outlaws. The normal processes of law and order could not keep up with the many quarrels and shootings which occurred. Forty or fifty men were shot, with few assailants being brought to justice through legal channels.

In the first years of the Civil War Holcomb Valley was a favorite recruiting ground for Confederate volunteers. Although California remained loyal to the Union, secessionist sentiment was strong in San Bernardino County. Dissatisfaction of many Southern Californians with the policies of the state government, dominated by the much larger population of the northern mining counties and the Bay Area, had led to proposals to divide the state. The imposition of a property tax was especially distasteful to many of the original Hispanic owners of the southland. In 1859 a proposal to divide the state was passed by the state legislature, and in a subsequent state referendum the measure got considerably more than the required

Third Street in San Bernardino about 1880 was unpaved and quiet. This view is looking east from E Street and features Quong Tung Hang's laundry. (SC, SBRA)

two-thi
approv
Howev
disregai

Duri
the stro
Valley.
Bernar
Confed
the chu
San Be
secessi
Sherm
Bernar
and su
were n

Sher
tales a
primar
conting
Sumne
army,

We are
secessi
over th
boldly
the ord
southe
endeav
have a
Morm
Englis
while
right i
desper
Monte
Los A

Alth
situati
investi
Carlet
soldie
law a

V.
Railroads, Orange Groves, and Desert Mines

During the three decades following the Civil War, San Bernardino County experienced phenomenal growth. This growth was stimulated by the construction of railroads linking Southern California with the rest of the nation. In the San Bernardino Valley the citrus industry flourished. Land developers laid the foundations for new communities and agricultural colonies and promoted the valley as a land of sunshine, orange blossoms, and healthful living. Taking advantage of bargain railroad fares, thousands of Easterners came to settle the new communities. The subsequent building boom accelerated lumbering activity in the mountains. In the deserts, mining was the key to growth. Mining of chemical salts such as borax from the desert's dry lakes became a major industry. But the most profitable mines of this period resulted from a series of discoveries of precious metals—silver and gold—which brought thousands to mining boom towns.

Although San Bernardino was the only real city in the county during and immediately after the Civil War, a number of small rural settlements were already in existence. East Highlands had been settled by Frederick Van Leuven and the Cram family during the Mormon period, and it gradually grew to a larger community, organizing its own school district in 1869. Lugonia and Crafton were settlements on the bench south of the Santa Ana River, east of the Old San Bernardino Mission District.

About 1870 a new community came into existence along the Santa Ana River southwest of San Bernardino. Encouraged by 1866 state legislation that promised a generous subsidy to foster a silk industry, a group of Los Angeles promoters organized the California Silk Center Association and bought a portion of the Jurupa Ranch. After a brief high-pressure promotion to plant mulberry trees, raise silkworms, and sell their eggs, the state subsidy was withdrawn, the potential silk boom collapsed, and the promoters sold their holdings to the Southern California Colony Association headed by Judge John S. North. North, a native of Tennessee and a good friend of President Lincoln, had come west as the appointed surveyor-general of Nevada, and then served for a time as the chief justice of the Territorial Supreme Court. In 1870 North sent out a call for colonists. His colony was first called Jurupa, but its name was soon changed to Riverside.

The development of other valley communities awaited the coming of rail transportation. During a 12-year period beginning in 1873, San Bernardino County was the scene of much railroad construction. By 1886 the San Bernardino Valley had gained access to the East through two transcontinental rail systems.

The first railroad into the county was constructed by the Southern Pacific, an offshoot of the Central Pacific, the company which had built the western portion of the first transcontinental railway. In 1873

Facing page: *More than one engine was needed to pull the long trains through Cajon Pass. Courtesy, Southern Pacific Transportation Company*

Southern Pacific began construction of a line eastward from Los Angeles. Since San Bernardino was the only settlement of size in the interior, its citizens felt that any railroad connecting Southern California with the East would logically pass through their city, located as it was below both Cajon and San Gorgonio passes. Late in 1873 representatives of the Southern Pacific asked San Bernardino to donate some land and purchase $100,000 in Southern Pacific bonds to insure the railroad's entry into the city. The city's businessmen held a meeting to consider the request and formed a committee to negotiate with Southern Pacific.

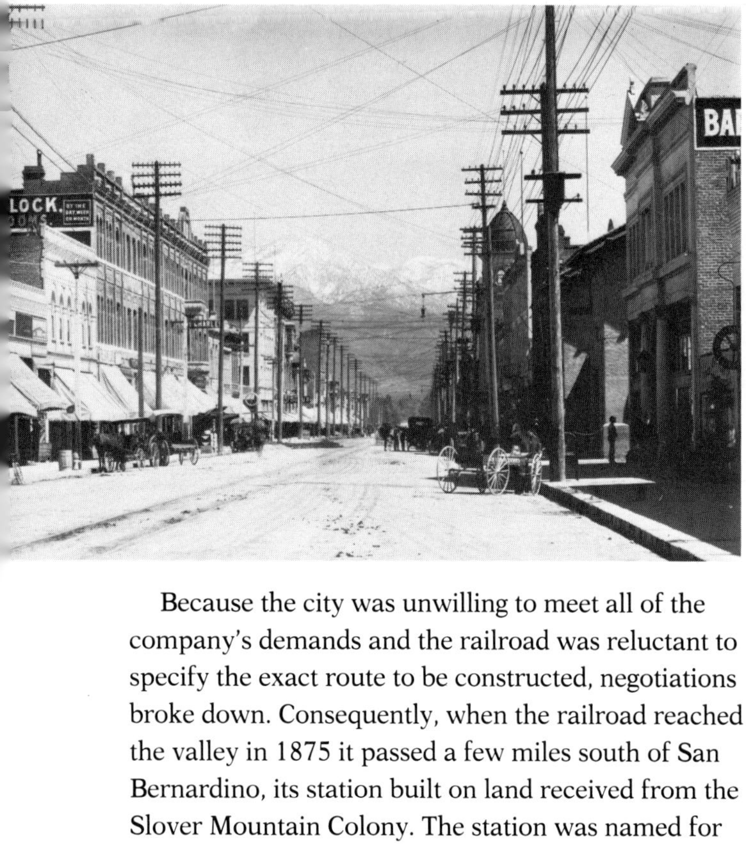

Third Street leads past Hotel Stewart and its tower on the right in San Bernardino at the turn of the century. (SPS)

Because the city was unwilling to meet all of the company's demands and the railroad was reluctant to specify the exact route to be constructed, negotiations broke down. Consequently, when the railroad reached the valley in 1875 it passed a few miles south of San Bernardino, its station built on land received from the Slover Mountain Colony. The station was named for David D. Colton, a Southern Pacific official. The first rail service between Colton and Los Angeles was limited to one train a week.

The Southern Pacific was also building a line from the San Francisco Bay area into Southern California as a part of a proposed southern transcontinental route. As originally planned the line was to go through the San Joaquin Valley, over Tehachapi Pass to the Mojave Desert, through Cajon Pass and the San Bernardino Valley, over San Gorgonio Pass and through the Coachella and Imperial valleys to Yuma. The Southern Pacific found its way blocked at Cajon Pass, however, for the most obvious route, through West Cajon, was already controlled by the Los Angeles and Independence Railroad, a small company planning a route across the desert to the newly opened silver mines in the Panamint Mountains. Thus thwarted, the Southern Pacific built through the Antelope Valley and Newhall Pass into the San Fernando Valley and Los Angeles. Los Angeles encouraged the move by levying a direct tax to raise $600,000 for the Southern Pacific Company. This line connecting northern and southern California was completed in 1876, and together with the extension to Colton, gave the San Bernardino area its first rail access to San Francisco and the northern transcontinental route. The Los Angeles and Independence Railroad never completed any major construction and the company was eventually acquired by the Southern Pacific, which now kept the rights to West Cajon only to keep out competition.

The Southern Pacific continued to build its line eastward from Colton to Yuma, and by 1881 San Bernardino County had access to a second transcontinental route, traversing the southern United States.

Congress also authorized the Southern Pacific to build a railroad across the desert from Mojave, on the San Francisco-Los Angeles route, to Needles, on the Colorado River. This line was to connect with one being built westward across New Mexico and Arizona by the Atlantic and Pacific Railroad (later Santa Fe).

The railroad dominated the town of San Bernardino, as is reflected in Napoleon B. Hale's advertising signs in 1906. (SPS)

Top: *The Needles roundhouse with 14 stalls was probably built in 1883 for the Southern Pacific Railroad. The Atlantic and Pacific Railroad acquired it in October 1884. On the right is the water tank. This view is circa 1890. Courtesy, Santa Fe Railway*

Bottom: *The first 10-stall roundhouse and 60-foot turntable, and machine and blacksmith shops of the California Southern headquarters were erected in 1887. In 1902 a new machine shop 200 feet by 120 feet was built. This machine shop view is circa 1926. From the Steele Collection. Courtesy, San Bernardino Public Library, (SC, SBPL)*

Such a desert line would give the Southern Pacific control over all rail routes into California.

Construction on the Mojave-Needles branch began in February 1882. Much of the work was done by Chinese laborers. They were taken in wagons to various points along the surveyed route and dropped off so that the roadbed was built in sections. In October 1882 the railroad reached the little mining settlement of Waterman on the north bank of the Mojave River. About ten miles farther east additional facilities were planned, with a coaling station, a telegraph and ticket office, and other passenger

accommodations. This settlement was named for John Daggett, a lieutenant governor of California who had mapped the new town and built the first house. A whimsical engineer named a series of small stations and sidings along the route in the mid-Mojave with names in an alphabetical sequence—Amboy, Bagdad, Cadiz, Danby, Essex, Fenner, Goffs, etc. The Mojave-Needles branch was completed in April 1883.

The Southern Pacific monopoly of rail travel in Southern California was soon challenged. In the late 1870s a competitive railroad, the California Southern, began construction of a line from National City in the San Diego area to San Bernardino. Completion of the line necessitated a crossing of the Southern Pacific tracks at Colton, but when construction reached that point in August 1882, the Southern Pacific denied permission to cross. The resulting court struggle lasted more than a year. To discourage any extra-legal action on the part of the California Southern or its sympathizers in San Bernardino, the Southern Pacific parked locomotives and cars on the track at the proposed crossing point, moving them only for passing trains. Guards were hired to prevent the installation of the necessary crossing "frog." After a year of squabbling the San Bernardino sheriff obtained a court order enjoining the Southern Pacific from further interference. Enthusiastic San Bernardino citizens armed with pickaxes and other tools accompanied the sheriff to Colton, where the court order was read. The order was not resisted, the Southern Pacific tracks were cut, a crossing frog spiked down, and a work train moved across it. The first California Southern train reached San Bernardino on September 13, 1883, to touch off a community celebration.

Another step in breaking Southern Pacific's railroad monopoly was the acquisition of the Mojave-Needles branch by the Santa Fe System, successors to the Atlantic and Pacific Railroad, which had completed its line to Needles. Dissatisfied with its transshipment arrangements with the Southern Pacific, the Santa Fe threatened to build another railroad across the Mojave Desert that would terminate on the coast at Port Hueneme in present Ventura County. Rather than face this competition the Southern Pacific in 1884 agreed to sell its Mojave-Needles right-of-way and existing rail facilities to the Santa Fe.

The Santa Fe further challenged Southern Pacific dominance by acquiring control of the California Southern in 1885. But it could not become a transcontinental competitor with Southern Pacific unless it gained direct access from the East or north

The original wooden station at Needles was a small one, but was enlarged in 1904, as shown here. Shortly after this it burned and was replaced by the present station. Courtesy, Santa Fe Railway

into Southern California. The Southern Pacific appeared to have all routes blocked, controlling the San Gorgonio and West Cajon passes, as well as the route directly north of Los Angeles.

The Southern Pacific monopoly was broken through the knowledge and efforts of Fred T. Perris, chief engineer of the California Southern. Perris was familiar with the topography of the Cajon Pass area and was aware that West Cajon was not the only possible access route into the valley. After meeting with some representatives of the Santa Fe System in San Diego, he conducted them on a tour of the Cajon Pass area. To thwart Southern Pacific personnel who followed him, Perris drove his buckboard, loaded with his guests and surveying instruments, through San Gorgonio Pass and into the Morongo Basin. Convinced that he was considering a Morongo route, which would have to utilize San Gorgonio Pass, the Southern Pacific party turned back. Perris then drove on through Old Woman Springs and the Lucerne Valley to East Cajon. There he showed the Santa Fe representatives the feasibility of a route about a thousand feet lower in elevation than West Cajon. The rights to the area were secured, and construction began on a line to connect San Bernardino with the Mojave-Needles branch at Waterman on the Mojave River. When this construction was completed in 1885, a second transcontinental line into Southern California became a reality.

Although the Santa Fe had intended to expand the facilities at Daggett as a division point, it found buying the needed additional land was far too expensive. The railroad employees, anticipating the company's need to purchase the land, had acquired much of it themselves as a speculative investment. Santa Fe then decided to move the division point west to Waterman Junction. There a large tract of land was acquired, a roundhouse built, and yard facilities constructed. The new settlement was renamed Barstow, for the president of the Santa Fe, William Barstow Strong.

Santa Fe's railway network spread as other connector lines were built between San Bernardino and Los Angeles. San Bernardino soon became identified as a Santa Fe town. In 1886 construction began on maintenance shops, a depot, and divisional offices on land provided by the city in the present Mount Vernon area. A number of short lines were also built to link San Bernardino with other points in the valley.

Railroad construction was only one stage in the accelerating economic development of the San Bernardino Valley. Another stimulus to growth was the increasing importance of citrus agriculture. The San Bernardino Valley possessed factors especially favorable for citrus culture—a soil of decomposed granite with good drainage, available water, abundant sunshine, and cool winter nights.

Oranges had been planted in the San Bernardino area in the 1850s, but major production followed the introduction and cultivation of the Washington navel orange. In 1873 Luther and Eliza Tibbetts of Riverside received from the U.S. Department of Agriculture two orange trees which had been budded from a mutant tree in Bahia, Brazil. The fruit from these trees were large, sweet, and seedless. The Tibbetts were soon besieged by nurserymen requesting cuttings, and from these parent trees the Washington navel orange industry developed. Increasing yields led to lower prices, and this in turn stimulated advertising and new marketing procedures. The first of several citrus fairs was held in Riverside in 1879. The first packing houses were built in the early 1880s, with oranges being graded and sized. An Orange Growers Protective Union was formed in 1883, and by 1886 it was sending representatives east to arrange for marketing the crops.

The fame of San Bernardino County oranges

Facing page, top: *Lucas Weiskoff drove the mule car in San Bernardino in 1889. The cars started in 1885 and stopped service in 1901. Their route ran from 3rd and K streets, east on 3rd Street, north on E Street to Hooperville. (SC, SBPL)*

Bottom: *Oscar Kohl married Emma Andreson in 1892. Oscar's brother Walter came to the wedding and fell in love with Emma's sister, Frances, and with the Harlem Motor Train. The train was in trouble financially because of the high cost of coal. Walter married Frances and acquired the railway in 1895. They converted the engine from coal to oil. (SC, SBPL)*

INSIDE
CITY STREET RAILWAY

Top: *The Santa Fe brought jobs and development to San Bernardino, which came to be known as a Santa Fe town. This 1910 view of the first Santa Fe depot shows the bustle of the busy station. This depot was constructed in 1886, and burned in 1916. (SPS)*

Bottom: *In 1918 this mission-style Santa Fe station opened to replace the depot that burned. This view is circa 1920. (SBPL)*

Top: *The hoist gang and electricians prepare to lift the body of a diesel locomotive from the trucks at the Santa Fe's San Bernardino shops. Steam locomotives can be seen beyond the diesel in this view from the late 1940s. Courtesy, Santa Fe Railway*

Bottom: *This view of the Santa Fe Railway's computerized classification yard in Barstow looks northeast to the mountains. The yard was opened in 1972. Courtesy, Santa Fe Railway*

spread nationwide. Citrus entries from the county won three gold medals at the Cotton Exposition in New Orleans in 1884. A citrus fair in Chicago in 1886 featuring San Bernardino County products attracted 75,000 people. Such publicity was a powerful magnet, drawing newcomers to Southern California.

The completion of the railroads linking the southland to the rest of the nation, together with the growing importance of citrus culture, made possible the spectacular land boom of the 1880s. San Bernardino County, and especially the valley area, was touted as a Garden of Eden, with the ideal climate for agriculture, for health, and for enjoyment. The boom was promoted by both the competing railroads (Southern Pacific and Santa Fe), and by local developers.

An intense rivalry for the passenger market erupted in 1886 between the Southern Pacific and

The Rialto Hotel is typical of the "boom" hotels that were built in the late 1880s in the towns along the railroad. (SPS)

Santa Fe. Passenger rates, which had been about $125 for a journey from the Missouri Valley to Southern California, plummeted to $100 as soon as the Santa Fe entered Southern California. For the next several months each line alternately cut their rates. In the early spring of 1887 the fare from Kansas City to Los Angeles had been reduced to $24, then $16. On one crazy day in March, the Southern Pacific met the Santa Fe's rate of $12, then in hours the fare dropped to $8, then $6, and $4, until at noon Santa Fe was offering the trip for $1. Such rates were very short-lived, but the rivalry did result in a great population influx into the southland.

About 30 new communities were started in the county during the boom period, about half of which survived. Many developments failed, or had their

Bottom: *To attract passengers on the Harlem Motor Train, the Kohl brothers developed Harlem Springs. They constructed bathhouses, a plunge, a dance floor, a roller-skating rink, and a steam merry-go-round. This view from the 1920s shows an improved bathhouse. (SC, SBPL)*

Top: *Fred T. Perris came to San Bernardino from Australia in 1853. He surveyed the Cajon Pass railroad route, and broke the Southern Pacific monopoly, allowing the Santa Fe to link San Diego, San Bernardino, and Barstow by rail. Courtesy, Mrs. Opal Perris*

EDUCATION IN THE COUNTY

The first building of the University of Redlands was erected in 1909. The front and back of the building were designed alike so that the campus could develop in either direction. Courtesy, A.K. Smiley Public Library

Education has been a concern of the citizens of San Bernardino County from the time of settlement by the Mormons. The first permanent school building in the county was built by them near Warm Creek in 1854. The Warm Springs Elementary School of the San Bernardino Unified School district is still located at that site. After the population boom of the 1880s and 1890s, 55 elementary school districts were organized in the county. Children usually were expected to walk to school, substantial distances in some cases. When improved public transportation developed, schools could be farther apart and unification of some small districts became possible.

Until the 1880s any education beyond the elementary level had to be supported by private means. In the mid-1860s a "collegiate school" to prepare students for college work was run by J.C. Alsop in the former home of Mormon settler Jefferson Hunt on San Bernardino's 5th Street. Gradually the number of such schools increased. In 1870 St. Catherine's Academy was started at the corner of 5th and E streets by the Sisters of the Immaculate Heart. Paine's Academy and Business School was established in San Bernardino in 1873.

In 1881 David Sturges, then county superintendent of schools, founded the San Bernardino Academy and Business College, a private school charging tuition. In 1885 N.A. Richardson, the principal of a San Bernardino elementary school, began offering regular secondary-level classes, and four years later San Bernardino turned out its first graduates from a public high school. San Bernardino High School was officially organized under state law in 1891, and a public high school building was built at 8th and E streets. In the same year Redlands, Lugonia, and Crafton school districts united to form a Redlands High School District. Colton High School dates back to 1895, and both Ontario and Chino organized high school districts in 1897. In 1901 Ontario joined with Upland to form a union high school district.

In 1915 San Bernardino High School classes moved to new buildings at 18th and E streets, leaving the old high school to become an intermediate school. The old building was badly damaged by an earthquake in the summer of 1923. It was condemned, razed, and replaced with a new building dedicated to David Struges, Sturges Junior High School, which finally closed in 1968.

The first college in San Bernardino County was planned by the Chaffey brothers as a part of their Ontario colony. Twenty acres were set aside for an agricultural college campus, and the cornerstone of a college building was laid in March 1883. Management of the college was placed under the direction of the Board of Trustees of the University of Southern California, then only a small Methodist college in Los Angeles. The union with USC was dissolved by mutual consent in 1906 and the school, now Chaffey Union High School and College of Agriculture, continued to function on its own. In 1916 the college reorganized to become the county's first junior college.

San Bernardino and Colton were next in establishing a junior college district. In 1926 a college was organized under the leadership of N.A. Richardson. While construction was under way on a campus located midway between downtown Colton and San Bernardino, classes were held in the local high schools. The new campus was occupied in the fall of 1927. Student population growth in the years after World War II resulted in the expansion of the San Bernardino Valley College campus and the construction of many new buildings. A second campus, Crafton Hills College, was built in Yucaipa and welcomed its first class in the fall of 1972.

The Barstow Community College

Warm Springs School opened in 1857 in an adobe building. A log building served from 1864 to 1873. This clapboard school was built in 1874. Warm Springs School now has a modern building on Sterling Avenue. (SPS)

was the first college to be organized in the desert. It began offering evening classes at Barstow Union High School in 1960, followed two years later by day classes at the First Methodist Church. Construction of its own campus began in the spring of 1963, with the students moving in a year later. The Victor Valley Community College, also organized in 1960, moved to its own campus in 1965.

The University of Redlands was the first four-year institution of higher learning in San Bernardino County. In 1907 Jasper Newton Field, the minister of the First Baptist Church of Redlands, took the lead in convincing an American Baptist search committee to consider a local site for a new Baptist college. A gift of land from Karl C. Wells, an endorsement by the Redlands Chamber of Commerce with a pledge of $50,000 from the citizens of Redlands, and the support of the neighboring communities of San Bernardino and Colton were factors in ensuring the choice of Redlands as the site for the college. Reverend Field was appointed as its first president. By 1909 an administration and classroom building was completed, allowing 9 professors and 52 students to begin classes. More buildings were constructed before World War I, dormitories were added in the 1920s, and the University of Redlands gradually took on its present form. It has developed a reputation as one of the outstanding liberal arts institutions of the nation.

The Loma Linda Sanitarium, opened by the Seventh-Day Adventists in 1905, expanded in 1909 to become the College of Medical Evangelists. This was the precursor to Loma Linda University, which was organized in 1961 to consolidate the medical, nursing, and paramedical programs. A seven-story medical center completed in 1967 houses the hospital, classrooms, laboratories, and offices, and serves as the educational heart of the Seventh-Day Adventist medical network, which extends all over the world.

The newest of the institutions of higher learning in the county is the California State College at San Bernardino. Among the youngest of the 19 colleges in the California State University and College System, Cal State-San Bernardino opened its doors to freshmen, sophomores, and juniors in the fall of 1965. Initially offering six degree programs to 300 students, the college has grown to an enrollment of over 5,000 students, with a curriculum offering 36 baccalaureate and 9 master degree programs.

San Bernardino County now offers a wide variety of educational opportunities at both public and private institutions at all levels of learning. Also within close commuting distance from the metropolitan area of the county are other institutions of higher learning—the University of California at Riverside and the Claremont Colleges just across the county line in Los Angeles County.

names changed, or were absorbed by neighboring communities. Ioamosa, Grapeland, Urbita, Rosena, Rochester, North Ontario, Gladystra, Drew, Brookside, Arrowhead, Messina, Lugonia, and Mound City are place names now largely forgotten. Boom period communities that survived include Etiwanda, Ontario, Redlands, Chino, Rialto, Mentone, Highland, Bloomington, and Hesperia. Mound City became Loma Linda, Lugonia became a part of Redlands, and what was North Ontario became Upland.

Exaggeration and dishonesty were not unknown in sales promotions aimed at potential Eastern buyers. One promoter brought oranges from the San Bernardino Valley to Hesperia in the high desert and wired them onto Joshua trees. The region was then advertised as the only place in Southern California

where oranges were indigenous. Subdividers in both Urbita and Mentone alluded to their famous "beach."

The San Bernardino Valley was touted as a health resort. Such claims, dating back to the 1860s, emphasized the virtues of the climate and the curative powers of the many natural hot springs. In 1863 Dr. David Smith built a road to the Arrowhead Springs and constructed a small building to serve as a treatment house. This building was enlarged in the 1870s to house a number of guests in single rooms. These facilities were replaced in the 1880s by a 40-room, three-story hotel. Two more 40-room units were added in the boom period, providing a total of 120 rooms. These buildings burned before the turn of the century and were replaced by a second hotel structure in 1900. Promotional literature not only emphasized the beneficial results of bathing in the waters of the hot springs, but stressed their curative powers when taken internally:

The waters of the hot springs . . . hold, in a more perfect solution than the ingenuity of man can devise, certain simple yet powerful minerals which, when taken into the stomach, quickly find their way into the blood and neutralize the germs of obstinate and malignant diseases.

Crafton, in the eastern end of the valley, also gained fame as a health resort in the 1870s. Dr. Peacock, a San Bernardino physician, persuaded Myron H. Crafts to take in a sick man who could find no other suitable accommodations. The invalid did so well that others soon sought to follow his example, and Crafts found himself operating a sanatarium. "Crafton Retreat" also served as an early convention center, hosting meetings of the Pacific Press Association and the General Assembly of the Congregational Churches of Southern California. Crafts offered 40 acres of land to the latter group for a college site, but the Assembly decided to build a college in the Pomona area instead.

Boosters heralded each of their communities as an ideal health center. Colton was "free from all malarial influences, and has probably as desirable a climate for invalids as any place on the coast." "If there is any place on earth with a perfect climate, that place is Crafton!" Riverside was the "asthmatics paradise," and San Bernardino was "the garden of Southern

Facing page, top: *The arrowhead which has become a symbol of the county and the city is a natural formation. (SBCMA)*

Facing page, bottom: *George Chaffey placed Euclid Avenue stretching eight miles from the foothills south. Courtesy, Ontario Public Library (OPL)*

Above: *The Ontario bandstand, shown here circa 1903, in the center of Euclid Avenue, stood high above the ground. In 1905 the lower part of the stand was removed so that the stand was much shorter. The bandstand was moved to Nugent Park in 1909. (OPL)*

SOUTHERN
Towne-Allison Drug Co.
Store No. 4
4 State Stores
EASTMAN FILMS
The Rexall Store
SUNFREZE
CALIFORNIA DAIRIES INC
HOTEL

ANTLERS HOTEL
ABSOLUTELY FIREPROOF
ANTLERS HOTEL
COFFEE SHOP
Restaurant
Antlers
ANTLERS HOTEL
HOTEL
Liquors
Barber Shop
Antlers

Facing page, top: *Railroads made tourism big business in San Bernardino County. Old hotels were renewed, and new hotels sprang up. The Southern Hotel was built on the site of the old Bella Union in San Bernardino in 1889. Hotels occupied this southeast corner of 4th and D streets for 90 years. (SC, SBPL)*

Facing page, bottom: *The Antlers Hotel, shown here in 1953, stood on E Street. Its interior featured antlered animal heads mounted on the walls. (SC, SBPL)*

The Starke Hotel stagecoach stopped for a picture in front of the Garner Block. (SPS)

The Stewart Hotel was built in 1887, and in one of the worst fires in the area's history, burned down in 1892. This building replaced it in 1893. Inside the hotel (right) were a handsome cigar store, a bank, a Santa Fe ticket office, and other fine shops. The top floor of this building burned on Thanksgiving Day, 1935. (SC, SBPL)

Pine's Hotel, a two-story adobe building with 30 rooms, opened in 1858 at the corner of 3rd Street and Arrowhead Avenue. August Starke bought the hotel, and in 1870 added an adobe wing of 25 rooms. In 1880 the 50-room brick hotel shown here replaced the adobe. For many years Starke's Hotel was a center of social life in San Bernardino. (SC, SBPL)

California" whose climate was "good for rheumatism." In Ontario "there is not an acre of marsh or fen; not a rod over which malaria dare hover; scarcely a foot which the health giving sunshine does not bless."

Two of the first communities to be developed in the 1880s were Etiwanda and Ontario. Both were creations of George Chaffey, a Canadian-born engineer who came to Riverside in 1880. The following year, in partnership with his brother William, he purchased a part of the Garcia Ranch about 15 miles west of San Bernardino. Here he established an agricultural colony and named it Etiwanda after an Indian chieftain of the Great Lakes area. The land was divided into ten-acre parcels, and a sales promotion was carried on in the Midwestern United States and Canada. Within eight months 140 lots had been sold.

One of the keys to Chaffey's success as a developer was his creation of a "mutual water company" in which each landowner became a stockholder. The mutual water company acquired all the water rights for a fixed area and insured each land parcel an equitable share of water regardless of its location in the settlement or its distance from the water source. With an assured supply of irrigation water the little settlement of Etiwanda flourished.

Chaffey put his engineering skills to another use. He set up an electric generator run by a water wheel in Day Canyon, and used the current generated to illuminate his house. He installed an electric arc light on a tower above the roof of his house which could be seen at night from San Bernardino and Riverside.

The success of the Etiwanda community led to a larger development a few miles farther to the west. In 1882 Chaffey purchased 6,000 acres below the mouth

of San Antonio Canyon. Here he developed the famous Ontario colony, named after his native province in Canada. All basic improvements were installed before any land was sold. Streets were laid out and water made available to every parcel of land. A large boulevard, 200 feet wide and 8 miles long, passed through the center of the tract to the foothills. This thoroughfare, Euclid Avenue, was planted with trees especially resistant to heat and drought. One square mile was set aside as a townsite, with half of the area deeded to trustees for the endowment of an agricultural college. Twenty acres along Euclid Avenue were set aside for the college campus. To insure a "better" class of residents, Chaffey insisted that each deed to property contain a clause forbidding the sale of alcoholic beverages.

The Ontario colony was a huge success, its growth stimulated by the land boom. People came from all

Left: *Ontario used a mule car on the eight-mile long Euclid Avenue from 1887 to 1896. The unusual feature was a platform that was pulled out for the mules to ride on the downgrade. (OPL)*

Above: *A streetcar ran down the center divider of Euclid Avenue in the 1920s. Courtesy, Upland Public Library*

This North Ontario packing house used "Upland" labels. This photo is unusual in that it shows only men in an occupation in which women became very important. (OPL)

over to study this method of colonization. A model of the colony was exhibited at the St. Louis World's Fair in 1904.

Ontario began as an agricultural, primarily fruit-growing settlement. Citrus culture developed rapidly, but the olive industry was also important. In 1892 the C.C. Graeber Company was organized by two brothers from Indiana. This firm still continues to process and can olives, maintaining the same high standards that insured them initial success. The Armstrong Nurseries also date back to the 1890s.

Public transportation on Euclid Avenue was provided by a mule-drawn railway car. Two mules would pull the car up the two percent grade from Ontario to San Antonio Heights at the base of the mountains. The car returned back to Ontario, down grade, by gravity, with the mules riding on a special platform. The trip up to the end of the railway took an hour; the ride back, only 20 minutes. The round-trip fare was 25 cents.

As in Etiwanda, water was supplied to the settlers through membership in a mutual water company. However, Chaffey kept the rights for the use of the water to generate electricity. This was to implement a plan, not immediately fulfilled, to furnish electricity to the colony's settlers. With the construction of a generating plant by the San Antonio Light and

The Ontario Power Company built a power house, nicknamed the "Stone Castle," in 1895 in San Antonio Heights. Earl Richardson, who later developed the Hotpoint iron, was put in charge of the power house. He and his wife and daughter lived in two tents pitched beside the plant. (OPL)

Top: *Richard Gird persuaded the Oxnard brothers to build the American Beet Sugar factory in 1890. Courtesy, Chino Valley Historical Society*

Bottom: *This electric substation was built in 1909 on Euclid Avenue. Courtesy, Upland Public Library*

Electric Power Company in 1891, Ontario could claim the first commercially successful hydroelectric plant in the West. Electricity produced was used in Ontario, Pomona, and Riverside, and soon a 28-mile power line was built to San Bernardino.

In 1886 the Chaffeys sold their interest in the Ontario Land and Improvement Company and migrated to Australia to meet new challenges. George Chaffey was drawn back to California around the turn of the century and continued his involvement in irrigation plans, this time in the Imperial Valley.

In 1887 the Bedford brothers purchased a tract north of Ontario on the Santa Fe right-of-way. There they created another development, naming it Magnolia, but the area became better known as North Ontario. In 1902 this settlement changed its name to Upland.

As the Chaffeys were to the development of Etiwanda and Ontario, so was Richard Gird to Chino. The Chino Ranch suffered difficult times following the death of Isaac Williams in 1864, and the ranch and some additional lands were purchased in 1881 by Richard Gird, a millionaire who had made his fortune in the Tombstone mining district of Arizona. Gird imported dairy cattle, building up a herd of 200 milk cows, a prelude to Chino's more recent role as the dairy center of Southern California. In 1887 he subdivided half of the ranch into ten-acre farms and set aside a section of land for the townsite of Chino. A narrow-gauge railway was built to connect with the Southern Pacific line at Ontario. Gird also established a newspaper, the *Chino Champion,* and housed it in the new business block of the city.

Gird had dreams of making Chino an industrial center as well as an agricultural one. He organized the Chino Valley Manufacturing Company, planning to develop an iron and steel industry, complete with blast furnaces and rolling mills. The iron ore could be obtained from discoveries made in the Cronise and

The mountains are the backdrop for 2nd Street, in Upland. The Fruit Exchange office is in the lower right corner. Oranges and lemons were the main crops. (OPL)

N. KLINDT
GROCERIES
AND
CROCKERY
With
BRADLEY'S PAINT
PRINTING
ROY CREIGHTON
UPLAND
SECOND-HAND

Kelso areas of the Mojave Desert. But the collapse of the land boom at the end of the 1880s put an end to his plan for an iron industry—the necessary capital for development was no longer available.

Gird was more successful in developing a sugar industry. Becoming interested in growing sugar beets, Gird in 1891 persuaded the Oxnard brothers to build a sugar beet factory. Specialized machinery was imported from Germany. Gird gave the Oxnards 2,500 acres of land and agreed to plant much of his own land to sugar beets. By 1895 the Chino area was planted to over 5,000 acres of beets, a figure that was doubled two years later.

In the eastern valley the community of Redlands owed its origin to two far-seeing developers, Frank E. Brown and Edward G. Judson. In 1881 they bought 320 acres from the Southern Pacific, then added more until they had acquired about 4,000 acres south of Lugonia and the Mill Creek Zanja. They named their planned community Redlands, after the reddish color of the earth, and began a vigorous promotion campaign publicizing the area with a picturesque map showing the names of the principal streets, (which had not yet been surveyed). To provide water, the developers organized the Redlands Water Company, purchased 50 shares of Santa Ana water from the South Fork Ditch, and had a six-mile ditch dug to transport the water to Reservoir Canyon, where it was stored behind an earthen dam.

It soon became apparent that if Redlands were to prosper it would need more water than could be provided by the 50 shares of South Fork stock. Upon the recommendation of Dr. Ben Barton, a pioneer physician, Brown checked out Big Bear Valley in the San Bernardino Mountains as a potential reservoir site and found it ideal. Brown secured a 20-day option and in that time got sufficient financial support to organize the Bear Valley Land and Water Company. He gathered $30,000 to purchase the needed land. Additional money was raised to build a dam, construction of which began in June 1884.

Construction of the Bear Valley dam was a major engineering effort. A temporary earthen dam was first built upstream to retain the water of Bear Creek while the lower part of a permanent masonry dam was built in the rocky gorge at the outlet of the valley. Approximately 100 men were employed on the project. Granite blocks were quarried from the nearby hillside. Horse and mule teams hauled cement and heavy supplies from Colton and San Bernardino,

traveling through Cajon Pass, Lucerne Valley, and up the Cushenbury Grade—a round trip of 10 to 12 days. Some lighter supplies were carried by pack trains up the Santa Ana Canyon and over the mountains by the Clark Grade, a route that took them to nearly 8,000 feet in elevation.

The dam was completed in December 1884. It was 335 feet across the crest and 64 feet in height. The cost of the project was $75,000.

Now an adequate water supply, guaranteed by the Big Bear project, insured the continued growth of Redlands and the citrus area of the eastern valley. The building of a Santa Fe branch line to Redlands cemented Lugonia and Redlands into one community.

Above: *The Bedford brothers built the Magnolia Villa in 1887 as a focal point for their land development. (OPL)*

Facing page, top: *Richard Gird bought the Chino ranch in 1881. In 1887 he subdivided the ranch and platted the town. Courtesy, Chino Valley Historical Society*

Facing page, bottom: *A dam built in 1884 made Big Bear Lake. The dam of rock and cement in a single arch was only 53 feet high and could not impound enough water to fill all the obligations of the water company. Another company, the Bear Valley Mutual Water Company, was formed, and in 1910 built a new dam which raised the water level to 72 feet. Courtesy, Joe Elliott*

In an election held in November 1888, the old Lugonia and the new Redlands were incorporated under the name of Redlands.

Redlands soon became the country's most famous winter residential city, especially after the arrival of the Smiley brothers in 1889. Albert and Alfred Smiley, wealthy resort owners from the East, purchased 200 acres in Redlands on the heights overlooking the San Bernardino Valley and San Timoteo Canyon. Here they built their homes and developed the area into Canyon Crest Park, more popularly known as Smiley Heights. The Smileys planted over one thousand varieties of trees and shrubs and Smiley Heights became one of the great showplaces of the southland. Tourist trains stopped so that passengers could tour the estate and admire the plantings and the scenery. Writers waxed eloquent, as illustrated by a contemporary account in *Out West* magazine:

This magnificent park is, without question, the most original in conception, the most perfect in detail, the most fascinating in the scenery which it commands, of all the beautiful places made possible by the

marvelously fertile soil and balmy climate of Southern California.

Smiley Heights was visited by three U.S. presidents—William McKinley, Theodore Roosevelt, and William Howard Taft.

Many other wealthy families from the East and Midwest made Redlands their winter home, building their mansions on the heights overlooking the valley and the city. Some journeyed westward each fall in their private railroad cars. A few purchased additional land to become the owners of orange groves, becoming a part of a new rural-urban aristocracy, unique to Southern California.

In 1892 the Redlands Electric Light and Power Company built the world's first successful three-phase hydroelectric plant below the mouth of Mill Creek Canyon. The dynamos, built by the General Electric Company, then a small Eastern firm, were driven by undershot Pelton waterwheels, and produced more electricity than was being used in all Southern California at that time.

Another valley development was planned by the Semi-Tropic Land and Water Company, organized by two Los Angeles bankers in 1887. The company purchased 28,500 acres of land west of Lytle Creek

This excursion car of the San Bernardino Traction Company stopped in front of Redlands City Hall for this 1908 photo. The car seated 90, nearly double the number of passengers on a regular car. There were two of these cars; they were eventually scrapped in 1928. Courtesy, Charles McLaughlin

POLITICAL DEVELOPMENT

Throughout its history San Bernardino County has experienced both changes in its size and arguments over the location of its seat of government. The city of San Bernardino has been the county seat since the county was first organized in 1853. At that time it was the only populated center, and it incorporated as a town the following year. The Mormon Council House served as the first courthouse. In 1862 the county purchased the Charles Glasier home, between 3rd and 4th streets on "E," and remodeled it for use as a courthouse. In 1874 it was replaced on the same site by a two-story building with a central tower and dome at a cost of $25,000.

With the boom of the 1880s, when many new communities came into being, the need for a new courthouse became apparent. In 1887 the county supervisors placed a $175,000 bond issue on the ballot for the construction of a new courthouse in San Bernardino. Although the measure gained a majority of the votes cast, it did not receive the two-thirds necessary for passage. The greatest opposition came from the Riverside community, but other towns such as Redlands and Colton opposed the new construction because they had hopes of gaining the county seat for themselves. A second bond issue for $75,000 to build a Hall of Records was proposed by the supervisors and also failed. The Board of Supervisors then imposed a direct tax, the income of which was used to build a Hall of Records adjacent to the 1874 courthouse. This new building of local Mentone sandstone and Colton marble was completed in 1891.

The arbitrary action of the supervisors intensified the intracity rivalries and led eventually to the formation of Riverside County. An anti-San Bernardino faction, mostly from Riverside, first circulated a petition to move the seat of government, but no election was called when it was disclosed that many signatures were fraudulent, some having been copied from a San Francisco directory. Colton then made a bid for the county seat, offering a block of land and pledging a $200,000 building, but this was not acceptable to either San Bernardino or Riverside. In January 1891, Riverside dissenters called for the creation of their own county. Such a bill was introduced in the state legislature but was defeated because of the opposition of the San Bernardino County supervisors. A second attempt in the legislature to split Riverside from San Bernardino County was successful in February 1893. The new county was created from a large portion of northern San Diego County and the extreme southern part of San Bernardino County, which included the San Gorgonio Pass communities of Beaumont and Banning as well as Riverside.

The old courthouse, a white two-story wooden building, was built in 1874 for $25,000. The sudden expansion of San Bernardino County in 1886 made the old building inadequate. The new courthouse was finally finished in 1898 and was joined to the old courthouse with a walkway. (SPS)

After a second bond issue to build a new courthouse in San Bernardino failed, the supervisors imposed another direct tax to raise the necessary money. The new courthouse, when completed, was a three-story building of red Mentone sandstone, located on the southeast corner of Court and "E" streets, in front of the 1874 building. The building with its clock tower was demolished in 1928 after the construction of a new courthouse on Arrowhead Avenue in 1927. The old courthouse clock, in storage for over 40 years, is now housed in a special enclosure in front of the San Bernardino City Convention Center. A massive new county building, completed in 1984, has been added to the complex of county buildings now in use.

The Phinney Block built in Redlands in 1893 housed the Board of Trade. It was lavishly decorated for President Theodore Roosevelt's visit in 1901. Since the board, or Chamber of Commerce, moved out, the building has been used for different enterprises: a bottling company, upholsterer, offices, and restaurant. Courtesy, A.K. Smiley Public Library

and made plans for three townsites. Rights to some Lytle Creek water were obtained and a canal and water distribution system built.

Rialto, one of the three townsites, was first settled by a group of Kansas Methodists headed by Reverend T.C. Miller who proposed to establish a "congenial" colony and a college. The town was laid out along the new Santa Fe railroad linking San Bernardino to Los Angeles. In 1888 a second settlement was platted southwest of Rialto. It was named Bloomington by an official of the company, who was apparently impressed by the profusion of wild flowers in the area. Except in the proposed business section, the land was subdivided and sold in 20-acre tracts. The community of Rosena (present Fontana) was also laid out, but no development took place at that time, perhaps because of the lack of a reliable source of water and the collapse of the land boom, the result of depression and overdevelopment that affected all of the southland.

With the collapse of the boom of the 1880s, the Semi-Tropic Land and Water Company was unable to meet its financial obligations, and much of the property was taken over by its San Francisco creditors. Rialto and Bloomington survived as small communities, both largely dependent upon citrus culture. In Rialto, the proposed Methodist colony did not survive and the college never materialized, but several of the original families remained as permanent residents. In Bloomington about 200 acres were planted in citrus, a school was built, and a small business district was laid out.

Loma Linda had very inauspicious beginnings. When the Southern Pacific was building its railroad through the San Bernardino Valley a small station was built a few miles east of Colton and named Mound Station. In 1875 a Mound City Land Company was incorporated but failed in its attempt to establish a community. Another try was made in 1887 with the organization of the Mound City Land and Water Company. A resort hotel was built on the small hill which gave the area its name and a townsite was planned around it. Again the venture was not successful. Around the turn of the century a group of Los Angeles businessmen and physicians organized the Loma Linda Association and purchased the site. They refurbished the hotel and landscaped the area in the hope of developing a resort hotel catering to health-seekers. Their hopes did not materialize, the hotel closed in 1904, and what had been Loma Linda became "Lonesome Linda" to many valley citizens. The following year the property was purchased by the Seventh Day Adventists who eventually developed what was at first only a "sanitarium and vegetarian hotel" into a great medical center and university.

Even after the peak of the great land boom, development continued eastward. The townsite of Mentone was laid out on the Santa Fe Loop Line by the Pacific Land Improvement Company, a subsidiary of Santa Fe. The drought of the 1890s and the lack of

a dependable source of irrigation water discouraged early attempts at orange growing, but eventually this small community east of Redlands was surrounded by groves.

Most of the San Bernardino Valley communities which were established in the 1880s and 1890s owed their growth during the subsequent decades to citrus agriculture. An "orange belt" was created extending from the eastern San Bernardino Valley westward into Los Angeles County and southwest through Riverside and Corona into Orange County. Oranges became the most important agricultural commodity in San Bernardino County, a position held from 1890 through World War II.

Although Colton originated as a railroad town, it, too, owed much of its early growth to the citrus industry. By 1889 it claimed to be the leading citrus shipping point in California, with 581 carloads of fruit being carried by the Southern Pacific. The following year over 800 carloads were sent east. In 1892 the Colton Fruit Exchange, a growers' cooperative, was formed. This became the Southern

President McKinley visited Redlands May 8, 1901, and was driven behind a team of matched white horses to Casa Loma Hotel. The hotel opened February 25, 1896, and became a girls' dormitory for the University of Redlands around 1950. After a last sentimental dinner on April 22, 1955, the hotel was torn down. (SBCMA)

California Fruit Exchange a year later. A large packing house, known as the "Pavilion," was built at 10th and I streets, with the grading and packing machinery installed on moveable bases so that they could be pushed aside, permitting the building to be used as a community center.

Most of the early groves were from 10 to 25 acres, with many of the owners being elderly and conservative types who had "retired to an orange grove." Membership in the fruit growers' exchange permitted "leisure farming," with the exchange being able to handle any phase of production—cultivation, irrigation, spraying, picking, packing, and shipping.

Lemons and grapefruit were also grown. Lemons, more susceptible to frost damage, were often grown upslope from the oranges, and were more commonly grown in the county's "West End." Although grapefruit thrive on the summer heat, they, too, were more frost-sensitive and were more successfully grown in Riverside's Coachella Valley.

Another contributor to the agricultural economy in the San Bernardino Valley was the grape industry. Although the famous vineyards in Cucamonga were not started until the 1900s, the Muscat raisin grape was introduced in 1870. George Lord introduced this grape in the hope of promoting a raisin industry, having noted that the local climate was apparently similar to those areas of Spain where the bulk of the world's raisin crop was grown. The raisin industry proved quite successful and many acres were planted to Muscats. Some growers made up to $500 an acre on raisins, but $200 to $250 was a more common return. Production in San Bernardino County declined, however, when vineyards in the San

This post card shows lemons harvested in an orchard. Courtesy, Norman Sturgess

Joaquin Valley, where better drying conditions existed, came into production. Many local vineyards were rooted out and replaced with navel oranges.

The building boom of the 1880s accelerated lumbering activity in the San Bernardino Mountains, mostly in the area north of the crest between Mormon Springs (Crestline) and Hunsacker Flat (Running Springs). Large steam-powered sawmills were located in Grass Valley, Little Bear Valley (now Lake Arrowhead), Strawberry Flats, Kuffel Canyon, and Burnt Mill Canyon. Each year they produced between five and six million board feet of lumber, mostly pine.

The last area of the mountains to experience large-scale logging was an 8,000-acre tract of timber along the mountain crest at the head of City Creek. This operation, the largest in the county's history, was started in the 1890s by the Michigan Lumber Company, which sold out to Robert E. Brookings in 1898. A mill was built at Fredalba, below Running Springs, just off the present City Creek road. Several miles of narrow-gauge railway along the crest linked the areas of clear-cutting with the mill at Fredalba.

Four- and six-horse teams hauled the lumber down a steep, dangerous road built by the company through City Creek Canyon to the valley. Some of the lumber went to a box factory built in the early 1900s at Molino, on the Santa Fe loop line just east of Highland. About 50 men were employed there manufacturing packing boxes for the many citrus packing houses of the valley.

Bottom: *Lumber was cut in the San Bernardino Mountains as early as 1852 to build the new Mormon settlement. Part of the lumber was sold in Los Angeles to help pay off the Mormons' mortgage on Rancho San Bernardino. (SC, SBPL)*

Top: *Brookings Lumber Company bought the Highland Lumber Company in 1898, and improved the mill at Fredalba. At first they used wagons to haul the logs but later they built a narrow gauge railroad. The company ceased lumbering about 1911 after most of the timber was cut. (SBCMA)*

Randsburg in 1897 near the prosperous Yellow Aster Mine bustled with loaded wagons in the street. The structures look flimsy, and indeed in 1898 the town burned and had to be rebuilt. (SC, SBPL)

The Brookings operation in the mountains ceased after the Fredalba mill burned in 1910. The railroad was scrapped, the equipment sold, and the company moved on to Oregon. In future years concern with watershed protection and recreational usage would reduce lumbering activities in San Bernardino to the selective cutting of diseased or fire-damaged trees.

Mining was the key to development in the desert throughout the late 19th century; in fact, the value of the county's mineral production exceeded that of agriculture.

Silver mining was of great importance to the economy, especially in the last decades of the 19th century. Silver ore was first discovered at Ivanpah in the Clark Mountain region in 1865. During the 1870s Ivanpah was the chief silver-producing region in the state. At first, lacking processing facilities, the rich ore was transported by team over 250 miles to San Pedro from where it was shipped overseas to smelters in Wales. Stamp mills and a reduction plant were finally built at the mines. Ivanpah had a reputation for being a quiet, law-abiding town, but in keeping with Western mining camp tradition, even here the saloons remained open around the clock. Activity continued for over a decade, but by 1885 the principal mines had closed and the camp was abandoned.

Silver deposits were discovered and worked at several other areas of the county, but the two most exciting and profitable mines of the 19th century were developed in the region north and northeast of Barstow. The first of these was discovered in 1880 by John Porter and Robert Waterman, who was later to become governor of California. Elected lieutenant governor in 1886, he became governor in September 1887 upon the death of Governor Washington Bartlett. Waterman served out the remainder of the term but did not seek re-election because of poor health.

The Waterman Mine was located a few miles north of Grapevine (present Barstow). Teams hauled the ore about four miles to a stamp mill constructed on the north bank of the Mojave River where the little settlement of Waterman began. When the Southern Pacific Railroad first came through Waterman in 1882, about 100 men were employed at the mill and the mine. Between 1880 and 1887 the Waterman Mine produced 40,000 tons of ore which yielded about $1,700,000 in silver. The mine closed in 1887 after a drastic drop in the price of silver.

The biggest mining boom in San Bernardino County was set off in 1881 by the discovery of rich silver ore in the Calico Mountains, northeast of Barstow. The first mine to be developed was the Silver King. At first its ore was taken 40 miles by wagon to Oro Grande for processing, but stamp mills were soon built in the area. By 1890, at the peak of activity, mills at Calico and Daggett totaling 150 stamps were in operation.

The town of Calico sprang up along a narrow ridge with canyons dropping away on either side. The first buildings along its one main street were all wooden, but after two destructive fires, several were rebuilt of adobe or rammed earth. Some of these structures survived to form the nucleus of the present Calico "Ghost Town." The population of the town grew to over 1,000, with miners living in lean-tos, tents, and caves. Although Calico had its saloons, gambling dens, and dance halls, it was not as "wild" as many Western mining camps. It was a law-and-order town peopled by hard-working miners, many of whom had their families with them. By 1885 Calico could boast of a schoolhouse, church services, temperance lectures, a literary society, and a dancing school. It had its own newspaper, the *Calico Print.*

Calico had its share of village characters, but one of the most loved was Dorsey, a black-and-white shepherd dog who attained fame as the only four-legged mail carrier in the postal department of the United States. For three years Dorsey carried the U.S. mail from Calico to the nearby Bismarck Mine. With small mail sacks strapped to his back, the dog was all business and would not be distracted from his appointed rounds.

In the period between 1883 and 1885 the Calico mines accounted for over 80 percent of California's total silver production. The operations in the Calico

Top: *"Old Dinah" belonged to the Pacific Coast Borax Company. It pulled as much ore as two teams and was used to haul ore into Daggett. Its engine burned a ton and a half of coal on the 12-mile trip and it took an engineer, a fireman, and a brakeman to run it. After a year, the company returned to mule teams. (SC, SBPL)*

Bottom: *Borax was hauled from the Calico district in 16-foot wagons. The teams had two horses next to the wagon and as many as 18 mules ahead of them. In this 1890 view, Ed Pitcher stands beside the wagon. Charlie White is the driver. (SC, SBPL)*

district continued well into the 1890s. But the price of silver dropped from $1.13 an ounce in 1894 to 57 cents in 1896, and with the exhaustion of the high-grade ores, silver mining virtually ceased. During the 15 years of major production Calico yielded silver with a total value estimated at from $13 to $20 million.

Gold mining in the county, like silver, has had its ups and downs. The discovery of gold in the Mojave River Valley in the 1870s led to the establishment of the mining town of Oro Grande. Discovery of gold-bearing ore in the New York Mountains in the northeastern part of the county produced the town of Vanderbilt, a name synonymous with great wealth. Most active around the turn of the century, some mining at Vanderbilt continued into the 1950s. There was a minor gold rush to the Dale district, southeast of Twentynine Palms, in the mid-1880s. The best-known mine developed there was the Virginia Dale, with mining continuing off and on throughout the early 1900s. A gold mine at Doble in the San Bernardino Mountains overlooking Baldwin Lake was owned and operated by E.J. "Lucky" Baldwin in the late 1800s.

The principal source of gold in San Bernardino County has been the Bagdad-Chase mines, accounting for over half of the total recorded gold production in the county since 1880. These deposits were discovered in 1889 by John Suter, a Santa Fe employee searching for sources of water for the railroad. A ten-mile branch railroad was built to the mines, connecting at Ludlow on the Santa Fe main line. The station and post office at the mines was called Stedman, named for the Rochester, New York family who provided substantial financing for the mining project. The living area at the Bagdad-Chase mines was also known as Camp Rochester, but sometimes nicknamed "Copenhagen" because of the large number of Scandinavians who sought employment there.

The greatest gold strike in Southern California was made in Kern County, just across the San Bernardino County line. This discovery was made in 1895 by the Burcham brothers, San Bernardino butchers-turned-prospectors, in what became known as the Rand District, named after the great South African mining area. Their mine was the Yellow Aster, Southern California's most productive and longest-lived gold mine. The typically Western boom town of Randsburg grew up below the mine. Half of the town burned in 1898, was rebuilt, and burned again a few months later. The mining district was linked to the Santa Fe tracks with the construction of a branch line from Kramer to Johannesburg, "Joburg," a community adjoining Randsburg. San Bernardino was the major outfitting and supply center for the Rand development as it had been for most other Mojave Desert mining ventures.

Borate minerals have also figured prominently in San Bernardino County mineral production. In 1860 John and Dennis Searles, prospecting for gold in the Slate Range, discovered the dry lake which now bears their name, and noted the deposits of salts on the lake surface. A decade later, after the borax discoveries in nearby Nevada and Death Valley, the Searles brothers returned to the area and established claims on the northern end of the lake. They organized the San Bernardino Borax Mining Company, which produced over a million pounds of borax in its first year of operation.

In the 1880s borax discoveries in the Calico Mountains added to the other mining activity already under way in that district. A colemanite (calcium borate) deposit was discovered here at the very time that the earlier discovered borax deposits in Nevada and Death Valley were nearing depletion. The colemanite was mined at Borate in the eastern Calico Mountains, and a calciner plant to "roast" or dry out the ore was built about four miles north of Daggett, northeast of Calico Dry Lake. The latter site was named Marion after Francis Marion "Borax" Smith, who organized the Pacific Coast Borax Company in 1890 and acquired the Calico claims. Smith later purchased the Searles brothers' plant and promptly closed it down to avoid competition.

The mining camp at Borate was only 12 miles from the railroad at Daggett so that transporting the borax minerals was much less of a problem than it had been at Death Valley. Death Valley borax had to be hauled 165 miles through the desert of northern San

Bernardino County to the railroad at Mojave. The haul from Death Valley was made by the famous 20-mule teams, the first of which was put together by Ed Stiles, a veteran San Bernardino teamster. Each 20-mule team pulled two huge wagons and a 1,200-gallon water tank. Some of the wagons, capable of carrying 12 tons of borax, were built by the Bright and Chute Wagon Works in San Bernardino. The wagons were manned by a crew of two, a teamster and a swamper, the latter being responsible for doing the cooking and other camp chores. The round trip from Death Valley to Mojave and return took 20 days.

After the Calico discoveries some of the mule teams were diverted from Death Valley to the shorter Borate-Daggett run through Mule Canyon. Seymour Alf of Daggett built two borax wagons and contracted to haul ore. In 1894 a steam tractor, "Old Dinah," was brought in to replace the mule teams, but it did not prove successful. Four years later, in 1898, the Borate-Daggett short-line railroad was built to carry the ore to Marion and Daggett. From Daggett the ore was shipped on to Alameda in the Bay Area for final processing.

The Calico borax mines reached peak production in 1902, but then the output rapidly declined. In 1907 new colemanite discoveries were made in Inyo County near Death Valley Junction, and the Pacific Coast Borax Company transferred its operations there. Daggett's economy suffered as a consequence. In 1900 Daggett was larger than either Victorville or Barstow, supporting three stores, three saloons, two Chinese restaurants, a hotel, a drugstore, and a lumber yard. By 1907 business was reduced to one store, one saloon, and one restaurant.

Profitable new discoveries and mining developments continued to be made into the 20th century, so mining continued as a strong part of the county's economic base. However, the coming of the automobile was to make the desert more accessible for a number of other uses as well.

From its early pioneer days to the start of the 20th century, San Bernardino County had experienced tremendous development and change. Railroads, orange groves, land developers, mines, and lumber had all contributed to the building of new communities, the influx of settlers, and the continued expansion of the economy. This trend of growth continued into the 20th century. But with the new century came further changes and new forms of development, including industry and urbanization in the valley, recreation in the mountains, and military bases in the desert.

In 1887 the Homestake Mine was restaked as the Rose Mine by James Smart. The name refers to the high iron content of the soil, which gave it a dull rose color. A five-stamp mill processed 15 tons a day. In 1898 it was enlarged but was mostly worked out by 1906. The mine was one of the major producers in the mountains. (SBCMA)

EYMANN-GOERZ

VI. The Automobile, New Industries, and Urbanization

With the 20th century came the automobile, and a new kind of growth for San Bernardino County. Road construction opened up the mountains and deserts to recreation and tourism. During the early years of the 20th century, agriculture in the valley expanded and diversified; new agricultural industries moved there after being crowded out by urbanization in Los Angeles County. World War II, however, was another turning point for the area; it brought heavy industry to the valley, and in following years a big increase in population and urbanization, and a consequent decline in agriculture. World War II also saw the beginning of the military as a strong economic presence in San Bernardino County. Although mining activities continued in the desert, military bases and retirement communities added to the diversity of lifestyles.

For the average person living in the San Bernardino Valley in the early 20th century, the changes to come would probably have been difficult to imagine. Life in the valley then was still strongly rural and agricultural, with the landscape dominated by orange groves.

However, in the winter of 1913 an event occurred that almost destroyed the orange industry in the eastern valley. The first years of orange production had corresponded to a period of warm winters, so there had been little attention paid to frost protection. The drying Santa Ana winds had sometimes been a problem, and in the middle valley extensive windbreaks of cyprus and eucalyptus had been planted. The eastern valley had suffered less from the violent winds, but in January 1913 there came a spell of subfreezing weather. On three consecutive days the temperature remained below 20 degrees all night. Many owners lost everything and had to start over again.

Killing frosts occurred in several subsequent years, but they did not have the disastrous effect of the 1913 freeze. Orchard heaters or smudge pots came into common use, with as many as 75 to 100 used per acre to protect against the winter frost. Radio frost warnings, broadcast regularly throughout the coldest months, sent hundreds of workers into the groves at night to "smudge." The result was an air pollution nightmare, so in recent years wind machines rather than smudge pots stand guard over many of the remaining groves in the valley.

The successful publicity efforts at fairs and expositions that had contributed so much to the expansion of the citrus industry during the previous century continued in the 1900s. In March 1911 a National Orange Show was held in a tent at San Bernardino's 4th and E streets. This citrus exposition was the brainchild of Harry Perkins, and it was eagerly supported by the Chamber of Commerce and well publicized by the local newspaper. The response was so good that it was continued as an annual event,

Facing page: *The story goes that the driver of this delivery truck in Upland was frightened by a team of runaway horses. The officer at the scene was Louis Cronmeyer, the first motorcycle officer in the Upland Police Department. He was nicknamed "Two-gun Louie." Courtesy, Upland Public Library*

interrupted only during World War II. In 1922, after incorporation, the National Orange Show acquired a permanent site of 43 acres at Mill and E streets. This was increased to its present 135 acres with several permanent buildings and a stadium constructed for year-around use. The National Orange Show has developed into a true regional fair with entertainment, commercial exhibits, and numerous displays no longer restricted to the citrus industry.

The citrus industry continued to prosper through World War II. Orange acreage in the county exceeded 50,000 acres in 1945, with a production valued in excess of $50 million. Citrus production steadily declined after that time as orange groves gave way to urban and suburban development.

After oranges, grape culture was probably the agricultural industry for which San Bernardino County was best known early in this century. The alluvial fan of Cucamonga Creek, spreading out into the valley below the San Gabriel Mountains, became Southern California's principal grape-growing district.

In 1902 Secundo Guasti, an immigrant from Italy, set out grapevines in what was a desolate wasteland south of Cucamonga. From these beginnings developed the world's largest vineyard under one management—approximately 6,000 acres growing over 25 varieties of grapes for commercial use. Annual crops in excess of 20,000 tons were picked, with over 400 tons of grapes being stemmed and crushed daily during the harvesting season. Most of this vineyard, like the orange groves in the valley, has given way to housing and commercial development.

The Chino area underwent considerable agricultural change in the 20th century. During World War I the American Beet Sugar Company moved its refinery operation to Oxnard, in Ventura County, but soon other agricultural activities took its place. Libby, McNeill, and Libby opened a cannery. The walnut industry became very important to the area in the 1920s. As dairies were forced out of Los Angeles and Orange counties by urbanization, they moved into

Facing page, top: *The 1908 street fair featured automobiles and an electric light display. Courtesy, Inland Empire Postcards*

Facing page, bottom: *The picture of this Upland hardware store was taken on the eve of electric service. Courtesy, Upland Public Library*

Above, left: *The Centennial of the naming of San Bernardino was elaborate with horse races, a midway, and Spanish balls. (SBRA)*

Above, right: *The Towne, Allison drugstore at 3rd and D streets grew along with the town of San Bernardino. It is shown here circa 1920. (SPS)*

San Bernardino County's West End, and the Chino Valley became the largest concentrated dairy center in the nation.

Rosena, or Fontana, the proposed settlement of the Semi-Tropic Land and Water Company, finally came into existence in the 20th century. In 1905 A.B. Miller and three associates leased land from the Fontana Development Company. They cleared the land and planted it to grain. An irrigation system was installed and in 1910 a large tract was planted to citrus. Under Miller's direction, in 1913 the Fontana area was subdivided into smaller plots, but the area remained primarily an agricultural settlement until World War II.

Agriculture in Fontana had many facets, with poultry raising especially important. In 1919 commercial poultry production provided the livelihood for only ten families, but by 1926 that number had been increased to 500. The raising of domesticated rabbits became sufficiently important that the U.S. Department of Agriculture established an experimental station there. Hog ranches also prospered, with hogs being fed on garbage hauled out from Los Angeles. On the eve of World War II Fontana boasted of being the home of the Wade Hog Ranch, largest in the world, which raised 50,000 pigs at one time.

The 1911 National Orange Show at 4th and E streets was in a tent, but boasted an impressive entrance. Courtesy, Norman Sturgess

Early citrus fairs were held in Riverside and Colton. In 1911 the National Orange Show was first held in a tent on the northwest corner of 4th and E streets. Three thousand people attended. A box of oranges could be purchased and shipped directly from the orange show to friends in the east. (SC, SBPL)

Top: *From 1912 to 1918 the National Orange Show was on the southwest corner of 2nd and E streets. Snow, sleet, and rain fell on all but two days of the 1913 show. The Santa Fe Railway supported the show with this handsome "orange" locomotive in thanks for the shipment of fruit over its rails to the eastern markets. (SC, SBPL)*

Bottom: *On Main and Sultana streets in Ontario, a large cannery was built in 1901, and a second cannery was built in Cucamonga. In 1917 the peach canneries supplied the largest share of peach pits to the Army to make charcoal gas masks in World War I. (OPL)*

Top: *The Mission Winery was built in 1910 and was designed by Arthur Benton, architect of the Mission Inn of Riverside. Garrett Brothers took it over in 1912 and renamed it the Virginia Dare Winery. It closed in 1962 and was damaged by fire in 1964. A portion of the buildings will be incorporated into a commercial development. (OPL)*

Bottom: *Secondo Guasti came to Los Angeles in 1883 and ran a hotel. In 1900 he formed the Italian Vineyard Company with 16 other Italians. The company bought South Cucamonga and added acreage until it was the largest vineyard in the world. The company built a church, store, and housing for the workers. (OPL)*

The importance of agriculture in the Fontana area declined dramatically with the coming of the Kaiser Steel Mill during World War II. Coke ovens, smelters, and rolling mills replaced the hog ranch; smog from these industries damaged the citrus, other industrial establishments moved into the region, and Fontana became identified as the center of heavy industry in the county.

Today the rural character of San Bernardino County is best preserved in the extreme eastern part of the San Bernardino Valley, in the Yucaipa area, and in some parts of the Mojave Desert where water is available. Orange groves are still producing in East Highlands, Crafton, and Mentone. Scattered groves still exist on the bench south of the Santa Ana River.

The Yucaipa Valley, although growing rapidly in population, still offers a degree of country living, and until recently, it remained primarily an agricultural area. The Yucaipa portion of the original San Bernardino Rancho was acquired from the Mormons by James Waters, an ex-mountain man, who developed it into one of Southern California's largest and most prosperous farms, raising livestock and grain to be shipped to the newly discovered goldfields in western Arizona. In 1869 Waters sold the ranch to John Dunlap, a Texas cattleman, who with his sons

The hog farm of Fontana was replaced by the Kaiser Steel Mill, as the economy of San Bernardino shifted from agriculture to heavy industry. (SPS)

farmed the Yucaipa area for many years. In 1910 some of the larger holdings were subdivided, with many of the new owners planting apple orchards. By 1916 over 4,000 acres in the Yucaipa Valley were planted to apples, and for about two decades the name Yucaipa was synonymous with apples. The Yucaipa Apple Show became an annual event. Low prices and the lack of markets in the depression years of the 1930s almost ended the apple industry, and most of the orchards were replaced with peaches, plums, and cherries. Apple orchards remain at the higher elevations of Oak Glen, where the fruit is still sold directly to those who drive out from the urban areas each fall. After World War II the poultry industry was introduced, and it has grown to be of great importance in the economy of the Yucaipa Valley.

Today San Bernardino County's agriculture is not restricted to the valley area. Along the Mojave River and below the northern slopes of the San Bernardino and San Gabriel mountains where water is available, certain types of agriculture thrive. Ranches growing alfalfa for livestock feed, as well as a number of poultry farms, are located in the Mojave and Lucerne valleys.

A few large cattle ranches are found farther out in the desert, but most of the Mojave is not well suited to livestock ranching. The Lanfair Valley, north of Essex, provides somewhat better grazing conditions, because of its higher elevation and denser vegetation.

San Bernardino County remains an extremely important agricultural area, although eggs and dairy products have long since replaced grapes and citrus as the most valuable sources of farm income. But the continuing urbanization of the San Bernardino Valley can only result in agriculture playing a less important role in the county's future economy than it has played in the past.

In the desert, as in the valley, the 20th century saw the continuation and expansion of an earlier economic activity—mining. New mining discoveries in the 20th century included the Kelly Mine at Red Mountain—the largest single source of silver in California. The deposit was discovered in 1919 by two prospectors grubstacked by a former sheriff of Kern

County, John Kelly. During the 1920s the mine recorded a silver output valued at about $16 million. Ore valued at over $150,000 was grubbed with picks and shovels from a "glory hole" during the first two months of the mine's operation before shafts were sunk and modern machinery installed. Declining silver prices and escalating mining costs reduced the Kelly to only intermittent activity after 1929. The Rand District, site of Southern California's most productive gold mine, also yielded another metal of great value—tungsten. The tungsten discoveries were made in 1904 about five miles from Randsburg, south of Red Mountain in San Bernardino County. The area

The Kaiser Steel Mill in Fontana was rushed into production in World War II nine months after the financing was approved, and started work December 30, 1942. In another four months the first ship plates were made. The company mined iron ore at Eagle Mountain, Riverside County, shipped in coal from Utah and New Mexico, and quarried limestone at Cushenberry near Lucerne Valley. The mill continued in production after the war, until it phased down in the late 1970s because of low profits. (OPL)

was determined by the U.S. Geological Survey to contain the nation's largest known bodies of the tungsten ore, scheelite. The mining camp was called Atolia, a name suggested by combining the names of two miners, Atkins and DeGolia, who built the first tungsten mill in 1907. The big tungsten boom came during the years of World War I when the metal was in great demand to harden steel. Then the population of Atolia exceeded 2,000. Ore prices were high, as much as five dollars a pound. This led to the problem of "high grading" by individual miners who secreted pieces of the richest ore to sell privately. A story is told of one miner going off shift who had a very noticeable limp. When questioned about it, he complained of rheumatism, but examination disclosed about 50 pounds of high-grade scheelite hidden in his pants leg. Another miner is said to have tripped and fallen and was unable to get up again because of the weight of contraband ore hidden in his clothes. Mine owners soon instituted elaborate surveillance methods. Miners had to change clothes before and after each shift. Lunch buckets could be taken into the mines, but they had to be sent to the surface and inspected after lunch, to be picked up on the surface when the miner left shift each day.

More recently rare earth minerals have been recovered in the Mountain Pass area, adjoining Interstate 15. Discovery of these valuable minerals, which are used in many high technology processes, was made in April 1949. In August 1951 even larger deposits were found on the nearby property of the Sulfide Queen Mine. The claims were acquired by the Molybdenum Corporation of America, which built milling and chemical plants on the site to obtain concentrates of these rare earth oxides. Today the Mountain Pass area provides the major share of the western world's rare earths production.

Searles Lake was the site of renewed activity in the 20th century. In 1908 the California Trona Company was organized to recover soda deposits found on the surface of the lake, but the project proved unprofitable and the company went bankrupt. When potash in commercial quantities was discovered in the lake brine, the American Trona Company took over the assets of the bankrupt company and built a plant to recover the mineral. The first carload of potash was shipped out on a newly constructed 31-mile branch railroad in the fall of 1916. As processing techniques improve, other salts from the lake brine, including soda and borax, were recovered. The American Trona Company reorganized in 1926 as the American Potash and Chemical Corporation. This in turn has been taken over by the Kerr-McGee Chemical Corporation. Kerr-McGee also operates another facility at Searles Lake producing soda and borax, organized by "Borax" Smith in 1920 as the Westend Chemical Company.

The opening of the rich borate deposits near Kramer in 1927 made all other borax mining operations in the country uneconomic. Lower production costs, together with the vast quantity of ore available, transformed borax from a costly specialty item to a staple industrial commodity. Although these deposits are located just across the county line in Kern County, the operation at Boron has had a significant impact on the San Bernardino economy.

Slover Mountain has been the site of another profitable extractive industry—the quarrying of limestone and the making of cement. Lime kilns were in operation there as early as the 1850s. Later the Colton Marble and Lime Company quarried marble from the south slope of the mountain. Slover Mountain marble went into some of the mansions of San Francisco's Nob Hill.

Cement began being manufactured at Slover Mountain in 1891, with an output of about 50 bags a day. With the completion of a new plant in 1894 the California Portland Cement Company began an operation that continues to the present time. The shape and size of Slover Mountain has changed considerably since the time when it rose over 700 feet above the surrounding valley.

Three other major cement plants began operation in the 20th century. The Golden State Portland Cement Company began making cement at Oro Grande in 1910. In 1923 the plant was taken over by the Riverside Cement Company, which continues operations today. The Southwestern Portland Cement Company at Victorville began production in 1916, using limestone from quarries northeast of the city. The Cushenbury quarry in the San Bernardino Mountains above Lucerne Valley was opened in the late 1940s to furnish limestone for the Kaiser Steel Plant in Fontana. Kaiser-Permanente built a 24-million-dollar cement plant at Cushenbury, which went into operation in 1957. A 29-mile railroad connects the quarry and cement plant with the Santa Fe line at Hesperia.

Other minerals that have added to San Bernardino County's economic well-being include the rocks, sand, and gravel recovered from the dry stream channels and washes and used in the construction industry. Rock salt, calcium chloride, gypsum, and celestite are recovered from Bristol Dry Lake, south of Amboy. San Bernardino County has been and continues to be a treasure trove of mineral resources.

Transportation, as well as mining, has molded the character of many desert communities. The coming of the automobile had a great impact on desert development. Increased automobile use early in this century stimulated a movement to improve the desert roads, which in turn encouraged travel and immigration into Southern California.

Travel across the Mojave Desert before World War I was an adventure to be long remembered. A trip from San Bernardino to Needles averaged about four days. The routes, unsigned until 1914, closely paralleled the railroad tracks whenever possible. A public movement to improve the roads was spearheaded by the Automobile Association of Southern Californa.

In 1923 the California Division of Highways established a district office in San Bernardino. The District Engineer, E.Q. Sullivan, began a program of highway modernization. Highway roadbeds and alignments across the desert were improved, with hard surfacing of roads to Needles and Las Vegas completed in the early 1930s. The road from Needles to San Bernardino and Los Angeles was designated as a part of the "Old National Trails Highway" (Route 66) and became the route to California for thousands of emigrants and travelers from the South and Midwest during the 1930s and 1940s. Settlements along the highway such as Needles, Barstow, and Victorville owe much of their prosperity to this continuous stream of traffic across the desert.

The improved roads and increased automobile use of the early 20th century also opened up both desert and mountain areas to a great influx of tourists, who came to enjoy the scenery and recreational opportunities. Recreational development, especially

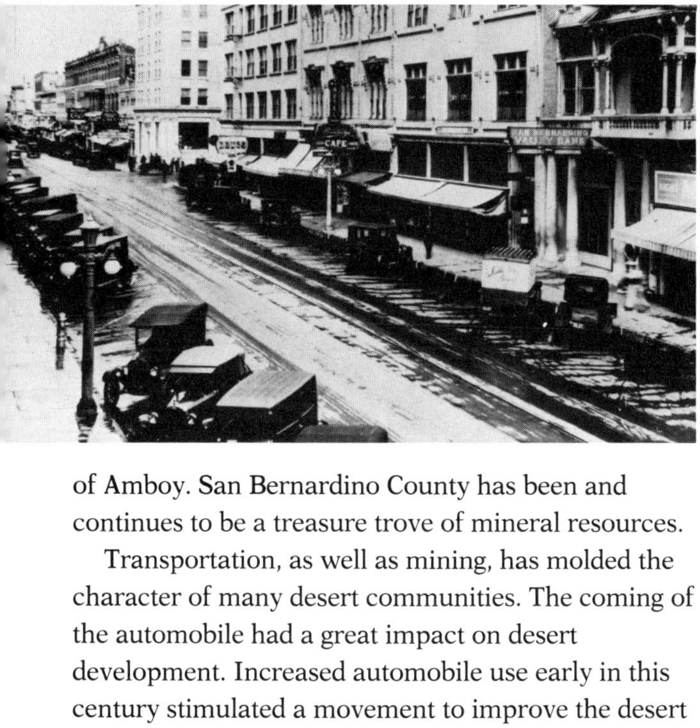

The Armory Building, the first building on the right in this 1926 picture, was the first home of Harris Company Department Store. Farther down the street is the Palace Hotel. (SC, SBRA)

The National Trails Highway crosses the railroad and Mojave River where they wind through the Narrows at Victorville. This bridge served from 1892 to 1928 when it was replaced by the Rainbow Bridge. The freeway now swings past the site. (SC, SBPL)

POPULATION GROWTH IN THE COUNTY

San Bernardino County's population had increased decade by decade, from less than 4,000 in 1870 to more than one million in 1984. The most rapid rate of growth occurred in the 1880s when the population more than tripled from less than 8,000 to more than 25,000. The decade showing the greatest population increase was the 1950s when over 220,000 were added to the county's rolls. This figure, however, apparently will be exceeded in the 1980s.

The growing urbanization of the county has been paralleled by the establishment of new municipalities. San Bernardino, the first city in the county to incorporate (1854), was for many years the only city. In 1887 Colton became the county's second city. Redlands followed a year later. The West End communities of Ontario, Upland, and Chino organized municipal governments in 1891, 1900, and 1910 respectively. Rialto incorporated in 1911 and Needles became the desert's first city in 1913. For a period of over 30 years these eight were the county's only cities, but after World War II the rapid growth of other communities led to a progression of incorporations—Barstow (1947), Fontana (1952), Montclair (1956), Victorville (1962), Adelanto and Loma Linda (1970), Rancho Cucamonga (1977), Grand Terrace (1978), and Big Bear Lake (1980). Seventeen cities now exist within the county, with a few unincorporated areas still aspiring to municipal status. San Bernardino has always been and continues to be the county's largest city, but the West End communities are presently experiencing the most rapid growth.

in the mountain areas, awaited the construction of safer two-way roads. The mountain roads that had been built for logging or dam construction provided the nucleus of what became one of the most publicized highways of the West, the Rim-of-the-World Drive. Dr. John Bayliss of San Bernardino initiated the idea of joining the existing mountain roads into a continuous loop from the valley up into the mountains and back again into the valley. A "Rim-of-the-World Association" was formed, and the county supervisors were induced to construct a few more roads to fill the gaps.

The roads that already existed included the old switchback road up Waterman Canyon, which had been further developed and extended into the Little Bear Valley (Lake Arrowhead) area, a toll road between Green Valley and Fawnskin in the Big Bear Valley, and a road to Big Bear Valley by way of the Santa Ana Canyon and Clark's Grade. The Brookings Lumber Company's railway right-of-way provided another part of the mountain loop. To complete the circuit it was then only necessary to build a road linking the railroad right-of-way to Lake Arrowhead to the west, and another road linking with Green Valley to the east.

The result was a 101-mile scenic loop, completed in 1916 after two years of construction. The route of the road, unpaved but advertised as "ideal for automobiles," was modified even before it was officially opened. Heavy flooding in the winter of 1916 washed out much of the existing Santa Ana portion of the road. At the urging of the Redlands business community, an alternate route was proposed—up Mill Creek Canyon and Mountain Home Creek to Glen Martin (Angelus Oaks), then down into the upper Santa Ana Canyon to join the old road below Clark's Grade. Since the county had insufficient funds either to finance the repairs on the Santa Ana Canyon road or to build the suggested alternative, volunteers from Redlands took up the challenge of building and improving the Mill Creek route. On some days as many as 300 volunteers were at work, wielding axes, shovels, and picks, pushing wheelbarrows, or driving Fresno scrapers.

On July 18, 1916, the Rim-of-the-World Highway was dedicated with appropriate ceremonies. John Steven McGroarty, noted California poet and author, and later a congressman, delivered the dedicatory address and unveiled a monument at Pinecrest to the "101 Mile Drive on the Rim-of-the-World."

The road was an immediate tourist attraction. Over 2,000 automobiles traveled the road in 1916, and soon a motorized stage line was in operation bringing visitors from San Bernardino and Redlands to mountain resorts. Access to the mountains by automobile stimulated the development of the

mountain communities. Homesites proliferated along the mountain crest and in the Lake Arrowhead and Big Bear Lake districts.

Lake Arrowhead came into being as the result of the failure of an irrigation project. In 1891 a group of Ohio businessmen, impressed by the success of the Big Bear Water Project in bringing water to the San Bernardino Valley, acquired the recently logged Little Bear Valley as the site for another mountain reservoir. Construction of a dam on Little Bear Creek in the Mojave River watershed began in 1893. The dam was completed, diversion tunnels were built, and plans were made to generate hydroelectric power as the water was dropped into the San Bernardino Valley. These plans came to an abrupt halt, however,

Top: *The Vendome Bar at 458 W. 3rd Street in San Bernardino opened in the late 1920s and managed to weather the Prohibition days by serving soft drinks and lunches, and selling tobacco. It was in business into the 1950s. (SPS)*

Bottom: *These 1926 motorists enjoyed the improved roads, which opened the San Bernardino mountains to tourists eager to explore the scenery and mountain recreation. (SC, SBPL)*

when in 1908 the state supreme court, in response to a suit filed by residents along the Mojave River to the north of the mountains, ruled that the water could not be diverted from one watershed to another. The irrigation project was abandoned.

After 1921 the property was acquired by new owners from Los Angeles with the intention of making the area into a residential and recreational region. The Little Bear Reservoir was renamed Lake Arrowhead, real estate was subdivided and sold, and Arrowhead Village came into being.

In the 1930s a number of movies were made on location in the Lake Arrowhead area. Arrowhead Lodge became a favorite "in" spot for many of the Los Angeles and Hollywood elite. The lodge hosted such big-name entertainers as Charlie Chaplin, Clark Gable, Myrna Loy, Claudette Colbert, Eddie Cantor, and Marlene Dietrich. Groucho Marx stayed there and complained of being so cold one night that three blankets and a chambermaid couldn't keep him warm.

In 1946 the lake and much surrounding property was purchased by the Los Angeles Turf Club. More recently an organization of resident property owners took over the ownership and management of the lake itself. In the 1950s and 1960s business at Arrowhead Village declined and the costs of upkeep and rehabilitation of the old buildings became prohibitive. Except for one building, the old Arrowhead Village was razed in 1979 and an entirely new complex was built to take its place.

Another recreation site in the mountains was created when a reservoir was built on the north side of the mountains as part of the California Water Project, storing water brought by the East Branch of the California Aqueduct into Southern California. A dam was built in the 1960s, creating Lake Silverwood in the valley formerly occupied by the small mountain settlement of Cedar Springs.

The introduction of snow skiing into the San Bernardinos and San Gabriels brought many more visitors to the mountains. Although a few mountain

Max and Perry Green believed trucks could operate in the mountains. Theirs was the first motor stage west of the Hudson River. Only the Fifth Avenue coach line in New York City antedated the Mountain Auto Line. (SPS)

Facing page, top: *The Arrowhead Springs Hotel built in 1904 was very successful in attracting guests seeking mineral baths or a restful winter vacation. (SC, SBPL)*

Facing page, bottom: *Lake Arrowhead resort shops were built in an alpine style. These buildings, shown here in 1927, were razed in 1979. (SC, SBPL)*

residents were using skis as early as the 1870s, skiing did not become a recreational sport until the 1920s, when cross-country skiing came into vogue. In 1928 the Edelweiss Ski Club was organized in San Bernardino and began excursions for its members. The first ski ascent of Mount San Gorgonio was made in 1931, and in 1934 the "Edelweiss Ski Hut" was built to serve cross-country skiers on the mountain.

The sport of ski jumping was introduced into the area by John Elvrum and Halvor Halstad, both Norwegian immigrants and competitive skiers. The first ski jump in the mountains was built in 1929 at Big Pines and was managed by Halstad. A world's record jump was set there on the first day of competition in February 1930. Another jump was constructed at Lake Arrowhead in 1934, followed by others at Running Springs and Big Bear.

CULTURAL LIFE IN THE COUNTY

The San Bernardino County portion of the Inland Empire has had a rich cultural history. As the county's oldest community, the city of San Bernardino has experienced well over a century of cultural achievements. San Bernardino's Opera House, built in 1882 at Court and D streets, was for many years perhaps the finest and most elaborate theater in the southland. The 900-seat theater played host to such entertainers as Maude Adams in *Peter Pan,* Madame Schumann-Heink, Lillian Russell, George M. Cohan, and Sarah Bernhardt. Performers considered San Bernardino the best show town on the coast. Before the Opera House was torn down in 1927 to make way for an extension of Court Street, Will Rogers, Harry Lauder, Mae West, the Barrymores, the magicians Houdini and Blackstone, and scores of other entertainment greats had performed there.

Many of San Bernardino's early civic functions were held in the Pavilion in Pioneer Park. This large wooden building, built in 1891, served as a site for dances, parties, benefits, and political meetings. It burned in 1913, eventually to be replaced with a Municipal Auditorium. This building was recently razed to make room for a five-and-a-half-million-dollar city library, named for Rabbi Norman F. Feldhym.

From the 1920s until World War II, San Bernardino might have been called the "motion picture preview capital of the world." All major Hollywood studios used local theaters—the Fox, the Ritz, and the California—for unannounced showings of new productions, often before the final cuts. Many actors appeared among the preview audiences, including such stars of the time as Clark Gable, Spencer Tracy, Joan Crawford, and Wallace Beery. Sometimes a Hollywood group, including actors, producers, writers, and directors, would come to San Bernardino on privately chartered Pacific Electric "red cars" to attend a performance.

Today the city of San Bernardino's cultural achievements are measured, not by monumental buildings, but by the activities of many organizations. Art associations, theater groups, historical societies, a symphony orchestra, and a concert association all contribute to the cultural climate. Many of these activities are coordinated through the Arrowhead Allied Arts Council.

Ontario became known throughout the southland because of an unusual social event—an annual All-States Picnic. First held in 1939 and continued into the recent past, it was the brainchild of Carl Holmer, Ontario's city manager. Picnic tables arranged by state on the Euclid Avenue Parkway provided an opportunity for people to meet and mingle with others from "back home." Since much of Southern California's population was made up of migrants, this was a very popular event.

Of all the valley communities probably Redlands had become most closely identified with cultural activities. The Redlands cultural spirit originated with the city's early residents, of whom several were wealthy patrons of the arts. The activities of the Smiley brothers brought many other people of wealth and influence into the community. In 1898 Albert Smiley donated a library building and a downtown park to the city. His twin brother, Alfred, was instrumental in planning the winding scenic road above the city now known as Sunset Drive. Another wealthy family, the Englands, created Prospect

Twin brothers Albert and Alfred Smiley, shown here in front of Albert's home, came to Redlands in 1889. They developed Smiley Heights, a favorite destination for tourists in the horse and buggy days and on the special railroad excursions. Albert K. Smiley also gave the city a public library in 1898. Courtesy, A.K. Smiley Public Library

James W. Waters, a former mountain man, built an opera house in 1882. Mrs. Martha Kiplinger, Waters' daughter, managed the opera house until the 1920s. Some of the finest stars and musicians appeared here. (SC, SBPL)

Park, a private botanical garden, in 1896. This has since become a city park, as is Sylvan Park, built on the site of an old brickyard in 1912. The "Redlands Spirit" has been fostered by many civic organizations. Some, such as the Contemporary Club and the Redlands Horticultural and Improvement Society, date back to the 1890s. The Redlands Community Music Association, under the leadership of Mrs. Grace Mullen, first sponsored a series of free musical performances in Library Park in 1924. So began the famous Redlands Bowl concerts, which are held each summer. In 1930 the Redlands Bowl Prosellis Building was given to the city by Mr. and Mrs. Charles White. In 1932 the Lincoln Memorial Shrine was donated by Mr. and Mrs. Robert Watchorn in memory of their son. The shrine contains Lincoln and Civil War memorabilia and is operated as a part of the Smiley Library.

The reputation of Redlands as a home for millionaires who looked somewhat condescendingly upon neighboring communities naturally evoked a certain amount of envy and criticism. Harold Bell Wright, a popular early 20th-century author, who served for a time as the minister of Redlands' First Christian Church, sarcastically described the social caste system of "Fairlands" in his 1914 novel, *The Eyes of the World:*

In Fairlands the social rating is largely marked by altitude. . . . Plebian businesses, together with those who do the work of Fairlands, occupies the lowest levels in the corporate limits. The heights are held by Fairlands' Pride. Between these two extremes, the Fairlanders are graded fairly by the levels they occupy. It is most gratifying to observe how generally the citizens of this fortunate community aspire to higher things; and note that the peculiarly proud spirit of this people is undoubtedly explained by this happy arrangement which enables everyone to look down upon his neighbor.

No one in Redlands missed the point that it was their community that was being alluded to.

Redlands is also the home of the San Bernardino County Museum. This institution developed from the efforts begun in 1952 by the San Bernardino County Museum Association. This organization, under the leadership of Dr. Gerald A. Smith, enlisted support from other persons and groups, and in 1957 opened a museum facility in Bloomington. In 1961 the buildings and collections of the association were given to the county to operate as a free public museum. The encroachment of the Southern Pacific Freight Classification Yards made it necessary to abandon the Bloomington site, and in 1974 the museum moved to a newly constructed building in Redlands on donated land adjacent to Interstate 10.

The Lincoln Memorial Shrine was built in 1932 for Robert Watchorn, its donor. The architect was Elmer Grey, who also built the Beverly Hills Hotel and the Pasadena Playhouse. The shrine contains Lincoln memorabilia and a library of books about Lincoln and the Civil War. Courtesy, A.K. Smiley Public Library

The popularity of downhill skiing was ensured by the construction of the first ski lift in the mountains, a "sling lift," built in 1934 at the site of a summer camp at Fish Camp (now Snow Valley). A similar lift was erected at Big Bear Valley in 1938. In 1941 the Snow Valley ski area was acquired and managed by John Elvrum, and in 1948 the Snow Valley Corporation was organized and the first chair lift installed. Improvements and expansion continued, and other ski developments kept pace in Big Bear Valley, Green Valley, and at Big Pines. The recent introduction of snow-making equipment at some resorts has made skiing possible even under unfavorable natural snow conditions. Although the mountains of San Bernardino County can never rival the ski areas of the Sierra or the Rockies, they draw tremendous numbers of winter visitors because of their proximity to the great population centers of Southern California.

In the combined winter and summer seasons, the

August Winkler came to San Bernardino in 1860 and built 18 buildings; this one, considered his best, on 3rd Street between C and D, was constructed in 1884, just two years before he died. An Italian architect designed the handsome bathhouse and soda works. In 1902 O.A. Allen bought the building for his iron works. Shown here in 1905, the building was torn down in the early 1960s. (SC, SBPL)

San Bernardino Mountains received twice as many visitors annually as the nation's most popular national park. The typical visitor comes to the mountains on a one-day outing, and nearly all are residents either of the San Bernardino Valley or of the greater Los Angeles Basin.

The desert has attracted its share of tourists, who come to explore ghost towns and enjoy the unusual scenery. Both Death Valley and Joshua Tree National Monuments, established in 1933 and 1936 respectively, lie partially within San Bernardino County. Mitchell Caverns, located in the Providence Mountains, is presently the only state park in the

Top: *Ground was broken for the Ontario Motor Speedway with great hope and excitement September 24, 1968. The first race was September 6, 1970, and the last race was November 15, 1980. The ground was cleared to build a large office, hotel, and store complex. (OPL)*

Bottom: *Motorists used the free auto camp in Meadowbrook Park on 3rd Street in San Bernardino in the 1920s. Now it is the site of the Meadowbrook Apartments. Courtesy, Norman Sturgess*

FIRST ANNUAL
RED MOUNTAIN
ROUNDUP
RODEO
SAT. SUN. MAR. 29-30
Sheriffs Office
Justice Court
Brand Inspector
State Relief
Red Cross
Military Police
Constables Office
Notary Public

county. The U.S. Bureau of Land Management's California Desert Plan has designated an area lying between Interstate Highways 15 and 40 as the East Mojave National Scenic Area, a region many would like to see attain national park or national monument status.

Beginning in 1969 San Bernardino County developed a series of ten regional parks. One of them, Calico Ghost Town, is the most visited tourist attraction in the desert. Other desert county parks are Park Moabi (a marina on the Colorado River) Mojave Narrows near Apple Valley, and Morongo (a high desert oasis now leased to the Nature Conservancy). Other parks closer to urban centers are: Glen Helen, where two nationally publicized rock festivals were recently held; Prado, the site of the 1984 Olympic shooting competition; Cucamonga-Guasti, a small urban park in the West End of the valley; and Yucaipa, a 240-acre park catering to picnickers, campers, equestrians, swimmers, and fishermen. Lake Gregory and Mojave Forks are the county's two mountain parks. Together, these parks are visited by nearly two million people annually.

The desert also hosts its share of "snowbirds," those residents of the northern and Midwestern United States who seek the sun during the winter months. The population of Needles on the Colorado River increases by about 25 percent in the wintertime. More recently the desert has attracted permanent residents who seek an escape from super-urbanized living. Many have emigrated to communities in the high desert to the north of the San Bernardino Mountains. In 1945 Newton Bass developed the new residential community of Apple Valley adjacent to Victorville. A few years later Hesperia experienced a development revival. Farther to the east, settlements at Yucca Valley, Joshua Tree, Twentynine Palms, and Morongo Valley grew as retired and semi-retired families moved into the area

The Sheriff's office building in Victorville could be a stage set for a western. Edward Dolch was constable of Hesperia and later of Victorville, from 1910 to 1928. The building was finally moved to Roy Rogers' Museum in Apple Valley. (SC, SBPL)

seeking the healthful desert sun and air.

Another development since World War II has been the establishment of various military sites in the desert areas. San Bernardino County's relationship with the military dates back to the last century but has developed in recent years into a major support for the region's economy, in the valley as well as the desert.

When the state legislature authorized an increase in militia strength in 1887, San Bernardino was one of the communities seeking to organize a militia unit. State funds were limited and competition was keen, but San Bernardino's unit was approved. The fact that the unit was named the "Waterman Rifles," and that San Bernardino's best-known citizen, Robert Waterman, had just become governor of the state, probably worked in the city's favor. A few years later, in 1892, a citizen militia group was also organized in Redlands.

Both the San Bernardino and Redlands units, now designated as National Guard companies, saw service in the Philippines during the Spanish-American War. Units were called to San Francisco in 1906 following the disastrous earthquake and fire. In 1916, during the period of Mexican revolutionary unrest, they were sent to Arizona to guard the international border at Nogales. In World War I, the guard units were again "federalized" and sent to France, where they participated in the Meuse-Argonne offensive. Upon returning home after the war the county's National Guard companies disbanded and no local units existed for a period of over ten years. A new San Bernardino guard unit was organized in 1930 and did guard and relief work following the Long Beach earthquake of 1933. Both Redlands and Ontario developed National Guard units in the 1940s.

Before World War II there were no permanent military installations in the area, except for March Field in neighboring Riverside County. But World War II brought about a flurry of military construction throughout the whole Inland Empire, and ever since that time the military has been a significant contributor to the area's economy. March Field personnel more than doubled in 1940. Across the highway from March Field over 5,000 men were employed in the fall of 1940 building Camp Haan to house anti-aircraft training units. At its peak Camp Haan was the base for as many as 80,000 men. It was abandoned after the war, but March Air Force Base has retained its importance as a base of the Strategic Air Command.

The army, seeking a suitable site for an artillery and anti-aircraft range, selected a vast area in the northern part of San Bernardino County, closed it to public entry, and designated it as the Mojave Anti-Aircraft Range. Camp Marr, a tent camp about 35 miles north of Barstow, was built to house the personnel coming from Camp Haan for field training. In 1942 the camp was renamed Camp Irwin after a World War I artillery officer. At the end of the war Camp Irwin was deactivated, only to be reopened again during the Korean War as a proving ground and maneuvering area for mechanized units. In 1961 it was given permanent status and renamed Fort Irwin. It was temporarily closed ten years later, coincident with a cutback in defense spending, and was used for a time as a California National Guard training center. Once again it has been reactivated as a center for desert warfare training.

The bombing of Pearl Harbor in December 1941 had an immediate impact upon the region. Within days General Joseph Stillwell of the Western Defense Command established headquarters in San Bernardino's California Hotel. Troops were quartered in the Municipal Auditorium. The National Orange Show grounds became a storage depot. Shortly after the outbreak of the war a medical battalion was stationed temporarily on the Valley College campus,

Facing page: *The Orange Show in San Bernardino was an extravaganza during World War I, as indicated by this graceful 1918 poster. Courtesy, California State College, San Bernardino*

EIGHTH NATIONAL
ORANGE
SHOW
SAN BERNARDINO
California
FEBRUARY 20 TO 28, 1918.
EXCURSION RATES ON ALL RAILROADS
"CALIFORNIA'S GREATEST MIDWINTER EVENT"
WESTERN LITHOGRAPH CO. LOS ANGELES CA

Above, and facing page: *The boxes for the first shipment of oranges to St. Louis in 1877 were branded "Wolfskill California Oranges." In competition and with pride, ranchers continued to label their boxes with their names and with images of nearby scenery. The California Fruit Growers Exchange, formed in 1893, adopted the trade name "Sunkist," and they began to use different*

labels to differentiate quality and size. Max Schmidt in San Francisco introduced lithography and used heavy stones imported from Bavaria. By 1930 the peak of citrus box labels was reached when growers changed to cardboard boxes, and the fanciful labeling came to an end. Courtesy, Floyd J. McDonald

The All-Year Club of Southern California was formed in 1921 to promote tourism in the summer as well as the winter. One of the favorite images included orange trees and snow-covered mountain peaks. This one taken near Redlands in 1949 has the backdrop of San Bernardino peak. (SBCMA)

Heritage House and the Christian R. Harris Memorial Hall were dedicated May 20, 1983. The house was built in 1891 by George E. Otis, a superior court judge. The hall was named for Christian Harris, first president of the San Bernardino Historical Society and past president of the Pioneer Society. (SBRA)

Top: *The San Gabriel Mission sent Father Francisco Dumetz east in 1810. He reached the Indian village of Guachama, west of Redlands, on May 20, the feast day of San Bernardino de Sienna. (SBCMA)*

Bottom: *Fort Piute, built in 1867, was the most eastern fort on the Old Government Road that led from Barstow to the Colorado River. The fort was built from volcanic rock and mud mortar. It was occupied by the U.S. Army for only three years. Courtesy, Arda M. Haenszel*

Facing page, left: *The discovery of gold in Holcomb Valley brought in hordes of prospectors in the early 1860s. Courtesy, John Elk*

The California Theatre at 562 W. 4th Street, north of the Central City Mall, was built in 1927. Will Rogers made his last stage appearance here before his fatal airplane trip. The theatre is now the home of the Civic Light Opera and the San Bernardino Symphony Orchestra. (SBRA)

Artesian wells were common until population demands lowered the water table. The Antil wells were bought by the City of San Bernardino and this picture was taken in 1906. This postcard became famous because it was reprinted so often, each time with a different background. Courtesy, Norman Sturgess

Two men in old military costumes posed on the ruins of Fort Piute during the Bicentennial. On the left is a man in the uniform of the First Dragoons of the 1850s. The man on the right is wearing a cavalry lieutenant's uniform of the 1860s. Courtesy, Arda M. Haenszel

Miners in the Holcomb Valley unearthed $350,000 of gold in one year. Local law could not keep up with the influx of miners and outlaws, and 40 or 50 men were killed from 1861-1862. Courtesy, John Elk

The Calico Bottle House, a popular attraction at Calico, was built in 1951, using mostly wine bottles. Courtesy, John Elk

Right: *The romance of an old silver mining boom town is preserved through careful attention to details in Calico ghost town. Courtesy, John Elk*

Above: *The ghost town of Calico was bought and developed into a tourist attraction by Walter Knott. Now a San Bernardino County park, it is the most popular tourist destination in the desert. Courtesy, John Elk*

Facing page, top: *The Arrowhead Avenue courthouse, built in 1927, serves San Bernardino County. Courtesy, John Elk*

Above: *Skiers from Los Angeles and nearby communities flock to the many ski resorts in the San Bernardino Mountains.*

Facing page, bottom: *Sailors enjoy the clear blue water of Big Bear Lake. Courtesy, John Elk*

SAN RNARDINO COUNTY COURT

Lake Arrowhead has been a popular retreat for tourists since its glamor days of the 1930s. The lake and forests provide summer and winter recreation. Courtesy, John Elk

Green Valley is five miles north of the Rim-of-the-World Highway, between Running Springs and Big Bear Lake. Big Bear Wagon Road, built to bring lumber down the mountain to the mills in Highland, passed by Green Valley. In 1924, the dam was built to create the lake. Courtesy, Paul Curty

Rim-of-the-World Highway climbs the San Bernardino Mountains, allowing travelers to watch the sun set below the mountain summit.

with personnel housed in the gymnasium.

San Bernardino County, like much of the rest of California, was caught up in the post-Pearl Harbor anti-Japanese hysteria that led to the mass evacuation of all persons of Japanese ancestry from the region. The news that "enemy aliens" were to be banned from certain areas under the Western Defense Command was greeted enthusiastically by many residents of the Inland Empire. An editorial in the San Bernardino *Sun-Telegram* disclosed an economic interest in the evacuation:

Japanese control of the vegetable industry of California is doomed and there will be no tears shed over the passing of what has amounted to the greatest monopoly in the history of the west.

Although Governor Culbert Olson gave assurances that "no Japanese-American will be mistreated. They will be treated as human beings," other officials appeared less tolerant. The clearing of the entire coastal area of all Japanese was urged by many Congressmen. San Bernardino County District Attorney Jerome Kavanaugh promised that non-citizen Japanese landowners in the county would be prosecuted, enforcing an old alien land law that had not been enforced for many years. FBI agents, assisted by city and county officers, arrested seven longtime Japanese residents of San Bernardino on the suspicion that they were members of a Japanese secret society. The charges were never proved and the case was dropped.

An Executive Order on February 19, 1942 supported such activities by authorizing the army to exercise such control of the West Coast Japanese as was deemed necessary for national security. Three months later on May 19 orders were posted throughout the Inland Empire that all persons of Japanese ancestry residing in the San Bernardino and Riverside areas were to report on one of the two following days to a Civil Control Station (i.e., evacuation center) in Riverside, bringing with them only clothing, toilet articles and personal effects, and bed linens. Most of these people were transported to Manzanar, an internment camp in the Owens Valley, where they were confined for the duration of the war.

Several military installations were established in the valley during the war. The San Bernardino County Airport, which had just been built in the bottomlands along the Santa Ana River between San Bernardino and Redlands, was designated as an air depot site, and an additional 900 acres of private land was purchased in the spring of 1942 to expand the facility. This became the San Bernardino Air Depot of the Air Material Command. By December 1943 the base had over 300 buildings including warehouses, hangars, machine shops, and barracks. A civilian force of over 20,000 was employed there.

The flurry of building activity and the influx of population had a great impact upon the valley communities. The demand for construction workers throughout 1942 and 1943 created labor shortages in the agricultural sector and stimulated the demand for Mexican labor to work in the citrus groves and vineyards. A civilian housing shortage resulted in the construction of the first federal housing project in San Bernardino—Waterman Gardens.

Another effect of the military presence in San Bernardino was the disappearance of the notorious D Street red-light district. For many years San Bernardino officials had allowed the prostitutes to work without much interference. Business brought to the city by their clients was welcomed by many city merchants. Many of the prostitutes regularly contributed to community charities and could be depended upon for a large block vote at election time. In 1940 about 40 "houses of ill fame" were in operation, most of them older frame residences located on D Street south of Rialto Avenue.

With the influx of military personnel into the area, the army, concerned about the spread of venereal disease, threatened to declare San Bernardino off limits to its troops. This, along with negotiations then under way for the establishment of the air maintenance depot, was sufficient to move the city fathers to take action. On February 12, 1941 a shutdown of the red-light district was ordered and enforced, and most of the women packed up and scattered to other places of business. Some residents requested that D Street be renamed to remove the

The San Bernardino Mountains rise above Norton Air Force Base in the mid-1950s. Courtesy, U.S. Army

USAF

stigma from the city. This was not done, however, so the name and the memory lingers on.

A Quartermaster Depot, Camp Ono, was built in northern San Bernardino along Highway 66 (Cajon Boulevard). As the war progressed, Camp Ono also became an Italian prisoner-of-war camp. After the Italian surrender those prisoners who signed pledges that they were no longer hostile to the United States were permitted passes to leave camp for social visits or to do agricultural labor, usually in the vineyards. Although all of the prisoners were returned to Italy after the end of the war in Europe, some returned later as immigrants to the San Bernardino area. In 1946 Camp Ono was deactivated.

The San Bernardino Air Depot was ordered deactivated in 1947, but the cold-war climate and the pleas of San Bernardino citizens and their influential congressman, Harry Sheppard, resulted not only in its preservation, but in an expansion. In 1950 it was renamed Norton Air Force Base, honoring Leland F.

A Thor missile stood at the main gate of Norton Air Force Base in this 1965 photo. Courtesy, Norton Air Force Base

Norton, a San Bernardino pilot who had been killed in action in France in 1944. Since that time Norton Air Force Base has fulfilled a variety of functions for the Air Force and continues to provide a significant payroll in the east valley.

World War II military installations had perhaps an even greater economic impact on the desert area of the county. A large facility for the Marine Corps established in 1942 just east of Barstow served as a complete supply and repair center for all marine units assigned to the Pacific Fleet Marine Force. Thousands of military vehicles, weapons, and other supplies were warehoused there in the arid desert climate. It was eventually expanded to become a major supply and repair center for the Defense Supply Agency of the Department of Defense. A second branch facility was constructed near Yermo, and both, under one command, continue to employ many civilians from the Barstow area. Early in the war a county airport at Minneola, east of Daggett, was enlarged and converted into an arming and modification plant for bombers turned out by Douglas Aircraft, and this too provided another important wartime desert industry.

The sparsely settled desert environment provided the armed services with an ideal location for training troops and testing equipment. The army, anticipating desert warfare in North Africa, utilized a huge sector of the eastern California desert as a training ground. A vast Desert Training Center under the command of General George Patton had its headquarters just south of the Metropolitan Aqueduct's Iron Mountain Pumping Plant near the Riverside county line. A number of subsidiary camps were scattered throughout the eastern desert in San Bernardino, Riverside, and San Diego counties. The environmental destruction resulting from this mechanized desert warfare training can still be seen 40 years later.

Most of Patton's forces were gone by early 1943, but other military activity in the desert continued throughout the war. George Air Force Base near Adelanto provided training facilities for fighter pilots. A navy bombing range at China Lake in the northwestern part of the county was expanded in 1943 to become the 750,000-acre Naval Ordinance Training Station (NOTS), and some 16,000 construction workers and base personnel descended upon the area. A large share of this facility lies in neighboring Kern and Inyo counties. The army established the Muroc Bombing Range astride the Kern-San Bernardino county line, and on the surface of Rogers Dry Lake built a dummy replica of a Japanese cruiser, soon nicknamed the "Muroc Maru."

After the war ended some of the military facilities in the desert were deactivated, others were cut back to peacetime levels, and some actually expanded. George Air Force Base and Camp Irwin, closed after World War II, were reactivated with the advent of the Korean War. In 1947 the Naval Ordnance Training Station was enlarged by the addition of Mojave "B" Range lying wholly within San Bernardino County. A

The Barstow Mounted Color Guard is an honored tradition at the Marine Corps Logistics Base. Courtesy, Marine Corps Logistics Base

large Marine Corps Training Center was established north of Twentynine Palms in 1952. In geographic size, this facility is the largest military installation in the United States. The Muroc Bombing Range was transformed into Edwards Air Force Base. Here many experimental planes were tested and supersonic flight was first achieved. After the creation of NASA, Edwards became the home of the X-15, moon landers, and space shuttles.

Certainly the military has played a major role in the transformation of the desert. Today a vast amount of the county's desert lands are still dedicated to military activities.

World War II was also instrumental in bringing heavy industry into the San Bernardino Valley. Henry J. Kaiser, to satisfy the need for steel plate for his shipbuilding industry, proposed to build a totally integrated steel plant on the West Coast, utilizing Western iron ore and coal. In the spring of 1942 he borrowed money from the Defense Plant Corporation and the Reconstruction Finance Corporation for the construction of such a steel plant. Although originally planned for a coastal location at either Port Hueneme or Richmond, military considerations dictated that it be located at least 50 miles inland, well out of the range of shelling by enemy submarines. Eighteen hundred acres near Fontana, including the Wade Hog Ranch, were purchased, and in April 1942 a 2,500-man crew moved in to begin plant construction. In spite of problems arising from war priorities for some

Fort Irwin has an estimated post population of 8,413 civilian and military personnel. Hundreds of families live in these homes on the post. Courtesy, U.S. Army

Facing page: *Units training at Fort Irwin have been painting their unit symbols on these rocks for more than 40 years. This unique historical landmark is located just outside the main gate at the fort. Courtesy, U.S. Army*

materials, the first blast furnace was in operation by the end of the year. Christened "Bess" after Kaiser's wife, this blast furnace produced 1,200 tons of pig iron every 24 hours. Most of the iron ore for the steel mill came from the Eagle Mountain mine in Riverside County, 160 miles away. The coal came from mines in Utah and Oklahoma. A water reclamation system was developed at the plant so that only about 1,400 gallons of water were needed to produce a ton of steel, compared with the industry average at that time of 65,000 gallons.

By the end of the war the Kaiser plant had reached an annual production of 675,000 tons of carbon and alloy steel, 300,000 tons of ship plate, and 90,000 tons of structural steel. Kaiser was able to repay his construction loans in 1950 by "going public"—selling shares of stock in what had been a privately owned company. After the war the plant was further expanded with the construction of a hot-strip mill, an electric-weld pipe mill, and additional open hearths.

For over 30 years Kaiser Steel remained one of the biggest employers in the county and a major producer of the steel used on the West Coast. In 1965 over 8,500 people were employed at the plant. However, a number of factors—foreign competition, high labor costs, an outdated technology, and growing environmental concerns—resulted in a decreasing profitability, which culminated in the plant's closure at the end of 1983.

To many people Kaiser Steel's operation had been

a mixed blessing. Although adding greatly to the county's economy through its payroll and taxes, it was the major stationary contributor to the valley's air pollution problem, which may have discouraged other types of economic development. At the time the plant was built not much was known about the factors that would lead to Southern California's smog problem. It was not fully understood that in summer, especially, the valley suffered from a chronic inversion layer which trapped the pollution below it. When concern was expressed at the beginning of World War II about the smoke and fumes that would result from a steel plant in the valley, one of the county supervisors reacted by saying that what the county needed was "more smoke," since that smoke would mean industry, which in turn meant more jobs.

Electric irons are assembled in the 1907 building E.H. Richardson built for the Pacific Electric Heating Company. The factory kept introducing assembly line refinements and became a model for other industries. (OPL)

The Kaiser Steel Plant did encourage further industrial growth in the Fontana area as steel fabricating and chemical plants were added to a growing complex of heavy industry.

Other industries have played an important part in the economy of several county communities. In 1903 Earl Richardson organized the Pacific Electric Heating Company in Ontario and began manufacturing electrical appliances. When his wife pointed out the need for an electric flatiron with a "hot point," such an appliance was made. The plant, renamed Hotpoint, was eventually taken over by the General Electric Company. For over 60 years Ontario was the "Iron Capital of the World." The city of San Bernardino for many years looked to the Santa Fe as its principal industrial employer. Colton was a Southern Pacific town, but became the site of a large honey processing plant. Orange packing plants were a principal source of employment in many valley communities.

Geography has given the San Bernardino Valley a unique advantage as a base for both manufacturing and distributive industries. A complex of highway, rail, and air connections combine to make the valley cities important distribution centers. In the 1960s the construction of Southern Pacific's "Palmdale Cutoff," from Colton through Cajon Pass and the Antelope

Top: *The Pacific Electric Heating Company, makers of the first Hotpoint iron in 1904, quickly outgrew its first plant in the bank building at Euclid and Main streets in Ontario. In 1907 the Chamber of Commerce bought a livery stable and gave the building to E.H. Richardson, on the condition he would keep his company in Ontario. (OPL)*

Bottom: *E.H. Richardson's wife wanted an iron with a hot point to iron her little girl's ruffles. This model was manufactured by the Pacific Electric Heating Company before General Electric took it over. Hotpoint irons were manufactured in Ontario until 1981. (OPL)*

Solar One is the nation's first experimental solar power plant. It is a 10-megawatt electrical generating plant built on 130 acres in Daggett, approximately 12 miles southeast of Barstow. Only a short distance north is the old mining town of Calico and to the northeast is the site of the Early Man Dig. Courtesy, Solar One Visitor Center

Valley to Palmdale, permitted much freight traffic to bypass Los Angeles. It was built in conjunction with new freight classification yards at Bloomington, completed in 1973. The Ontario International Airport has grown to become one of the southland's principal passenger and air freight terminals, and provides a nucleus for the development now taking place in the West Valley area. The future promises much greater industrial and commercial growth. Lower comparative land costs, access to markets, an adequate labor pool, excellent transportation facilities, and conditions for living the good life all serve to ensure an expanding economic environment.

San Bernardino County has had a long and varied history. Within its borders have been found what many believe to be the oldest evidence of man yet discovered in the western hemisphere. Several Indian groups called it home before the arrival of the first Europeans. It has known Spanish conquistadors and mission priests, Mexican ranchers and Mormon saints. Miners, farmers, lumberjacks, and merchants have earned their living here, and in doing so they have made the county what it is today.

But what of tomorrow? San Bernardino and Riverside counties are projected to be the fastest-growing area in the nation. A population spillover from the metropolitan counties to the west has already led to explosive growth in the Ontario, Chino, and Rancho Cucamonga areas. The national migratory trend from the nation's North and East to the South and West will have a continuing and growing impact on California and on San Bernardino County. With such population growth will come additional urban problems demanding solutions. Problems and the people's reaction to them are the stuff that history is made of. The specifics of San Bernardino's future history depends upon the intelligence and foresight of its citizens and the wisdom of their leaders.

Partners in Progress

By Baxter J. Williams

Still often thought of as an agricultural area, steel-producing country, or just as a place to go for the weekend, San Bernardino County has a much more complex and diversified economy than is commonly recognized.

Today, teetering on the brink of the nation's most rapid development, the Inland Empire is the home of a broad spectrum of business activity ranging from comparatively new think-tank-type facilities to heavy manufacturing and distribution. That is by no means to say, however, that the old-time economic base of the area is fading away in its entirety.

Mining, perhaps among the county's first major pursuits, began in the mid-1800s with major gold and silver strikes in the mountains and desert. Though these mining areas have long since been exhausted or at least become unprofitable, rich deposits of limestone, potash, borax, rare earth minerals, and other chemicals remain vital to the economy.

In the 1880s irrigation gave rise to citrus and grape production, which would lead the area into agricultural prominence for many years to come. Despite the fact that, in recent years, thousands of acres of groves and vineyards have turned into residential areas and industrial parks, San Bernardino County remains a statewide leader in the production of both milk and eggs.

Recreational and tourist activities are also long and well established, dating back at least to the 1920s when numerous movie stars made their resort homes at Lake Arrowhead, and several speakeasies were popular gathering places in the San Bernardino Mountains.

Though times have changed, the high country continues to offer both snow and water skiing, fishing, boating, hiking, and camping. The desert, too, draws visitors from throughout the West who seek spring wildflowers, the red-rock canyons of the Colorado River, or simply the solitude of a slowly shifting sand dune.

Despite the unquestionable economic benefits of all these industries, it was the carving of the first Indian and Mormon trails, and the arrival of the railroads in 1875, that laid the early foundation for the present and future prosperity of the Inland Empire.

Many of the early, but well-worn, paths into the valley became the routes of major highways that now make San Bernardino County the eastern gateway to the greater Los Angeles area and provide a magnificent network of freeways between local communities.

All three transcontinental railroads operate main-line routes through the area, resulting in excellent freight service for industries. Equally important, each of the railroads has a major classification yard in the county, resulting in literally thousands of jobs for residents.

The highways and railroads combined with Ontario International Airport—one of the fastest-growing in the nation—to create an almost unprecedented comprehensive transportation system.

It cannot be denied that steel making, as in many parts of the nation, has taken a serious downward turn. But the county's overall economy is strong, with every indication that a period of phenomenal growth has already begun.

Even with the population having risen to more than one million, all credible forecasts are calling for growth rates of up to 20 percent in the immediate years ahead.

Why? There are many reasons, but an important one is the fact that San Bernardino County contains some of the most desirable, yet still reasonably priced, land available in Southern California.

By the year 1990 the complexion of the area will have undergone dramatic changes. The region will have prospered, matured, and become truly an economic cornerstone in the western United States.

Industries and businesses such as those described in the pages that follow will have countless new neighbors. But all will continue to be San Bernardino County's "partners in progress."

Facing page: *A freight wagon hauls a load of gold away from a mine on a dusty canyon road in the 1880s. (SPS)*

SAN BERNARDINO COUNTY MUSEUM ASSOCIATION

With a treasury totaling slightly less than $110, the San Bernardino County Museum Association was founded and began its now widely respected work in 1952. The group, which began with a community-based effort in Bloomington, had its organizational meeting in what was then the county agricultural building on May 13, 1952. Testimony to the long-term effectiveness and success of this organization is now clearly evident near Interstate 10 in Redlands, where an ultramodern county museum houses thousands of highly valued display pieces.

At the forefront were its first president, Dr. Gerald A. Smith, now museum director; and vice-president O.J. Fisk, who would years later donate $150,000 from his estate to help make a new museum possible. Others prominent in the formulative years were Dr. Walter C. Schuiling, Dr. Paul F. Allen, L. Burr Belden, Dean A. Painter, Eugene Shepard, Arda Haenszel, Herman Obrikat, Bobbette Sipe, Ruth Harris, attorney Thomas M. Eckhardt, and association treasurer George A. Klapp. Also deeply involved were Ruth Goodman, Jane MacLin, Gilbert Krebill, Ralph Binford, Clinton Schonberger, Frederick Gros, Emily Knight, Wilson Hanna, Ed Fisher, and Paul Young and Wesley Break, who were members of the San Bernardino County Board of Supervisors.

The association's clearly stated objective was to establish a museum—a place where the public could view and appreciate the county's rich historical and cultural heritage. Fifty-dollar contributions from the County Historical Society and San Bernardino Pioneer Society helped get the effort financially under way. After five years of diligent work, official dedication ceremonies were held in Bloomington, and the first museum was formally opened to the public on July 14, 1957.

The first county museum in Bloomington, as it appeared in the 1960s, provided a site for many popular indoor and outdoor displays from 1957 to 1974. The property is now part of the Southern Pacific Railroad classification yard, which is centered in Colton and sprawls over several surrounding communities.

This facility, located at 18860 Orange Avenue, was to be visited during the next 17 years by hundreds of thousands of adults and children who enjoyed both the indoor and outdoor exhibits. The original display area of less than 5,000 square feet was, however, being rapidly overfilled by an ever-growing collection of artifacts and, in the early 1970s, it became clear that the site would soon become part of the massive switching yard planned by the Southern Pacific Railroad.

On July 31, 1974, the county's first museum locked its door, but the association and the County Board of Supervisors had several years earlier undertaken a cooperative venture to assure the continuation and enhancement of the museum's valued contribution to society. The San Bernardino County-Redlands Public Facilities Authority was established and, with an $800,000 contribution from the association, a new, three-story facility was constructed.

More than 3,000 persons visited the new museum as opening ceremonies were held on November 22, 1975. Association president Ruth O. Harris participated in the official ribbon cutting as the $2.5-million, 50,000-square-foot structure was opened to the public.

Situated amidst the rapidly disappearing orange groves of Redlands and adjoining the historic Edwards Mansion, the museum is the home of countless attractions ranging from military weapons and railroad antiques to beautifully mounted North American mammals and the nation's most complete collection of bird eggs.

Now with more than 1,700 members, the San Bernardino County Museum Association celebrated its 32nd anniversary in May 1984. Its original objective reached, the association continues working throughout the county by conducting archaeological research, creating children's science and nature trails, and constructing a Teachers' Hall of Fame Museum.

TRW

General Bernard A. Schriever and Simon Ramo shake hands as Ramo, one of the founders of TRW, begins work on the Air Force missile program in 1954. The partnership continues as TRW plays an important systems engineering role in the development of the nation's ICBMs.

San Bernardino entered the Space Age in 1961 with the arrival of the first members of a team, the Air Force's Ballistic Missile Division and systems engineers from TRW. This team had pulled together since 1954 to develop the nation's ballistic missiles. Their immediate responsibility was to guide the flight tests and deployment of the Atlas and Titan liquid-fueled rockets. Leadership for TRW was in the hands of Dr. Richard D. DeLauer, who set a pattern of on-the-job technical excellence as well as personal and continued community involvement. Still dedicated to the nation's defense, DeLauer was appointed in 1981 as Under Secretary of Defense for Research and Engineering.

Office space for a limited number of TRW engineers was found in Building 520 on Norton Air Force Base. But as the size of the team continued to grow—over 100 engineers were at work by the end of the first year—the warehouse portion of the World War II building had to be converted to additional offices.

Although the primary purpose of these missiles was for defense, many of the boosters, some of which were stored at Norton, were used to place exploratory payloads in earth orbit. The environmental data they obtained was a vital step for follow-on satellite, moon landing, and the current shuttle programs.

In the fall of 1962 another large group of TRW employees came to the San Bernardino area to work on a new Air Force ICBM, Minuteman. Office space was not available on base, so the Civic Center Building on Fifth Street provided overflow offices for a short period. It was this group of employees that stimulated considerable growth in the local housing industry and family services.

The recession in the aerospace industry of the early 1970s had little impact on the San Bernardino area since the task of maintaining and developing Minuteman improvements continued to grow. TRW's payroll, for example, shows a steady increase from $2 million annually in early 1962 to about $35 million in 1983. Today TRW's Ballistic Missiles Division has redirected its effort from Minuteman to the development of the new ICBM, Peacekeeper, and is assisting the Air Force in the development of the new small ICBM recommended by the President's Commission on Strategic Forces.

The U.S. Air Force has not only found Norton AFB to be a suitable home for its ICBM headquarters, but has established a long working relationship with TRW as its systems engineering contractor.

GENESIS OF TRW

1901 *Cleveland Cap Screw Co. - manufacturer and welding company*
1926 *Thompson Products, Inc. - auto and aircraft valve producer*
1953 *Ramo-Wooldridge Corp. - developer of systems engineering*
1957 *Space Technology Laboratories - guided missile division of Ramo-Wooldridge Corp.*
1958 *Thompson Ramo Wooldridge Inc. - merger of R-W with its financial backer*
1965 *TRW Inc. - leader in defense, space, electronics, automotive, communication, and energy*

It may not look like it, but these early TRW employees were pushing the frontiers of technology with a new process for the manufacture of automobile valves. The same spirit of leadership in technology exists today at TRW.

LOCKHEED AIRCRAFT SERVICE COMPANY

With headquarters at Ontario International Airport, Lockheed Aircraft Service Company (LAS) is the oldest and most diversified operation of its type in the United States, and is the largest overseas division within the entire Lockheed organization.

The firm does not, however, manufacture airplanes as often thought. But it does do just about everything else imaginable, from aircraft overhaul and damage repair to reassembly and major modification. In most recent times, LAS has become a world leader in flight data recorders, which are used to determine the cause of aircraft incidents or accidents, data playback stations, and aircraft training equipment.

Lockheed expanded to Ontario from its original Burbank location in 1952. Early employees recall working in two small leased hangars and eating grapes picked from surrounding vineyards. Only four years later the firm's headquarters was moved to Ontario and the wheels of progress were set in motion.

Today Ontario is the largest Lockheed Aircraft Service Company facility in the world, with 27 buildings totaling 725,000 square feet. Sprawling over 86 acres, the complex houses 1,650 employees who are involved in work on nearly every type of military and commercial aircraft.

Whether the job involves only the electrical system or complete structural changes, the basic tenet at LAS is service for the customer. Time and time again, the company has proven that its experience in modification can produce a more efficient product at only a fraction of the cost required to manufacture a new aircraft.

LAS is clearly recognized as a pioneer in its field and is respected for successfully meeting the many challenges of an increasingly complex industry. If there is a reason why Lockheed is not more widely acclaimed it is because so many of its greatest accomplishments are highly classified and cannot be publicized.

The full story of LAS dates back considerably before Ontario to June 1938. It was then that expanding production by the parent corporation necessitated the inception of a customer-service department at Burbank.

Twelve men started the new function in a tiny rented office above the men's room in the Walt Disney studio. With tools, equipment, and personnel—mostly borrowed from other Lockheed divisions—growth was rapid.

The first job was creating the Lodestar by cutting the fuselage and adding a 66-inch section to a previous Lockheed model. LAS' management cites the project as the beginning of "airframe modification without degradation of flight integrity," which has been the hallmark of the company into the Jet Age.

The precedent for Lockheed's overseas dominance was, however, established early. One of the first major LAS assignments was the reassembly of 200 Hudson bombers purchased from the United States by England in 1939. Ultimately, some 1,300 employees worked on about 13,000 planes at Speke Air Force Base in Liverpool.

World War II also produced contracts for Lockheed at Sydenham Base and Langford Lodge Air Depot in Ireland as well as at Abbotsinch Base and Renfrew in Scotland. In short, the war paved the way for literally millions of man-hours of work in repair and maintenance, with LAS moving quickly thereafter to serve customers as well in peacetime as it had during the war.

Its wartime record well in place, Lockheed was retained almost immediately by a number of foreign countries—most significantly Iceland—for the entire operation and maintenance of Keflavik Airport. Many other European customers were served from MacArthur Field in Long

Lockheed-Ontario is the largest Lockheed Aircraft Service Company facility, with 27 buildings on 86 acres and employing more than 1,600 people.

Well over 50 percent of the world's flight recorders, used to determine the cause of aircraft incidents or accidents, are designed and produced at Lockheed-Ontario.

The majority of the programs for the 1980s and beyond involve highly technical and sophisticated modification activities, many in support of electronic warfare missions.

Island and Shannon Airport in Ireland.

The MacArthur Field operation was moved in 1949 to what is now John F. Kennedy International Airport, where LAS provided service to the world's leading commercial airlines for nearly 30 years—sometimes working on as many as 8,000 planes annually.

It was in New York that Lockheed workers converted a C-121 Constellation into the famous *Columbine* for President Eisenhower—complete with Mamie's notorious green and pink bathroom.

In previous years, Lockheed had produced the modified Douglas C-54 known as the *Sacred Cow* in the Roosevelt years, and the DC-6 *(Independence)* used by Harry Truman. John F. Kennedy, Lyndon Johnson, and Richard Nixon all had Presidential aircraft modified and maintained by LAS.

Starting with the 1960s the company became heavily involved in Greece, Zambia, and Saudi Arabia, with additional work in Germany and Japan. In Saudi Arabia, LAS fought against severe mountain cold, scorching desert heat, and devastating sandstorms to maintain the kingdom's fleet of C-130 Hercules cargo aircraft. For Saudi Arabia, LAS developed a complete airborne emergency hospital with short-distance takeoff and landing capabilities for remote areas combined with extensive in-flight life-support systems. In the decade that followed, assistance was extended to many other foreign countries, including Singapore and Iran until the fall of the Shah.

At home, Lockheed was busy converting the C-141 Starlifter, the most common sight at San Bernardino's Norton Air Force Base, into a flying laboratory for NASA (National Aeronautics and Space Administration). With more than six miles of new wiring, the modified aircraft can carry a 15,000-pound, porthole-mounted, infrared telescope to an altitude of 40,000 feet.

Scheduled for use in recording the passage of Halley's Comet in 1986, the project is typical of Lockheed's most difficult tasks—some requiring the addition of external devices for space tracking without interfering with necessary flight characteristics.

Major projects at Ontario, itself, have included fuel-saving alterations to the L-1011 and production of flight recorders now used by more than 100 airlines and in planes ranging from those built by Boeing and Lockheed to the European-made Airbus. LAS has carried out work on more than 120,000 aircraft from 22 countries, with highly skilled mechanics and technicians prepared for a full spectrum of planes with single-engine, piston-driven craft at one end and multi-engine jumbo jets at the other.

An international leader in aviation, LAS continues to supply support services to countries worldwide in their efforts to achieve technical security and economic stability throughout the world.

In 1956, just a few years after LAS' relocation to Ontario from Burbank, new hangars were constructed and the flight line filled in support of aircraft maintenance and modification programs for the U.S. military services.

MILLER'S HONEY COMPANY

An early photo of the Miller family with (top, left to right) Woodrow, Dell, and Raymond Miller; Dr. Irvin Miller; and Earl Miller. Seated (left to right) are Florence Miller Farish; Harriet and N.E. Miller; and Ilah Jane Miller McEwan.

Sitting in the yellow and red caboose he has transformed into an office, Woodrow Miller considers himself semiretired. It's true that in late 1983 Miller sold much of his honey-packing business to a son-in-law, but he continues to supervise honey production leases, properties, and investments in California, Utah, and Nebraska.

Woodrow wasn't the founder of the business. Actually, his father, Nephi E. Miller, started things "buzzing" back in 1894 when he accepted seven hives in trade for a few sacks of oats. It was Woodrow, however, with his courage and foresight, who brought the company from the brink of financial disaster during the Depression to where it is today—a great pioneer and leader in the honey and beeswax business.

In a good year the plant now packages more than two million pounds of honey and distributes a total of 105 different products to retail outlets throughout the world. Varieties range from Hawaiian honey in a cleverly designed hula-girl container to honey made from a particular blossom especially for diabetics.

At one point Miller maintained some 32,000 colonies of bees and owned every hive in Hawaii. Today the firm processes 85 percent of the honey sold in health-food stores throughout the nation.

Miller's key to success was, however, not in sales volume or sheer number of bees, but rather in an entirely new, then unheard-of method of honey production which involved transporting the bees back and forth between Utah and Southern California to produce two honey crops per year instead of one.

Bees work incredibly hard. A honeybee makes more than 150 trips between his hive and the blossoms to produce only a teaspoon of honey. Unbelievable as it may seem, it takes 160,000 bee hours, the equivalent of 18-plus years, to make a pound. If one bee lived that long, he'd fly a distance of three times around the world.

"If they can work like that," thought Nephi Miller in the early 1900s, "why should I let them hibernate during the winter?" In 1907 he traveled to the West Coast and came to the realization that would affect the entire honey-producing industry for years to come.

Soon the rail shipments were begun from Logan, Utah, to Southern California, making Nephi the world pioneer of migratory beekeeping. Although he lost a number of bees by working them year-round, he and his cattle cars full of hives followed the flower blossoms with new generations of bees being born en route.

All five sons had become involved in the lucrative business, but the Great Depression would force the senior Miller to divide his by-then-substantial holdings among the boys simply to survive the hardships of the times.

Woodrow Miller had taken to Washington politics and was a procurement agent for the Department of the Interior. But in 1937, with his father in deteriorating health, he headed west to direct the Colton portion of what remained locally of Miller's Honey Company.

The Colton location on West J

Miller's Honey Company, Colton.

An apiary in Utah. N.E. Miller, the founder of the family honey and beeswax business, is standing on the far left, and a very young Woodrow is on the horse.

In order to produce two honey crops per year, the Miller bees were transported back and forth between California and Utah. Here are Earl and Irvin Miller in Utah.

Street had been selected for its access to the all-important orange groves as well as to all three major railroads. Yet, when Woodrow arrived, things seemed literally hopeless.

The price of honey had fallen to three cents a pound, putting nearly all other producers out of business. An entire hive was valued at only five dollars, leaving Miller with a debt of $10 per colony. Economists termed honey making the worst business in agriculture other than raising goats.

Even his brother, Earl, who had turned his part of the business in Idaho into a 20,000-colony operation, advised Woodrow that it "wasn't worth pursuing any further."

Nonetheless, local bankers encouraged Woodrow to maintain the hives on which they held loans, offering attractive financial terms until he showed a profit.

And soon he did. In the 1940s conditions turned 180 degrees. During the war, sugar was in short supply, and beeswax was proved to be an irreplaceable lubricant for numerous weapons. Not long after, it was found that more than 50 important crops required pollination and that DDT had killed off nearly all insects capable of doing the job—other than bees.

Prices soared. Honey now retails for at least one dollar a pound and a hive is worth no less than $100. Earl came from Idaho to join Woodrow in the early 1960s and, now retired, remains a member of the corporate board of directors.

In 1950 Miller was forced by freeway construction to move from J Street to the current site at the corner of Laurel Avenue and Miller Drive. The plant, itself, is about 20,000 square feet, but storage facilities and other buildings a few blocks away bring the total to nearly 70,000 square feet.

Although the railroads are no longer used, Miller still ships its bees back and forth between other locations in Utah, Nebraska, and the Dakotas. Locally, the products are sold to a number of well-known markets including Jensen's, Stater Bros., Ralphs, and Alpha Beta.

In late 1983 the owner's son-in-law, George Murdock, took over the ownership and management of Miller's American Honey, Inc., which now handles all packaging and distributing of honey and beeswax.

Woodrow Miller is a member of the corporate board and continues the parent production company, now called Miller's Honey Hill Farms. Miller's efforts do not, however, stop with the business. He is known as a tireless worker in seemingly countless community projects and has even been recognized at the national level.

He is a former mayor of Colton, was a member of its city council for 20 years, and was a candidate for Congress in 1962. His long list of civic accomplishments includes terms as president of the National Orange Show board of directors, chairman of the board of trustees for San Bernardino Valley College, and president of the Colton Rotary Club.

Most impressive perhaps, Miller served as a special advisor to three Secretaries of Agriculture and was sent to the Soviet Union in 1959 by President Eisenhower to study insecticides.

He has been featured in *Reader's Digest* and *American Westways*, as well as in numerous agricultural journals and health-related publications.

Despite all this, it is top-quality honey and maybe even the honey bear gift container by which Woodrow Miller is most recognized.

Aristotle once referred to honey as "dew distilled from the stars and the rainbow—the nectar of the gods." Woodrow Miller must surely agree.

GRABER OLIVE HOUSE

One hundred and fifty tons of olives per year may not be overwhelming production by agricultural statistics. But quality, not quantity, has been the rule at the Graber Olive House since 1894 and is a key ingredient in the success of this four-generation business in Ontario.

Founder Clifford C. Graber set the high standards at the very beginning when he broke all the rules of olive growing by ripening every olive on the tree—a time-consuming and expensive procedure which means that pickers must return to each tree as many as seven times.

The result, however, is an unusually flavorful gourmet olive that is famous throughout the world. The olives may be purchased direct or as far away as Paris and Tokyo and are found in America's finest restaurants and specialty shops.

Cliff Graber arrived in Ontario from Clay City, Indiana, in 1892 with his brother, Charles. Then only 19, Graber began raising the fruit on a small-scale basis to sell with his other produce. In 1905 Clifford married Georgia Belle Noe, and the new Mrs. Graber was soon selling olives by the dipper from the olive vats.

Knowing that many customers would prefer olives uniformly sized, Cliff designed and built a wooden olive grader, the basic concept of which is still used to sort olives. Neighbors and friends worked with the family at harvest time.

Olive sales swelled around 1910. In addition to being sold fresh-cured direct from the vats, the olives were now being canned. Graber needed more land and in the 1920s moved his growing operation to Hemet in Riverside County, though processing, canning, and sales would remain in Ontario.

The cannery was enlarged in 1934, and nine years later Graber's two sons, Robert and William, took over the business in partnership with a brother-in-law. Cliff, however, remained active in the company until he died in 1955 at age 83.

Robert eventually emerged as sole owner and in 1963 moved the ranching operations to 75 acres of olive groves in the San Joaquin Valley, where it remains to date.

Throughout the years, the original Graber quality standard has never been compromised. To prevent bruising, a picker holds no more than three olives in his hand and deposits them in a padded bucket. The olives are never oxidized and no artificial coloring is ever used.

Robert now serves as chairman of the board and his son, Clifford II, has become president. Robert's wife, Betty, is vice-president in charge of Graber's two gift shops, and young Clifford III, great-grandson of the founder, has enjoyed helping in the plant since the early age of three.

Clifford C. Graber, founder.

During the October-to-January processing period, Graber hires about 60 workers and has given many Ontario students their first job. But by contrast, there are many long-term employees with one approaching 60 seasons with the company.

Now also a popular, year-round tourist stop, the Graber Olive House is a unique blend of old and new. At peak production, the plant pulsates with the vibrance of any modern factory. Yet, only yards away, turn-of-the-century structures built by the founder still stand strong, perhaps as a tribute to the heritage of Ontario's oldest existing business.

Robert D. Graber inspecting a vat of olives in the processing room at Graber Olive House.

FRED G. WALTER & SON

Dating back more than 60 years, Fred G. Walter & Son is truly a locally developed business which has prospered in San Bernardino under three generations of family management.

Today a specialized machine operation, the firm is located in new facilities situated west of Interstate 215 south of Palm Avenue. The founder's son, Robert F. Walter, heads the enterprise and is assisted by his own son.

Walter provides a full line of machine shop services but concentrates its business in the manufacture and repair of chemical processing equipment. Notably, major customers include chemical and cement plants in nearby desert areas.

After moving from Illinois to San Bernardino, Fred Walter learned his future trade with Parker Iron Works near Third and I streets. He established his own firm in 1922 at 518 Court Street, which is now part of Central City Mall. In his small, rented facility, Walter rebuilt engines and repaired commercial ice machines.

This building on South E Street in downtown San Bernardino was the firm's home from 1936 to 1982. Fred G. Walter & Son now occupies much larger facilities at 5770 Industrial Parkway in northwest San Bernardino.

By age 12, son Robert was already working in the shop and several of the early machines he ran remain among the 60 pieces of modern equipment in his present-day operation.

In 1936 the firm moved to new quarters at 170 South E Street, where it would spend the next 46 years. The building, at the beginning only 6,000 square feet, was made of used red brick salvaged from structures destroyed in the earthquake that devastated Long Beach in 1933. Since then it has been expanded to more than twice its original size.

Robert F. Walter, then serving in the U.S. Navy, is shown in 1945 with his father Fred G. Walter, founder of the family business. Robert is now president of the company.

Robert Walter had foreseen the firm's growth and this, combined with the evolving commercial nature of E Street, brought about his purchase, in 1967, of the five-acre industrial site on which the new plant now stands.

Fifteen years passed, but in 1982 Walter Machine undertook construction of the 35,000-square-foot, $1.5-million facility that is now its home. In sharp contrast to the earlier brick structure, this metal building lies directly in the path of San Bernardino's industrial growth and the Walters are optimistic about their investment.

The facility includes four overhead cranes with capacities ranging as high as 30 tons. What's more, Walter equipment rivals any locally available and features one of the area's plasma cutting machines for cutting stainless steel and hard-faced plate.

With current annual sales of more than $3 million, short-term plans include the employment of as many as 65 persons receiving a yearly payroll of $1.7 million.

In addition to the current principals, Robert F. Walter, Sr., and Robert F. Walter II, management also includes Dolores, the president's wife, who serves as secretary/treasurer, and daughter Mary Neises, who is a company bookkeeper.

Fred Walter's little shop of the 1920s on a now-nonexistent portion of Court Street has grown into a major business entity in San Bernardino, and hard-working family members guarantee greater growth in the decades ahead.

FONTANA PAVING, INC.

Currently producing more than 400,000 tons of asphalt per year, Fontana Paving, Inc., has become one of the Inland Empire's leading builders involved in the construction of highways, airports, shopping centers, industrial parks, and residential subdivisions.

With new executive offices at 15384 Arrow Highway in Fontana, the firm operates two asphalt plants—one also in Fontana and the other in Corona. The company employs 80 workers and reports annual sales approaching $20 million.

Although the local history of Fontana Paving begins in 1950, forerunners owned by the same family can be traced back as far as 1908 when E.R. Werdin and Co. was formed in Los Angeles.

Werdin, grandfather of Fontana Paving's current president, had served as superintendent of streets for the City of Los Angeles and later as head of Western Paving Co. In 1912 he incorporated L.A. Paving Co., which he owned and operated until his death in 1932.

His son-in-law, W. Reed Sprinkel, had joined the firm in 1926 and, with this experience, established Vernon Paving Co. in 1936. His own two sons, Warren Reed Sprinkel and Richard W. Sprinkel, became involved in the business 10 years later.

In 1950 the company moved one of its asphalt plants from Vernon to 8747 South Lime Avenue in Fontana, the 20-acre site of one of the two current Fontana Paving plants.

At the beginning, this was strictly a manufacturing facility where asphalt was produced and sold. That changed, however, in 1952 when Warren Reed Sprinkel (known as Reed) returned from the Korean conflict and began contracting for complete paving jobs from the Fontana location.

E.R. Werdin founded several firms in the early 1900s including L.A. Paving Co., a predecessor of the present-day Fontana Paving, Inc.

Walter Reed Sprinkel, father of Fontana Paving's current president, established Vernon Paving Co. in 1936, leading to the development of the local firm in the early 1950s.

Four years later Sprinkel, by this time president of the Fontana Chamber of Commerce, decided to change the name of his operation—and Fontana Paving was born.

Today, although the firms have been completely separate entities since 1980, both Fontana Paving and Vernon Paving are controlled by the Sprinkel family. Reed is president of the company he developed while Richard heads the original firm. Their father remained active as chairman of the board until his death in 1975 at age 80.

Although the basic product has remained largely unchanged, Fontana Paving has undergone several major improvements in its capability to serve customers. While the original Lime Street plant could produce only 800 tons of asphalt per day, there are now two plants each able to turn out 2,000 tons per day for a total five times that of the 1950s. To assure an adequate supply of raw material, both sites have their own quarries and rock crushers.

Also important is that each location now includes a hot storage facility which can hold as much as 400 tons of paving material. This means that a truck and trailer hauling 24 tons of asphalt can be filled in two minutes instead of the 12 to 15 minutes required to load directly from the plant.

Sprinkel moved the company's offices in 1970 from the Lime Street property to a building on Arrow Highway near Cherry Avenue. This location would, however, be only temporary, and in 1982 Fontana Paving occupied the modern, 4,500-square-foot structure it had built as its permanent headquarters.

By the time the firm celebrated its 25th anniversary in July 1981, an impressive list of projects had been amassed throughout a four-county area. Montclair Plaza, Tyler Mall, Ontario International Airport, Fontana's Southwest Industrial Park, and portions of Interstate 15 are only a few. Many others are similarly in this $1.5- to $2-million price range.

Reed Sprinkel, at age 16, operating a clam shovel on a construction project in 1938.

Reed Sprinkel, president and chief executive officer of Fontana Paving, Inc.

To carry out this work, Fontana Paving maintains a fleet of equipment consisting of Barber-Greene asphalt pavers, Hyster rollers, John Deere paddle loaders, and Caterpillar blades and rubber-tire loaders.

Sprinkel, however, takes greater pride in his employees and the fact that many have been with him for more than 20 years. In particular, he calls attention to Felix D'Amico, who was general manager for 23 years before his retirement in 1982 and still performs as a management consultant to the company.

The new management team is Hank Sipe, vice-president and general manager; George Koch, vice-president and superintendent of plants; Rick Vallecorsa, vice-president of construction/estimating; and Henry Bendzala, corporate accountant/office manager.

Like many of his employees, Sprinkel himself is active in public affairs and has frequently been recognized for his contributions to the community.

In 1974 he was named Contractor of the Year by the Engineering, Grading, and Contractor's Association and is a past statewide president of that organization.

Sprinkel was a member and past chairman of the State Contractor's License Board and is a past national president of the contractor's division of the American Road and Transportation Builder's Association.

He holds a degree in industrial management from the University of Southern California and received the Distinguished Flying Cross during his eight years in the U.S. Air Force. Sprinkel is a senior active member of the Rotary Club of Fontana and a past president.

Twice a delegate to the Republican National Convention, Sprinkel has chaired several campaign committees for the elections of Ronald Reagan for President and Pete Wilson for the U.S. Senate.

Reed's wife, the former Rita L. Inderbo, is a Southern California representative for the Royal Norwegian Embassy and is currently director of employee and public relations for Fontana Paving.

With nearly 40 years in the asphalt business, Sprinkel is optimistic about the future of his company. He points out that the recent residential and industrial growth of San Bernardino County has contributed substantially to his success and that he is sure this trend will be accelerated in future years.

McANALLY ENTERPRISES, INC.

McAnally Enterprises, Inc., now among the most prominent egg producers in the western United States, had a modest beginning in 1939 when president N.A. McAnally entered the poultry business. But what started as a one-man operation with fewer than 100 laying hens has grown to a five-state corporation with 600 employees and nearly four million chickens which produce more than 2.5 million eggs per day.

McAnally married his wife, Dovie, in Texas during the Depression and drought in 1933. Soon, however, they moved to Southern California and San Bernardino County where McAnally worked at a dairy farm in Ontario and later on a turkey ranch in Yucaipa. His first business venture involved the lease of 25 acres, also in Yucaipa, where he raised tomatoes in 1938 and 1939.

In December 1939 the McAnallys embarked on the undertaking that would make their name a standard in egg production. With $90 borrowed from their real estate broker, A.H. Heitman, they made a down payment on the 10-acre site in Yucaipa, which has been the backbone of their business and is now also their corporate headquarters. Located on Seventh Street immediately south of Yucaipa Boulevard, the property was then a grain field, and the $1,800 selling price included a small house.

With 95 chickens, McAnally began one of the area's first poultry ranches, and a year later hired his first employee at a wage of 30 cents per hour. The operation grew and prospered to the point where in 1953 the ranch included some 30,000 birds. Perhaps equally important, a total of more than 300 such ranches had begun production within a five-mile radius where 15 years earlier there had been only a few.

Worthy of note is the fact that San Bernardino and Riverside counties have the highest concentration of laying hens found anywhere in the United States. McAnally attributes this situation to the area's mild climate and the production of laying cages he developed and started manufacturing in 1949. Known as the "McAnally Production Line," this new system utilized wire laying cages and is still the basis of methods employed throughout the world.

Mr. and Mrs. N.A. McAnally in 1969, on the 30th anniversary of the establishment of their poultry ranch.

N.A. McAnally prepares for a ride with daughter Raye and son Larry on the tractor he built from miscellaneous parts in 1938.

For a time, McAnally manufactured and sold the cage, but eventually found it more desirable to produce it only for his own use and concentrate his efforts on expanding the business. Beyond this, McAnally built the second electric cart ever used in the poultry industry for gathering eggs. Although McAnally's application of the device is limited to his ranch, a number of similar vehicles, including the modern golf cart, have resulted for a variety of purposes.

Flash flooding damaged the ranch in 1944 and, in 1954, all the brooders were destroyed by a fire that swept the henhouse. Nonetheless, in 1962 McAnally Enterprises was incorporated and the business continued to

An employee at the McAnallys' Yucaipa ranch rides on one of the poultry industry's first electric carts while gathering eggs. The cart, built by N.A. McAnally, is a forerunner of the modern-day golf cart.

expand. In 1974 McAnally developed ranches in Arizona and New Mexico, and two years later in Kansas and Oklahoma, with Yucaipa remaining the headquarters of the organization.

Today McAnally Enterprises is one of few egg producers in the nation that is a fully integrated operation. The ranches produce their own feed, raise the chicks, process the eggs, and even maintain a fleet of trucks to deliver the product to market.

To feed the chickens, the firm owns four feed mills, the largest of which is part of the complex in Yucaipa. This original location also houses the corporation's executive offices as well as an accounting center and is linked by computer to all other McAnally ranches.

New corporate office facilities were enlarged on the Yucaipa property for the fifth time in 1970, finally totaling 10,000 square feet and replacing four previous structures that had, one by one, been outgrown as the company expanded into a nationally recognized giant.

Just as it was founded single-handedly by the McAnallys, the corporation continues as truly a family-owned and -operated business. In addition to first-and-only president N.A. McAnally, his son-in-law, dentist Carlton R. Lofgren, serves as one of several vice-presidents and his son, Larry L. McAnally, one-time vice-president, remains a major stockholder while conducting his business in Newport Beach.

What's more, the McAnallys point with pride to the six grandchildren they foresee as future management, and are quick to note that even some of their nonfamily employees have been with the firm for more than 25 years.

McAnally, too, has made substantial social and civic contributions. Not only has he been commended by health officials for his efforts to control the odor problem always associated with poultry, but in addition has assumed positions of leadership in several community-based organizations.

From 1952 to 1957, McAnally served as president of the Yucaipa Valley Water Company and, for 20 years, was a member of the board of directors for the Production Credit Association. Perhaps most important, McAnally was a key figure in the founding of the Southland National Bank, helping to establish branches in Hemet, Loma Linda, and Yucaipa.

His interests also include a collection of antique vehicles, which comprises 38 cars featuring a 1908 Buick and the last Chevrolet Corvair to come off the production line. Mrs. McAnally, likewise, is a woman of diversified interests and is active in both real estate and interior decoration.

Despite the McAnallys' numerous other involvements, their company's sales total more than $50 million per year, clearly the hallmark of the McAnally family and a major element in the development of the Yucaipa area.

H.M.C. ARCHITECTS, INC.

One of Southern California's most recognized and respected institutional architectural firms dates back to 1940, when Jay Dewey Harnish opened a small office just east of Euclid Avenue on B Street in Ontario.

H.M.C. Architects, Inc., formerly the partnership of Harnish, Morgan, and Causey, today is perhaps the area's most prominent and accomplished designer of medical and educational facilities.

Among a long list of such projects, Harnish points with satisfaction to Upland's San Antonio Community Hospital for which he did major architectural work from the early days of his career in 1939 until his retirement in 1978.

Looking back, Harnish can cite at least 10 major clients he worked with for 40 years or longer. He attributes the success of his organization to detailed service and active involvement from preliminary drawings to move-in day. "We were never afraid to walk the ground and get our shoes dirty," says the firm's founder.

Harnish and his parents moved to Upland for his mother's health in 1910. He attended local schools and later served active duty in France during World War I.

Upon returning from the Front, he earned his degree in architecture from the University of California at Berkeley and worked for a time in San Francisco. Later he became associated with the firm of York and Sawyer in New York where he did his first design work on hospital projects, laying the foundation for his future career.

Back in California during the Depression, Harnish designed sets for Metro-Goldwyn-Mayer and RKO Studios, eventually finding work, more to his liking, with Dewitt-Mitchem, a San Bernardino firm heavily involved with Works Progress Administration (WPA) projects.

As economic conditions improved, Harnish, now with a broadened architectural background, began to consider the possibility of establishing his own business and, in 1940, the forerunner of H.M.C. hung out its shingle.

From 1941 to 1945 Harnish's efforts were largely concentrated on the design of military housing. He mapped out projects in San Bernardino, Colton, Redlands, and Barstow, sometimes extending his practice as far as Trona and Needles. Among his still-known World War II involvements are Waterman Gardens in San Bernardino and Lugonia Homes in Redlands.

As the war drew to a close, Harnish anticipated a change in the nature of future construction and began to prepare himself and his five employees for the institutional work that would come with peacetime, and with which he had earlier been involved in New York.

H.M.C. Architects, Inc., noted throughout the area for its institutional and medical facility designs, created this building which houses the firm's offices at 500 East E Street in Ontario.

The highly specialized practice that eventually would become the firm's calling card began to materialize in 1945, when Harnish undertook architectural contracts at San Bernardino County General Hospital.

Ten years later he designed the hospital's tuberculosis unit, in the early 1960s he laid out the plans for its acute-care unit, and ultimately he received the assignment to do the now highly acclaimed burn unit.

San Antonio Community Hospital, Upland.

Kaiser Permanente Medical Center, Fontana.

Also on H.M.C.'s list of notable projects are Pomona Valley Community Hospital and Kaiser Permanente Medical Center in Fontana, a major health facility with which the firm has been involved since 1955.

In 1960 Harnish entered into the partnership that would produce the present-day concern. Jack Causey, current president, and M.C. Morgan became principals in the new organization as Rudolph Voss and William Swords assumed the position of major investors.

Since that time, in addition to its long-term, ongoing projects, H.M.C. has developed the plans for no fewer than 25 schools in the Ontario-Montclair area, 5 high schools in the Chaffey District, and 10 schools in Upland. Beyond this, the architects have undertaken extensive work for school districts in Fontana, Victorville, and Big Bear.

Outside the immediate area, the firm expanded its reputation in the early 1970s with impressive work at both the Hoag Memorial Hospital in Newport Beach, the Santa Ana-Tustin Community Hospital, and more recently, the Desert Hospital in Palm Springs.

When Harnish retired in 1978, his associates took on three new partners: James Chase, Kenneth Taylor, and Walter Siegl, who, with Causey and Voss, compose the company's current leadership.

Harnish, nonetheless, had made his mark in the community as well as in his profession. For eight years he served as a member of the State Board of Architectural Examiners and, since 1968, his name has appeared in *Who's Who in America.*

Locally, he was active in the Ontario Chamber of Commerce and was its president in 1939-1940. He was a leading member of the Chamber's aviation committee, which was instrumental in the city's purchase of the first increment of land to create Ontario International Airport. Interestingly enough, Harnish additionally did the architectural work on the airport's first terminal building in 1946 as well as the present terminal building.

Also prominent in the community was Harnish's wife, Jerene Appleby, who owned the *Ontario Daily Report,* the *Victor Press* in Victorville, and the *Escondido Times Advocate.*

One of the final projects Harnish undertook prior to his retirement was a 74-unit condominium complex on 20 acres in Rancho Cucamonga's elite Red Hill area.

Himself now a resident of the development he designed, Harnish is certain of H.M.C.'s future and watches with satisfaction as his former partners continue in the tradition he established.

Desert Hospital, Palm Springs.

FIRST AMERICAN TITLE INSURANCE COMPANY

The San Bernardino County office of what since has become one of the nation's top three title insurance firms had a unique combination of beginnings at Santa Ana, California, in 1889 and, later, locally in 1948.

Land Title Company of San Bernardino was incorporated on October 9, 1948, by two prominent area businessmen — Roy Chalmers, president of Arrowhead Title and Guarantee Company, and Walter Blount, owner of The Escrow Company. With 15 employees, the start-up venture began business in leased quarters at 369 Court Street, now in the mainstream of San Bernardino's downtown financial district.

Nearly 60 years earlier, however, First American Title Insurance Company had been born in neighboring Orange County when two small, but historically significant, companies were created. Their merger, brought about in 1894 by C.F. Parker, would produce Orange County Title Company, true forerunner of the present-day, nationwide giant.

In 1958 the Orange County Title Company acquired controlling interest in the 10-year-old Land Title Company of San Bernardino, and the name was officially changed to First American Title Insurance Company two years later.

Before this change, the growing San Bernardino firm had moved a short distance from its original location to what was known as the old Montgomery Ward building near the intersection of Arrowhead and Court streets. This structure was leveled in 1965 to provide a parking lot adjoining American Title's current four-story, million-dollar center which was under construction at 323 Court Street across from the county courthouse, once the site of a Mormon council house.

Throughout the years, the firm's principal objective has been to protect the ownership of real property against losses resulting from any defect in title. Microfilm, electronic indexing, computerized title plates, and all the latest technology are used to assure the accuracy of this process and replace the laborious task of manually searching files at the Hall of Records.

Among the seemingly countless local projects in which First American Title has been involved are several that serve to substantiate the company's stature in the history of the area. Perhaps most noteworthy are Campus Crusade for Christ, which now occupies the famous, old Arrowhead Springs Hotel; Inland Center and Central City shopping malls; nearly all of the downtown redevelopment project; the new San Bernardino County super block; the massive Rancho Mediterrania development on the Cooley Ranch property; and the Spring Valley Lake community in the high desert.

Commitment to the county has been further demonstrated by the opening of branch offices in Big Bear Lake, Upland, Victorville, and Yucca Valley.

Regional vice-president C. Wayne Wood, who heads the 150-member staff in San Bernardino, joined the original local firm at its inception in 1948 as a title searcher. Edward D. Young and Lorene Meek, both now vice-presidents, also were among the first employees.

First American Title Insurance Company now has assets of more than $100 million and offices in 44 states, but always has considered San Bernardino an important part of its organization.

To quote the firm in 1965, "We're proud of our pioneer past and the part we have played in the development of San Bernardino County. Our new home, located on land which has served as the center of county activity for more than a century, is a reflection of our faith in the community."

The San Bernardino County headquarters of First American Title Insurance Company is located at Arrowhead Avenue and Court Street. Once the site of a historic Mormon council house, the area is now the community's center of both financial and government affairs.

NOVACK'S AMERICAN METAL REDUCTION COMPANY, INC.

San Bernardino County's largest scrap metal-processing operation began four generations ago when Abraham Novack, still in his teens, came from Russia to the United States with his wife, Bessie, and their infant daughter. After a brief stay in Chicago, Novack and his wife (who by now had two children) moved to Santa Barbara. From there they worked up and down the coast of California buying and selling scrap metal. They foresaw a business opportunity upon learning that San Bernardino had no scrap metal-processing operation.

In 1916 the Novacks began their operation on the northeast corner of E and Mill streets, at what is now the heart of one of San Bernardino's major commercial districts.

This location would serve the community well until 1960. During those years, largely under the leadership of Bessie Novack and son Alex, a second site had been established during the mid-1920s on A Street (now Holt Avenue) in Ontario.

The 18 acres of rail-served property, which now ships approximately 400 tons of processed metal per day, was acquired in 1945. Still in Ontario, at the intersection of Milliken Avenue and Mission Boulevard, the current facility is accurately described by its owners and operators as a "factory without a roof."

Presently heading the firm are the founder's grandson, Donald Novack, chairman of the board, and his sons, Vincent, who serves as president, and Shawn, who is in charge of industrial purchasing.

Novack's receives most of its raw material from worn-out or outdated railroad cars and airplanes; surplus and used machinery; and material from demolition contractors, scrap collectors, auto dismantlers, and industrial suppliers whose scrap metals are by-products of manufacturing. The metal is put through various processes involving flattening, shredding, compressing, shearing, and cutting. A portion of the production is shipped to the Far East and Europe, but the largest portion is consumed domestically.

Today, with some departments operating around the clock, the plant receives trucks one after the other loaded with auto bodies, worn-out appliances, machinery, automobile parts, electric motors, copper tubing, and wire—in fact, everything imaginable that originated from metal products. In addition, there is industrial scrap that is delivered by trucks and roll-off units that are owned by a subsidiary company.

In 1983 alone, Novack's recycled more than 1.2 million pounds of aluminum cans, a process that involves a magnetic conveyor to separate the aluminum cans from other metal containers. A second processing step prepares them to be made into more beverage cans.

Novack's receives in excess of 100,000 tons of scrap per year, which is processed utilizing equipment ranging from automatic engine pullers to hydraulic shears, converting unusable material into a marketable product. Included in the equipment are a flattening machine that compresses auto bodies to a height of only eight inches and crushes 25 vehicles per hour, shears that can cut up railroad cars, high-compression metal balers, and other specially designed and built machinery and equipment.

Vincent (Van) Novack, the fourth-generation president of the business, takes pride in pointing out that the scrap metal Novack's buys would otherwise be filling up refuse disposal sites and permeating the countryside, roadways, and vacant lands, while resulting in the loss of hundreds of thousands of tons per year of our country's vital natural resources. Van notes with a sense of accomplishment that a truckload of nonferrous metal can be worth $30,000 or more. "Every metallic product in the entire world can be started with one-third to one-half processed scrap metals," says Novack. "Our company is becoming a bigger and more important part of that every year."

Abraham Novack, founder of Novack's American Metal Reduction Company, Inc.

SECURE SAVINGS AND LOAN ASSOCIATION

Secure Savings and Loan Association is a comparative newcomer to the San Bernardino County financial community, but one which, during its brief history, has demonstrated a civic spirit and record of accomplishment that place it prominently in the future of the area.

The firm was incorporated in September 1979 by 10 local investors whose objective was to serve the banking needs of Fontana and the county's central valley. The next two years would be spent marketing stock and obtaining insurance of accounts, but on November 16, 1981, Secure Savings and Loan was open for business in its original leased office space near the intersection of Arrow Highway and Juniper Avenue.

Colton dentist Delbert L. Van Voorhis had organized the undertaking and Colorado businessman Jerry Nash served, for a time, as the savings and loan's first president.

Other key figures making up the institution's founding fathers were John Boruchin, Fontana area residential and industrial developer; Tommy W. Hogan, a highly respected local coach and educator; Jess Mancha, well-known real estate broker and escrow company owner; Robert D. Raney, longtime building contractor; Marvin Reimer, president of Western Color Prints, Inc.; Sam Shapiro, a Canadian real estate developer; Nick Thomas, owner of Thomas Furniture Mart; and Lynn B. Whitesides, former owner of an aircraft parts manufacturing firm later purchased by Teledyne, Inc.

The organization was joined in 1981 by T. Edward Huckaby, now president, chief executive officer, and member of the board of directors. Huckaby brought to the firm a banking career dating back to 1946 and including top-level managerial positions with both Redlands Federal and Orange Belt Federal savings and loans.

At a time when even well-established financial institutions were experiencing uncertainties, Secure Savings and Loan entered the field with a strong start—showing a $9,000 profit in its first six weeks of operation.

By 1983 the still young and growing institution had acquired $11.5 million in assets and had opened its first branch office. The California Western Financial Services Corporation had been established as a subsidiary, and plans were under way to provide a full range of financial programs.

Having outgrown its facilities, but very pleased with the Fontana area, the firm constructed a new two-story office which would also serve as its permanent corporate headquarters at 16855 Arrow Highway. The move was made in the fall of 1983 and corporate executives pledge their continued support of the local area as anticipated expansion occurs.

"We fully expect to grow with our community," says president Huckaby. "And we are sincerely dedicated to the financial future of the Inland Empire."

Secure Savings and Loan Association, 16855 Arrow Highway, serves the banking needs of Fontana and the county's central valley.

THE BEAVER MEDICAL CLINIC

The Beaver Medical Clinic, a highly respected health care facility in Redlands, was established in 1947 by four physicians who had met while serving in World War II.

The staff now includes 28 physicians offering 13 specialties of medicine and serving a total of over 190,000 patients who have active records on file at the clinic.

Perhaps more important, the institution's founder, Dr. Meredith G. Beaver, embarked upon the clinic concept at a time when such facilities were subject to a degree of skepticism within the medical profession.

Dr. Beaver, a certified surgeon practicing in Redlands since 1932, constructed a medical building on the site of the present clinic at Fern Avenue and Cajon Street in Redlands. The year, however, was 1940 and military duty would soon temporarily disrupt his Redlands practice.

During the war Dr. Beaver and Dr. Joseph Hayhurst, a Redlands general practitioner, served with Dr. Espey F. Cannon, an internist, and Dr. Gordon L. Witter, an ophthalmologist, forming the nucleus for the team of diversified physicians that would become the Beaver Medical Clinic.

The new 55,000-square-foot Beaver Medical Clinic was built in 1974 and incorporates the original Redlands facility. Twenty-eight physicians currently serve approximately 190,000 patients at the clinic.

In order to do this, the foursome returned to Dr. Beaver's Redlands office. In 1946 they were joined by management consultant A. Leslie Richardson, also an Army associate, who spent the next 30 years with the clinic as its first administrator.

The original office, still part of the clinic, would undergo three major expansions and numerous modifications until 1974, when the current facility was built. Now totaling 55,000 square feet, the two-story clinic tactfully incorporates all previous offices and covers three-quarters of a city block.

The original offices of Dr. Meredith G. Beaver were constructed in 1940 and became the Beaver Medical Clinic in 1946, when Dr. Beaver and his three original partners returned from military service during World War II.

The Beaver Medical Foundation, established in 1961, has been successful in awarding funds donated by physicians to provide grants for medical research, professional education, and scholarships. By the time of his retirement in 1969, Dr. Beaver and his associates had witnessed both the emergence of their clinic as a leading medical facility and the acceptance of the multispecialty group practice concept.

The last of the four founders retired in 1979, and the original partnership was converted into a corporation. Dr. Beaver's early philosophy has never diminished and remains the key to the clinic's continued success. As phrased by a present-day colleague, the key factor is "offering the community a staff of certified specialists who complement each other's expertise with mutual support to provide the highest standard of medical care to the community."

Dr. Beaver and the physicians practicing today at the Beaver Medical Clinic share many common concerns. One, in particular, prevails: serving the health care needs of patients in the most professional, effective, and cost-efficient manner.

FUTURUS, INC.

Benjamin Anthony Kruce—a man who preceded himself by perhaps 25 years—began what newspapers have called "Upland's most unique business."

He liked to turn junk into something of value. Once he built a helicopter in his own garage. Today the enterprise he started and ran uses worn-out tires to produce some of the most long-lasting carpeting ever made.

Although recycling didn't become fashionable until contemporary times, Kruce was nearly obsessed with the idea from the time he was a brilliant young man. As his widow Mary puts it, "He always wanted to make something out of nothing."

"Tuff stuff," as many customers call it, is manufactured by Futurus, Inc., the company founded by Kruce in 1961. Some of the first carpeting he produced nearly 23 years ago remains in good condition at the entrance of Buffums in Pomona, and more recent material has been purchased by Saks Fifth Avenue, Macy's, Bullock's, May Company, and The Broadway.

A native of Ohio, Kruce began his career in Michigan at Pontiac Motors, later working for both Douglas and Northrup Aviation. By age 27 he had developed and was head of the Manufacturing, Research, and Development Department for North American Aviation.

His curiosity, deep-thinking, and inquisitive nature led him to experiment on his own with molding resins which he used to make luggage and an occasional fishing pole. By 1956 Kruce was using old automobile tires to make door mats and was experiencing a degree of success.

Then the big break came! The Broadway asked Kruce to produce a floor covering for its elevators that could not be penetrated by high-heeled shoes and would, therefore, reduce the risk of injury to women.

Benjamin Anthony Kruce (right), founder of Futurus, Inc., left his Upland plant for the last time in December 1982. With him are his former wife and partner, Mary, and the current corporate president, Fred C. Howard.

In 1961 Futurus opened its first plant in leased quarters at 1076 Ninth Street in Upland, moving five years later to larger facilities next door. Kruce continued to refine his process and the product was soon answering the call of an ever-increasing market.

Kruce built his own factory in 1976, an 18,000-square-foot structure at 1333 West Ninth Street, in the Upland Industrial Park, not far from his original location. Here, the business maintains an inventory of 18,000 used tires and employs approximately 35 workers.

As a result of Futurus' success, three other companies are now manufacturing similar products, and millions of truck, bus, and airplane tires that would otherwise have filled dump sites have been put to good use and are dignifying airports, hotels, and shopping centers throughout the world!

Benjamin Anthony Kruce died in 1983, but he had realized many goals. His curiosity was the driving force of his life and made his name known worldwide. Fred C. Howard, a veteran corporate manager from the East, now presides at Futurus and Mary (Kruce) Howard remains secretary/treasurer.

FREDRIC H. RUBEL JEWELERS

"A little bit of Beverly Hills in the midst of downtown San Bernardino." That's how Fredric H. Rubel describes the jewelry store his mother and father established in 1928.

Now located in the Central City Mall, Rubel offers a "guild" line of high-quality jewelry, featuring fine gems, Rolex watches, Lalique and Baccarat crystal, along with Lladro figurines.

The store began when Fredric Rubel's parents, Barney and Rose, passed through San Bernardino on their honeymoon, noticing several vacant shops on E Street. Having met while working for a jeweler in Los Angeles, the Rubels returned several months later to start their own business—then called Crescent Jewelers—at 345 North E Street.

Barney and Rose remained at that original location for 20 years, moving the store in 1948 a block up the street.

Barney Rubel retired for health reasons and his wife, Rose, continued to run the business. To this day she works in the store.

Their son and the current owner, Fredric, purchased an interest in 1962 and changed the store's name to the one currently used. Ten years later he moved the store to its present mall location, carrying only the highest-quality merchandise.

Fredric's wife, Joan, whom he married in 1957, works part time at the store. Fredric was joined in the business by his son David in 1981 and by another son Gary in 1982. All three are Certified Gemologists, Registered Jewelers, and members of the American Gem Society. The Rubels also have a daughter, Ellen, who is currently attending the University of California at San Diego.

The store, now with 11 employees, has an ever-increasing number of new customers as well as many on a long-term basis. Rubel's has a mailing list of more than 5,000 patrons.

Barney Rubel, founder of Crescent Jewelers, the forerunner of today's Fredric H. Rubel Jewelers.

Fredric is a past president of the San Bernardino Executive Association and has served eight terms as president of the Central City Mall Merchants' Association. He is a graduate of the University of California at Berkeley, where he met his wife. Their sons, David and Gary, hold degrees from UC San Diego and UCLA, respectively.

Fredric H. Rubel believes in providing unchallenged quality, custom design, and buying directly from diamond cutters according to his own high standards. He is perhaps most proud of his mother's nearly 55 years of work in the family business, and looks to its continued success in partnership with his sons.

ASSOCIATED ENGINEERS

Robert Mills (right), one of the original founders of Associated Engineers, discusses plans for a mobile home park with a draftsman in the "old yellow house," then located on the site of the firm's current parking lot.

Successful partnerships begin in many ways, but it is unique that a top-name firm should be the product of a carpool friendship that pulled together two young, but talented, engineers.

Robert E. Mills and Wayne P. Lill, sharing a ride to work, conceived Associated Engineers in 1955 and opened a tiny office in a rented room of an old home on Laurel Street in Ontario. Mills was previously Ontario city engineer and Lill had established a reputation in flood control, so it is not surprising that their young organization advanced quickly in the field of civil and municipal engineering.

Today Associated Engineers has to its credit some of the most widely acclaimed design jobs in the Inland Empire, including work on airports, drainage structures, sanitation facilities, and water systems.

Shortly after its inception the firm was joined by Lester "Red" Noreen, who complemented his partners with broad experience in highway routing, plant construction, and military airstrip layout.

In 1960 the threesome purchased and occupied what is remembered by many as the "old yellow house" at 316 East E Street, and later purchased the house next door, which was the residence previously owned by Ontario's well-known Bumstead family. The growth of Associated Engineers, however, was beyond the capacity of either structure and, in 1972, the current 5,000-square-foot office building was erected on the site of the former houses.

Mills and his partners placed special emphasis on preservation of the property's historic landscaping and, as a result of this concern, their working environment remains beautifully surrounded by crepe myrtles, elegant camellias, a sprawling fig tree, and a persimmon tree.

The true mark of achievement, however, lies in the vital part Associated Engineers has played in numerous jobs designed to improve the quality of life in San Bernardino County.

Perhaps most visible among these are two projects at Ontario International Airport, involving not only automobile parking and access, but aircraft taxiways and aprons as well. Major work on aviation facilities has also been carried out by the firm at Palm Springs Municipal Airport, Hollywood Burbank Airport, and the San Bernardino County airports at Chino and Big Bear Lake, contributing substantially to Associated's solid reputation for airport work.

Lill retired in 1981 with Mills remaining as president and Noreen supervising all survey parties and field operations. The original partnership, which was incorporated in 1969, has grown to 35 employees with a branch office in San Bernardino's new Commerce Center.

Mills' daughter, April Morris, is one of the firm's nine licensed Civil Engineers while his brother, Richard, owns a formerly affiliated company which provides geological and soil testing services.

Associated Engineers believes in being efficient, yet thorough. Robert Mills and his employees strive to cast a cost-conscious eye to every project, completing the engineering plans as expeditiously as possible according to the highest professional procedures.

A rented room in an old house at 425 Laurel Avenue in Ontario served as Associated Engineers' first office in 1955. The Rambler station wagon was used for survey work.

GRESHAM, VARNER, SAVAGE, NOLAN & TILDEN

In 1910 a young but rapidly rising attorney named William Guthrie opened his first law office in San Bernardino. Guthrie was an aggressive, self-educated individual from a prominent local family, but perhaps even he could not have envisioned what was to result.

During the next 70 years Guthrie's practice would evolve into the present-day firm of Gresham, Varner, Savage, Nolan & Tilden—quite possibly the county's leading firm in civil litigation and real estate. Many of the current attorneys are accomplished experts in their particular legal field, producing an impressive inventory of specialized services.

Guthrie's first office was in the Katz Building at the northeast corner of Third and E streets. With his business expanding rapidly, he moved in 1927 to the then-new Andreson Building at 320 North E Street, where he designed his own facilities on the fifth floor.

Although Guthrie retired in 1948, the firm stayed in the same building until 1966. At that time it moved to the newly constructed Lonergan Building, named for John B. Lonergan who was a respected partner from 1947 until 1978.

Located at 398 West Fourth Street, this building remains the firm's current quarters with attractive offices occupying the entire third floor as well as half of the second. Gresham, Varner, Savage, Nolan & Tilden now has nine partners, six associates, and a total of 33 employees.

Throughout its history the organization has always been headed by attorneys of prominence, both professionally and in their community. Guthrie served as San Bernardino city attorney for 18 years and was personally retained by Henry J. Kaiser when Kaiser Steel Corporation built its mill in Fontana in 1943.

William Guthrie opened his first law office in San Bernardino in 1910. The firm was the forerunner of what is today Gresham, Varner, Savage, Nolan & Tilden.

Jesse Curtis, who became Guthrie's first partner in 1937, was thereafter appointed to a superior court judgeship and ultimately advanced to the position of senior federal district court judge in Los Angeles.

By 1947 Guthrie had been joined by Lonergan and Donald W. Jordan, both now retired but still widely recognized. Jordan, though active in many areas, is perhaps best known for his work in banking and estate planning. Lonergan, on the other hand, was a leader in the state as well as county bar associations and played a vital role in the establishment of Division Two of the Fourth District Court of Appeal in San Bernardino.

It must also be noted that among the firm's current principals, both Allen B. Gresham and Phillip M. Savage have served as presidents of the County Bar Association, while John C. Nolan was president of the Legal Aid Society. M. William Tilden has extensive experience with the mining industry, and Bruce D. Varner and Savage have specialized experience in medical law. Varner and Gresham were both deeply involved in the city's redevelopment projects.

Additionally, the firm's areas of expertise extend to environmental regulation, military law, real estate, taxation, probate, and estate planning. Major clients include Kaiser Steel Corporation, California Portland Cement, Kerr-McGee, Pfizer, Saint Bernardine's Hospital, Southern California Edison, General Telephone, and Southern California Gas.

The firm has practiced law in the Lonergan Building, located at 398 West Fourth Street, San Bernardino, since 1966.

BOMATIC, INC.

The original Bomatic building at 236 Laurel Street in Ontario totaled only 2,000 square feet but served the new company well during its first two years of production.

When Borge Hestehave was growing up in Elsinore, Denmark, he always wanted to own his own business. He lived there through the period of German occupation and, afterwards, considered the possibility of moving to Australia, Canada, or the United States.

Today, more than 30 years later, he is the president of Bomatic, Inc., a firm he envisioned, created, and personally developed, based largely on his inventive spirit combined with a strong desire to succeed.

Located in Ontario, immediately south of the airport, the company molds a continuous supply of plastic containers purchased by some of the nation's most well-known companies in which to market liquids ranging from perfume to swimming pool chemicals.

Bomatic is one of few such producers that not only molds the containers, but also designs and manufactures its own molds. It's perhaps the only one that can claim to have conceived the technology behind its machinery.

In 1952, having earned a master's degree at the Engineering College of Copenhagen, Hestehave began his career by accepting a position in Santiago, Chile, which he believed would lead him to greater opportunity in the western world. He spent four years in South America building a toothpaste tube factory and training its employees at their new jobs.

But the time came for Borge to move on, as he knew it would. In 1956 he decided to relocate his wife and family to the United States, where they would settle temporarily with friends in Inglewood, California.

He worked as a tool-and-die maker and eventually gained his first blow-molding experience. The real beginning did not occur, however, until 1963 when Hestehave entered into partnership with Leonard Robinson, owner of a Northern California firm known as Magic-Cup. It was this team that would, in the next four years, invent and patent the now widely used injection blow-molding machine.

With his resulting reputation, Hestehave obtained a position designing and building his machine for Trans-Container in Upland where he was employed until late 1969. Again he entered a partnership, this time with longtime mold-maker and good friend Henry A. Myers.

Born of this partnership, Bomatic was incorporated and began production solely as a mold-making operation in a 2,000-square-foot leased building at 236 Laurel Street in Ontario. The firm had a modest beginning with Myers, Hestehave, several family members, and a mere two employees struggling to get a foothold in an increasingly competitive market.

By 1971, however, Bomatic had gained sufficient strength to buy a large, used blow-molding machine from Technical Plastics, original producer of Tee Pee gasoline containers. This purchase was accompanied by a move to a larger 5,000-square-foot facility at 1141 West Brooks Street where the company would courageously embark upon the blow-

Bomatic president and founder Borge Hestehave inspects a steel mold produced in his Ontario shop. Molds of this type now are valued at up to $100,000.

molding field.

In just two years Bomatic became the major supplier of Technical Plastics, once owner of the machine, and remarkably bought out its entire operation in 1975. During this time, son Kjeld, with a degree in mechanical engineering, had joined his father's firm and the two were matching wits to improve the product line.

Technical Plastics, now dissolved, was named Totem Plastics and serves, to this day, as a sales operation marketing a portion of Bomatic's products—namely the gasoline, kerosene, and water containers.

Well-established nationally by 1978, Bomatic undertook construction of yet a much larger building—a 26,000-square-foot facility on 2.5 acres near the intersection of Mission Boulevard and Vineyard Avenue. Located at 1841 East Acacia Street, the two-story structure serves as the current home of both Bomatic and Totem Plastics, housing all facets of the operation from processing of the raw material to final shipping.

Tiny polyethylene beads smaller than a BB are the basic ingredient. Once melted, the molten plastic is fed into a battery of molding machines to create an array of containers for uses ranging from Fabergé shampoo to gas tanks for McCulloch chain saws. Other major customers include Ajax, Beckman Instruments, Bentley Laboratories, Canon Business Machines, and Tomy Toys.

Bomatic's 60 employees operate 10 blow-molding machines, two injection machines, and two computers which are programmed to handle all accounting functions as well as inventory control. Equally important advanced lathe and milling machines produce the all-important steel molds—some with a value as high as $100,000.

To the rear of this clean, modern shop is a warehouse stacked nearly to the ceiling with cartons of plastic bottles awaiting shipment to Bomatic's customers. The company's own trucks are loaded for local delivery and to bring the product to other carriers for cross-country transportation.

Bomatic employs machinists, mold makers, engineers, quality-control personnel, set-up men, supervisors, packers, and shipping clerks. Hestehave, however, notes with pride that he and his son do all the design work of the machines.

Likewise, Bomatic is completely family owned and controlled. Borge's wife, Marianne, is vice-president in charge of personnel and quality control; Kjeld serves as vice-president with responsibility for production and sales; and daughter Judy is secretary/treasurer and office manager.

Now considering further expansion, Hestehave admits that a family-operated company requires diversified skills from each member. "But," he notes, "their personal pride and dedication create a high-quality product."

Lathes and milling machines provide the backbone of Bomatic's mold-making operation. The firm is one of the few plastic bottle manufacturers that produces its own in-house molds.

Containers for gasoline and other liquids were produced at one time by Bomatic for Technical Plastics, now known as Totem Plastics. Such items remain part of Bomatic's expanded line of products.

EVERETT/CHARLES

With offices throughout the United States and in three foreign countries, Everett/Charles administers its worldwide operations from a new corporate headquarters located in the northwestern corner of Fontana.

The 20,000-square-foot, two-story structure was completed in February 1982 and now houses the executive offices of chairman-founder Everett J. Long and many of his top-level staff members.

It is here that corporate policy is established while other management functions include accounting, communications, market research, quality assurance, technology development, and business planning.

In its manufacturing plants in nearby Pomona, Everett/Charles designs and produces highly sophisticated, computer-controlled test equipment, specialized electrical contact products, and reprogrammable factory automation systems. Though still young, the company employs almost 400 persons and reported annual sales of nearly $24 million in 1983.

Everett J. Long enters the block building on Grand Avenue in Pomona, which was the original home of the firm (1960-1963) that would become Everett/Charles.

Long started the firm in 1960 with partner Charles W. Burley, whose interest he would buy out five years later. Originally known as Long and Burley Laboratories, the business was largely a precision machine shop first located in a 1,600-square-foot block building at 1480 East Grand Avenue in Pomona.

Long and Burley had come to California in 1952 with the idea of beginning their own business, but some eight years would pass before their real beginning. During this time, Long spent several years as managing director for the Transducer Division of Consolidated Electrodynamics Corporation.

Born in Iowa, Long was raised in Canada—later working at jobs in New Mexico, Colorado, and back in Iowa. But it was in New Mexico that Long and Burley became acquainted and first discussed the possibility of their future partnership.

When they finally got under way, there were only two employees and shipments tallied a mere $13,000 during the first year. Strong indications of future achievement were soon evident, however, as this figure soared to nearly $100,000 in the following 12 months.

By 1963 the company had far outgrown its original shop and moved to larger quarters totaling 4,500 square feet at 1243 Transit Avenue in Pomona. This facility would be sufficient for a time, but three years later more space was again needed and Everett/Charles began moving into the 2800 block of Metropolitan Place in one of Pomona's industrial parks.

Rapid and steady progress would characterize the next decade, and a series of expansions resulted in the firm occupying some 38,000 square feet in the same area by 1977. What's more, employment had increased to 180 and plans called for still further growth.

This was to be a key year for the business and the beginning of a new era in its corporate history. To this point largely a supplier of equipment for the electronics industry, Everett/Charles now introduced its solid-state test system for bare printed circuit boards and, only months later, entered the worldwide market.

Manufacturing operations were relocated in 1980 to a new 60,000-square-foot plant built to specification by the concern at 2887 North Towne Avenue, leaving corporate offices on Metropolitan Place. Subsequently, an additional 40,000 square feet were constructed at 700 East Harrison Avenue, still in Pomona, bringing the firm's production facilities to their current level.

Perhaps most worthy of note, however, is the arrival of Everett/Charles in the San Bernardino County economic community. This took place in 1982 with the opening of new corporate headquarters near the Cherry Avenue entrance to Interstate 15.

Typically, the company's impressive Spanish-style building was the first to enter an industrially zoned area Everett Long and many Fontana

This Spanish-style complex houses Everett/Charles' corporate offices in Fontana. The building is heated and cooled by a system that utilizes energy gathered by the solar panels in foreground.

city fathers agree will become one of the county's most prosperous high-technology centers.

Long says he chose the six-acre site for its superb freeway access and proximity to Ontario International Airport, but admits that secondary considerations included the rural atmosphere and mountain scenery clearly in view from his office window.

In this setting, Long directs his corporation's three domestic subsidiaries: Everett/Charles Test Equipment, Contact Products, and Automation Systems. Additionally, overseas operations include a plant north of London, England; a sales and service center near Munich, Germany; and a limited-assembly facility in Yokohama, Japan.

Regional sales offices are spread throughout the United States in California, Texas, Illinois, Massachusetts, and Georgia.

Today nearly all of Everett/Charles' output is sold to other high-technology electronics firms to be used in the manufacturing or testing of their products. Though the line has become extremely diversified, including what the industry knows as robots, the company's foundation remains in the complex equipment that tests both loaded and bare printed circuit boards.

Everett J. Long founded the international electronics firm, Everett/Charles, which is headquartered in San Bernardino County.

So efficient are these devices that actual test time is only 400 microseconds per point, meaning that more than 24,000 points can be tested in less than 10 seconds.

Testimony to the increasing demand for these products lies in the fact that Everett/Charles has achieved a compounded annual growth rate of more than 30 percent each year since its inception. Further, Long has set an objective of $500 million in gross sales by 1995 and has every intention of being successful.

Everett Long, having developed a start-up local machine shop into a highly profitable international electronics firm, credits his company's success to a commitment to provide quality products and services while propagating concerns for its employees, for its customers, and for excellence in all its endeavors.

SCHEU MANUFACTURING COMPANY

Scheu Manufacturing Company, undoubtedly known best by many for its HY-LO citrus heaters, is a classic example of alert, aggressive management shifting gears quickly and making product modifications needed to meet the demands of an ever-changing market.

The company got off to a fast start in 1920, prosperously marketing an oil-burning orchard heater, predominantly to California's freeze-threatened, but very profitable and wide-spread citrus industry. Successfully marketing orchard heaters for years, eventually the desire to expand, a rapidly changing economy, and international oil pricing necessitated effective thinking at the corporate level.

Today a leading producer of temporary portable space heating equipment, the firm's earliest beginnings date back to 1907 in Grand Junction, Colorado. It was there that W.C. Scheu, grandfather of the company's current president, was tinkering with automotive parts and somehow found the answer to the needs of California orange growers.

In 1913 severe, freezing storms paralyzed Southern California and literally devastated its citrus crop, rendering unmarketable hundreds of thousands of bushels of otherwise valuable fruit. Growers pleaded with Scheu to demonstrate his oil heater on the West Coast and thus he journeyed to California to test his new burner.

The young inventor was met with overwhelming success and, by 1920, he had purchased a former packing plant in Upland from which to distribute his increasingly popular heater. Manufactured for Scheu in a number of eastern locations and shipped by rail to California, the crop-saving oil burner would, for years, dominate agriculture throughout not only the county, but also much of the western United States.

Scheu would ultimately design some 50 models of the burner and was, by the late 1930s, already working with the University of California at Davis to reduce the smoke produced by what had been affectionately nicknamed the "smudgepot." The very rewarding result of this research and experimentation was the HY-LO return-stack heater, which burns its emissions a second time to eliminate pollutants.

So prominent was the venture during the '30s that for a number of years it was a sponsor of radio's popular "Floyd Young Frost Report" and the "Standard Oil Symphony Hour."

In 1929 the founder's son, W.L. Scheu, became involved in the business and in 1944 took over as president. It was his decision in 1949 that his firm should manufacture its own products, thus bringing to an end the longtime relationship with American Can Company which had been producing the heaters in Toledo, Ohio.

Though the HY-LO and return-stack heaters would sell well for many years to come, W.L. Scheu was already toying, in the early 1940s,

W.C. Scheu, president and founder, 1925.

W.L. Scheu, president, 1944.

with the mechanism that would carry his organization into the 1980s and beyond. Called the Salamander, for the lizard-type creature which changes color to match its surroundings, the new heater was intended to provide warmth, thereby allowing construction crews to work in inclement weather.

With the introduction of the Salamander heater in the 1940s, sales spread across the nation, and by the 1950s, to Europe.

In 1951 Leland C. Scheu, grandson of the founder, joined the firm, followed closely, in 1959, by Allyn Scheu, the other son of W.L. Scheu. With father and sons, Scheu's line of portable heaters was soon expanded to include liquid propane, forced-air, convection, natural gas, and infrared models—some capable of producing as much as 350,000 British thermal units.

Winter hit Florida with unprecedented severity in 1963 and the company shipped a record 400,000 citrus heaters to struggling growers throughout the South. Nonetheless, the transition had begun that would, in the next 15 years, make agricultural heating a secondary product line and place the temporary space heaters in a paramount position.

The growing enterprise had added building space in 1948, 1951, and 1953. In 1962 Scheu bought out a longtime competitor, National-Riverside Co. In 1967 Leland Scheu became president and Allyn Scheu, vice-president, and in 1970 acquired California Orchard Heater Co.

A major fire had hit one of the Scheu structures in the early '40s, but in 1975 the firm suffered staggering losses when flames swept through its leased warehouse on A Street. The blaze was one of the worst in Upland history and destroyed more than $300,000 worth of inventory.

The company made a full recovery in the years that followed, at times employing as many as 350 workers. Today Scheu operates two manufacturing plants—60,000 square feet at the original location on Stowell Street in Upland and 30,000 square feet obtained in 1969 on Roberds Street in Rancho Cucamonga.

In 1976 Allyn Scheu, grandson of the founder, followed the family heritage and became its fourth president and his brother Leland was named chairman of the board of directors. Under their leadership, Scheu Manufacturing now has distributors in nearly every major city in the United States with major customers including Ace Hardware and W.W. Grainger, Inc. Heaviest sales are understandably in the eastern and northern states, but the heaters have also proven popular in such foreign countries as Australia, England, Israel, and New Zealand.

Leland and Allyn Scheu view the firm and its future with justified optimism and look ahead with anticipation to the opportunities that the future holds.

Leland C. Scheu, president, 1967.

Allyn B. Scheu, president, 1976.

LORAN, INC.

Loran, Inc., designs and manufactures exterior lighting fixtures such as the Powerliter (left) and the Footliter (right) for the customer who wants the exterior of his home as beautiful as the interior, and as functional by night as during the day.

What began as a hobby and "was fun" for William J. Locklin in the late 1940s has developed into Loran, Inc., one of the nation's most prestigious designers and manufacturers of outdoor lighting.

From his plant in Redlands, Locklin has masterminded lighting schemes for such notable locations as the White House rose garden, former President Nixon's San Clemente estate, and several world-famous hotels in the Hawaiian Islands. In late 1983 Loran was busy producing some 25 miles of lighting for the World's Fair in New Orleans.

William Locklin is the originator of low-voltage lighting for outdoor use where it has a number of important advantages. Most significant in his success story is the dramatic effects created by the lamps. Actually, Locklin is most proud of the systems in which the elements themselves are not seen and only their illumination is visible.

Born and raised in Lucerne Valley, Locklin saw action during World War II as a submarine chief electrician in the South Pacific. When he returned from combat, he worked for California Portland Cement and, by the late 1940s, was doing what he really enjoyed—electrical contracting.

In 1950 Locklin took charge of theatrical lighting for the Redlands Bowl, a job he relished for the next 20 years. It was, however, a visit to Palm Springs by then-President Dwight Eisenhower in 1953 that set Loran in motion.

The firm got started in the midst of an orange grove at the intersection of Fifth Avenue and Walnut Road near Redlands. The current 25,000-square-foot plant at 1705 East Colton Avenue in Redlands opened in 1963 after considerable growth, including Loran's incorporation.

Here, the company manufactures not only the lighting itself, but a variety of related products including timers, dimmers, and even the transformers that reduce power from the standard 110 volts to 12 volts. This low-voltage system has many selling features: They are more economical to operate, are safer, are easier to install, and even work well under water. "Lighting is the best deterrent to prowlers," says Locklin, "but what we really provide is a luxury item for the cultured customer who wants the exterior of his home as beautiful as the interior, and as functional by night as during the day."

These benefits have been taken advantage of by Swedish gardens in the community of Solvang, Disneyland in Tokyo, and at Six Flags Over Texas. Work is also under way at the 150-year-old Yankee Peddler Inn at Holyoke, Massachusetts, and at San Martin Islands.

Locklin notes that most of his business comes from outside the area: 40 percent on the East Coast and 20 percent in foreign countries, representing "new dollars for San Bernardino County."

Now with more than 50 workers, Locklin still retains the services of its 15 original employees. And "Bill" frequently answers the phone to accept orders. He's most often on the phone designing the garden lighting for a customer or custom designing a new fixture to meet a specific request. The most recent custom fixture is the Tiki Liter, a combination kerosene/12-volt torch for the Kahala Hilton.

DATA-DESIGN LABORATORIES

The emergence of Data-Design Laboratories as a successful high-technology company in Cucamonga is predicated on a straightforward business philosophy which says simply: "Build a quality product, price it competitively, and deliver it on time."

The firm's basic objective throughout its history has been to improve the position of its shareholders by expanding into fields that offer the greatest profit potential for the years ahead.

At present, this strategy has placed Data-Design prominently in four major areas: engineering services, communications, electronics, and emergency power and life-support systems.

Engineering services was the foundation on which Data-Design was formed in 1959. The firm's three principal founders—Kenneth L. McLellan, Thomas C. Beiseker, and Patrick G. Moore—had become aware of the Navy's need for documentation support and were soon to become deeply involved with the nation's most sophisticated underwater weapons.

Data-Design, along with such other major contractors as Lockheed, General Electric, and Westinghouse, has been a team contractor in the Navy's strategic nuclear weapons system program for 24 years.

Data-Design's first major contract for the Navy was with the Polaris program. In years to follow the company's expertise would be rewarded with contracts on the well-known Poseidon, Trident, Aegis, and Cruise Missile defense systems. In 1967 the growing organization started Hydrotronics, Inc., and thus entered the field of sonar and acoustical engineering for nuclear attack submarines.

Communications, one of Data-Design's fastest growing segments, began in 1979 when the company acquired United Scientific Corporation, located in Northern California's Silicon Valley. From its 60,000-square-foot facility, United Scientific serves a worldwide market with components for closed-circuit, cable, and satellite television systems.

Another success story is that of Aeroscientific Corporation, which is the backbone of Data-Design's electronics segment, established in 1969. This subsidiary has developed into a leading producer of high-density, multilayer printed circuit boards used by major computer manufacturers for products ranging from mainframe to personal computers.

Adding even greater diversity to Data-Design are emergency power and life-support systems made by two subsidiaries—Siltron Illumination, Inc., and Sierra Precision.

Acquired by Data-Design in 1970, Siltron provides a line of battery-powered inverters to furnish uninterrupted power for emergency lighting, fire alarms, communication systems, and security equipment.

Data-Design Laboratories' Aeroscientific Corporation subsidiary is a recognized leader in the manufacture of sophisticated multilayer printed circuit boards (PCBs) and back panels for the electronics industry.

Sierra Precision, started by Data-Design in 1970, manufactures a variety of high-pressure gauges and hoses used extensively in scuba diving and life-support systems.

Beiseker, one of Data-Design's founders and chief executive officer, is pleased with the firm's 24-year history of a compounded growth rate of 24 percent for sales and 22 percent for net income.

The company has expanded from a tiny, rented warehouse on Ontario's California Street into its current three-building, 70,000-square-foot headquarters at 7925 Center Avenue in Cucamonga. Data-Design now employs over 1,400 people and operates throughout the United States and in Ireland.

Company officials attribute this record of accomplishment not only to business diversification, but to aggressive management, flexibility, and financial liquidity, which allows Data-Design Laboratories to move quickly when opportunities arise.

SORENSON ENGINEERING INCORPORATED

"I never dreamed that first little machine would turn into this and take me all over the world," says Frank Sorenson, president of Sorenson Engineering in Yucaipa.

He speaks of the 200-employee precision machine operation he has developed since he began a one-man business with a single piece of equipment in the fall of 1956.

While growing to its current size, the company has also become highly specialized. Its major products are very complex electrical pins, sockets, instruments, and electronic component hardware for missiles, aircraft, and computers.

Sorenson parts have had many applications ranging from space suits to tracking systems. Accordingly, much of the work has been of a military nature, with major customers including Raychem, Hewlett-Packard, Hughes Aircraft, Texas Instruments, Bendix, Burndy, Amphenol, and most major connector firms.

The firm completed contracts on virtually all major missiles and, because of its high quality, was designated a sole-source vendor for electrical pins and sockets on the Poseidon project by Lockheed, who was the prime contractor. As Sorenson puts it, "We don't always have the lowest price—we're competitive—but we have one of the finest reputations for quality."

Frank grew up with a love for machinery. At age 17, when World War II began, he was running an engine lathe with great proficiency, making parts for Navy destroyers.

After serving in World War II, he returned home and began working with his cousin who owned a Davenport multispindle automatic lathe, recognized by many as the world's fastest screw machine. Sorenson made bolts for bicycles, roller skate parts, and plumbing accessories, but was never satisfied with the normal production speed. It was his output, above the norm, which gave rise to his early reputation as one of the best Davenport operators on the West Coast.

In 1950 Sorenson became the plant superintendent at Papermate, where he was one of five original employees who produced the first retractable ball-point pens. While with Papermate, Frank became familiar with the Swiss machine and its application to precision parts. The Swiss automatic lathes at Sorenson Engineering today represent a major part of the plant equipment.

In 1953 Sorenson moved on to Anja Engineering, where he became a vice-president and continued to gain experience with Swiss machines and other related equipment. He was in charge of manufacturing and building special high-speed automatic assembly and inking equipment for refills for ball pen points.

The real beginning, however, was still ahead. On his own, Frank had designed and built a machine for Winco Products that produced knitting needles from aluminum bar stock. During his working career, Frank had managed to save about $16,000 and, in 1956, decided to establish his own business. He purchased his first machine and support equipment for $10,000 and soon rented the basement of what was known as the Overcrest House on Yucaipa Boulevard near the freeway.

This 1,200-square-foot cellar of his home served the new company well as it grew rapidly during the next six years. Two major orders—one involving potentiometers for Fairchild Control and the other connector parts for Amphenol Western, a division from Chicago—produced a fast return on Sorenson's investment. In fact, during the first five years, business grew at a rate of 100 to 150 percent annually.

Frank Sorenson, founder and president of Sorenson Engineering Incorporated.

The current vice-president and general manager is Reinhard Thalmayer, who was 16 years old when he joined the firm in 1959. Sorenson had known Thalmayer through related sports activities at school with his sons. Thalmayer's interest in engineering and management led him to pursue further education, and he went on to obtain an AA degree in management at San Bernardino Valley College. This proved to be of immediate value as profits increased substantially.

By 1962 the company was running seven Swiss automatics and needed larger quarters. Sorenson Engineering incorporated at that time and moved to its current location at 32032 Dunlap Boulevard, then the site of the Lazy L Barbecue restaurant.

Beginning with 3,500 square feet, expansion has been steady with a large addition six years after the relocation. In 1984 the 15-acre complex included four buildings, totaling 40,000 square feet, and plans were being made for another major improvement.

Although the main shop already houses more than 100 highly automated machines, the new capital investment program is composed largely of additional equipment designed to create a more efficient flow of goods from raw material to finished product.

"We've got to think bigger and thoroughly streamline our total process to accommodate increasing demand," says Sorenson. He notes with pleasure that demand has increased so rapidly that the corporation doesn't have an active sales promotion program.

Having introduced several of his own innovations to the machine industry, Frank's many achievements have not gone unnoticed. He has been nominated by the U.S. Small Business Administration as national Vendor of the Year and was named the top candidate from the western region. In 1982 he received the Gold Micrometer Award from the National Screw Machine Products Association and has also been honored by Hughes Aircraft for 15 years of superior service.

Sorenson Engineering believes in advancing its employees within the organization. A surprisingly large number of operators in the shop are women and many are working to become fully qualified machinists.

The company maintains its own in-house training programs utilizing audiovisual presentations, and works in close cooperation with San Bernardino Valley Community College.

Sorenson also owned Baumac Inc. in Yucaipa, which produces fine-mist cooling systems for the poultry, egg, and agricultural products industry. Baurmac is now owned and operated by his two sons, David and Steven.

Frank enjoys a good reputation. Former County Supervisor Wesley Break once told him he had the type of industry the community wanted. "I've always tried to live up to that," says Sorenson. "At Sorenson Engineering, we sincerely care about our people. We have worked hard—very hard—but it's paid us well in many ways."

Sorenson Engineering Incorporated is located at 32032 Dunlap Boulevard in Yucaipa.

WILDEN PUMP AND ENGINEERING COMPANY

Air-operated double-diaphragm pumps are the only product of Wilden Pump and Engineering Company. The invention of its founder and chief executive officer, James K. Wilden, the air-operated double-diaphragm pump has earned worldwide acceptance and appreciation by industrial pump users as an extremely versatile and effective pump for the most difficult pumping jobs.

Wilden pumps handle highly viscous, abrasive, and corrosive materials with solids up to three-eighths of an inch, in addition to meeting requirements for a wide range of special pumping needs. This unique line of pumps has a multitude of applications: everything from peanut butter and pickle relish to highly corrosive and radioactive substances. As Wilden states it, "If it pours, it pumps!"

Other major advantages of the Wilden pump include the fact that it is portable and easy to install, self-priming, will run dry indefinitely without damage, is safe under explosive conditions, and is quiet and pollution free.

The enterprise began as the Wilden Company on the present site on January 1, 1955, when Jim Wilden began his own business in a metal building previously used for processing walnuts. The 10 acres belonged to Jim's father and contained a producing walnut grove. In the beginning, the firm's principal business was the production of custom hydraulic and pneumatic cylinders and valves for Kaiser Steel in Fontana. Jim worked days producing cylinders and valves, and evenings on a variety of design projects which he hoped would yield a product that would support a successful manufacturing company.

Jim Wilden was uniquely prepared for the task he had set for himself. He was 40 years old, a self-educated engineer with over 20 years of invaluable practical experience in mines, oil fields, steel mills, and other manufacturing disciplines. Even more important, he possessed a highly innovative and persistent character, qualities that would help assure his success.

From age six, he was raised only a few yards from the site of his present-day plant. He attended Colton Union High School where he concentrated his efforts in machine shop and mechanical classes, spending his spare time working on cars and designing guns in the small shop he built at home.

After graduation, he worked in the gold mines of Arizona and later in the oil fields of New Mexico, where he built a still to refine badly needed gasoline during the Depression.

When he returned to California in 1937, he was employed as a machinist for Riverside Cement Company, also serving as an instructor at Norton Army Air Field during World War II.

Most important, however, was his experience at Kaiser Steel where he worked from 1942 to 1945, and later from 1950 to 1955. As a millwright during the construction of the mill, he received an invaluable education in the principles of fluid power, a

Wilden Pump and Engineering Company, 22069 Van Buren Street, in Colton.

Jim Wilden, founder, was raised in Colton, attended Colton Union High School, and served as an instructor at Norton Army Air Field during World War II.

relatively new concept being introduced in American industry. This knowledge provided the basis for the design of a hydraulic mucking machine (mining equipment) which Jim designed and patented in 1953, and later for the air-operated double-diaphragm pump as well as a number of other projects.

In 1958, after years of development and painstaking trial and error, Wilden began commercial production of the Model M-16, the first air-operated double-diaphragm pump, and Jim began a one-man sales campaign to introduce his new invention to a skeptical market.

From this point forward, Wilden Pump and Engineering has concentrated on improving and expanding its line to maintain its position as the leader and standard in an industry that has grown to over 40 companies in 20 countries producing products based on Jim Wilden's M-16. Today Wilden produces five basic pump sizes in a wide range of materials including corrosion-resistant stainless steels, engineering plastics, and Teflon. The latest model is a polished stainless steel pump designed for the sanitary industries. Wilden has received USDA approval on this venture, and is looking forward to an exciting future in the food equipment market.

The metal "walnut shed" has grown to a 53,200-square-foot modern concrete facility in 1983, with a 38,000-square-foot expansion planned for 1984. This facility houses offices, warehouses, and a machine shop for Wilden's 75 employees. The machine facility is filled with modern computer-controlled machines customized for optimum production of Wilden parts, which helped Wilden achieve a "modern miracle" in maintaining the prices of standard pumps from 1974 to 1983.

A self-made engineer and inventor, Jim Wilden has taken up the challenge of solving the most difficult pumping problems and has succeeded.

Shown here are some of the pumps produced by Wilden Pump and Engineering Company for many diverse industries.

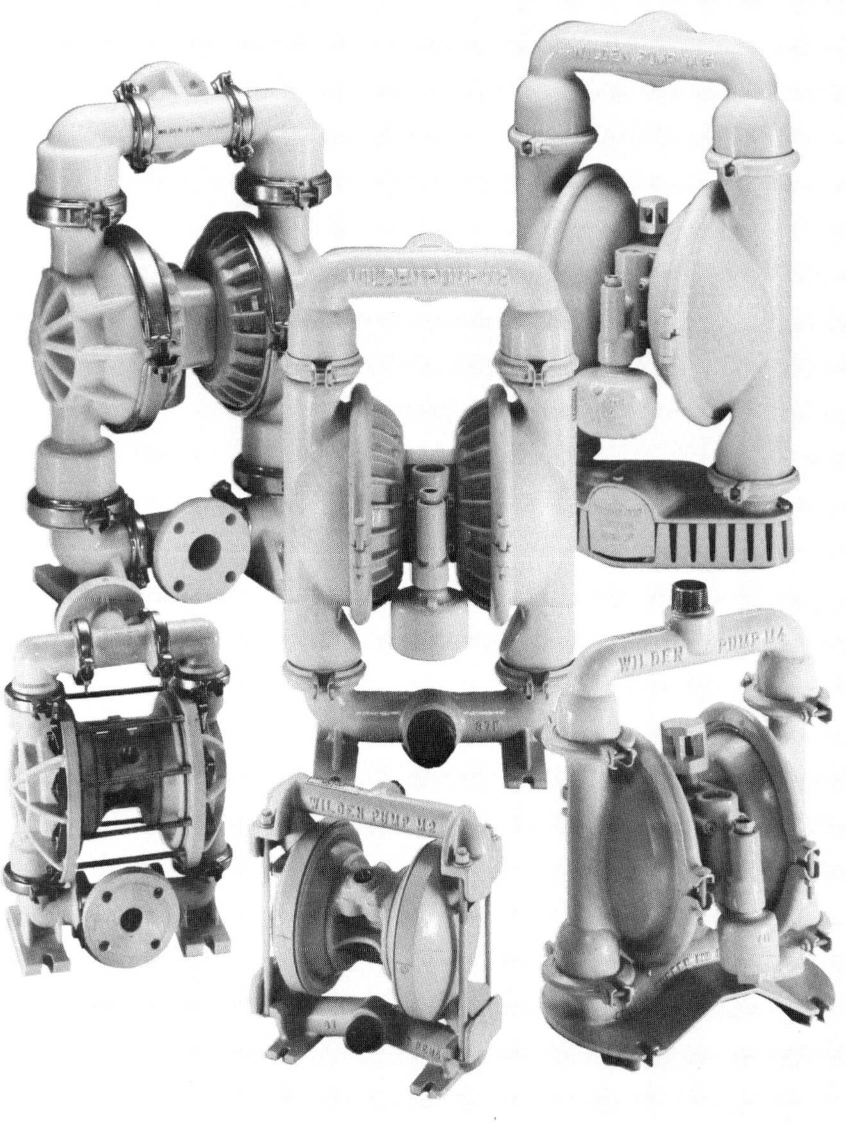

KEMPER MANUFACTURING, INC.

Today the world's most well-known producer of ceramic tools, Kemper Manufacturing began as strictly a kitchen-and-garage operation.

Located in the Chino area for more than 30 years, the highly respected company produces a popular line of specialized tools which to the untrained eye resemble dental instruments.

President John E. "Jack" Kemper founded the venture in 1947 through a unique combination of circumstances. The son of a midwestern minister, Kemper first came in contact with fine ceramics while in China with the U.S. Navy. After his discharge in 1935, he settled in Southern California to pursue a career in welding engineering with North American Aviation's experimental tool division.

The key element, however, was his wife Esther's interest in ceramic making and her instructor's expressed need for a then-unheard-of tool. Skilled in the trade, Kemper produced as well as designed the new tool, and, as orders increased, he found himself in business aided not only by Esther, but by their two daughters, Patti and Kathy.

Recognizing both opportunity and challenge, Kemper gave up his job and purchased the 600-square-foot building on Beach Street in Inglewood that was to be his first plant. Initial annual sales amounted to only $10,000, but two years later the business moved to Pomona and, by 1952, had established itself in the first of several increasingly larger Chino-area locations.

Kemper Manufacturing proudly celebrated its 25th anniversary in 1972, opening its new plant and offices totaling 16,500 square feet on 2.5 acres at 13595 Twelfth Street in one of Chino's attractive light-industrial districts.

John E. Kemper, founder and president of Kemper Manufacturing, has developed his Chino-based ceramic tool company from a home business into a million-dollar international operation.

The company currently employs more than 30 persons at this, its only facility, and reports annual sales substantially exceeding $1.5 million. Kemper has some 350 distributors throughout all parts of the world and the product line has grown to more than 350 different tools. All in all, the firm sells about five million tools per year.

Found in this varied array of products are brushes, carving tools, drills, knives, sponges, loops, and tongs. Many feature a fine wooden handle with a peculiar but precisely shaped wire at one end. Kemper's tools are used by such famous artists as Irving Burgues from Budapest, Douglas Downs of the United States, Gunther Granget of Germany, and Lazlo Ispanky from Hungary.

In 1966 Kemper purchased the Italian tool company owned by the acclaimed Anthony Rigotty who, in turn, shared his most sophisticated and guarded techniques.

For more than a decade Kemper has been assisted in his business by his son-in-law Herbert Stampfl, who is now vice-president. Stampfl is a past president of the Chino Chamber of Commerce; Kemper was president of the National Ceramic Manufacturers' Association and is a prominent trustee for the City of Hope. Interestingly, Kemper's credits also include winning the Navy Pacific Coast heavyweight boxing championship in the 1930s.

Jack Kemper explains that he designed many of his tools by observing great artists at work. In so doing, he has not only revolutionized the techniques of sculpting, but become a true artist in his own right.

MARK B. SHAW MORTUARIES

Mark B. Shaw Mortuaries, established by a Baptist minister in 1911, serves more families today than any other funeral home in San Bernardino County.

Owned by Richard J. Filanc, Jr., the firm has two locations—its main building at 1525 North Waterman Avenue in San Bernardino and a branch facility at 26985 Baseline Street in Highland.

Mark B. Shaw, founder of the mortuaries, was a colorful and popular figure in history, described after his death by the *San Bernardino Sun* as a "leading citizen, pioneer, former clergyman, soldier, and mortician." To this list one might well add politician, by virtue of the fact that Shaw served as a member of the County Board of Supervisors during 1917 and 1918.

Born in 1862, Shaw was a native of Nova Scotia where he had begun preaching by the young age of 18. Though often troubled by poor health, his religious work took him to many parts of the world and even to India where he spent four years as a missionary in the early 1890s.

Mark B. Shaw, founder of the mortuaries that bear his name, when he served as chaplain in the California National Guard during the early 1900s.

Shaw had visited San Bernardino briefly in 1889, but did not settle there permanently until 10 years later when he became pastor of the First Baptist Church. He is also well remembered as a chaplain in the California National Guard and as one of the organizers of the local American Legion post.

Shaw became involved in undertaking in 1909 and, two years later, opened his own mortuary at the northeast corner of Fifth and E streets. In 1912 he was joined by one of his four sons, Harold, and later by another son, Douglas.

In 1916 the funeral home was moved to 468 West Fifth Street, where it was to remain for nearly 40 years. Shaw died in 1922 at age 59, and Douglas took over the business until his passing in the mid-1950s.

His son-in-law, Richard J. Filanc, Sr., had been active in the firm since the late '40s. The company moved in 1954 to its current four-acre site on Waterman Avenue.

Filanc had one daughter and one son. In 1968 Filanc's son, Richard Jr., assumed leadership. Richard III, promises to carry the Mark B. Shaw Mortuaries through the fifth generation.

The history of the Filanc family in San Bernardino dates back to 1852 when Peter E. Filanc, a Frenchman by birth, settled in the area, eventually acquiring some 2,000 acres of ranchland. His son, Richard Sr., continued this and other real estate ventures, also starting the community's first cable television.

Today Richard Jr., in addition to the mortuaries, owns a mining operation, several ranches, and a number of commercial and industrial developments—some in Central California. He is proudest, however, of his funeral homes and notes that among his 30 employees are some who have been with the firm as long as 25 years.

Invited to membership in National Select Morticians, Filanc believes Mark B. Shaw Mortuaries provides a higher-quality, more personalized service, and that many of the families he assists will continue to return.

This vintage hearse was one of the first vehicles used by Mark B. Shaw Mortuaries.

HARRIS' DEPARTMENT STORES

Pillowcases were a dime and sheets cost 50 cents. Shoppers could buy a tie for a quarter or children's stockings for 12 cents a pair. Prices have changed drastically in 80 years, but the original ingredients that made Harris Company an institution in the Inland Empire remain unchanged.

There are now stores in five locations: San Bernardino, Riverside, Redlands, Indio, and Hemet. Despite this growth, the company's basic tenets are still fashion, quality, value, and service. Ever since Harris' was purchased by El Corte Inglés, a Spanish firm, in 1981, the full-line department stores have remained dedicated to both their customers and communities.

The Harris story dates back nearly 60 years before the opening of the first store when Morris Harris, a European merchant, fled to the United States from Germany. It was three of his 11 children—Herman, Philip, and Arthur—who started the company and ultimately established what is now the cornerstone of San Bernardino's downtown commercial district.

Herman had operated a small shop in Santa Ana, and Philip worked for his uncle, Leopold Harris, and his cousin, H.W. Frank, at the original Harris and Frank Store in Los Angeles.

The two brothers combined their assets to acquire a carefully chosen inventory valued at $4,700 and to rent a 2,200-square-foot storeroom in the old armory at 462 Third Street. Herman and Philip opened the Harris Company on April 18, 1905, with three employees, and history was in the making.

In its first advertisement the company told readers in part, "If courteous treatment, low prices, good goods, and honest methods are appreciated here, we will certainly have no difficulty in gaining your trade."

No difficulty, indeed! Within a year the little store gained almost immediate popularity, and greater floor space was badly needed. Arthur joined the business about that time, and Harris' moved across the street to a much larger building purchased from Joseph Israel.

After just three years of operation the threesome bought out Randall and Merriman in Redlands with Philip opening the store's first branch and remaining there as manager for the next 31 years.

This area, too, proved lucrative for the firm, and in 1915 the store moved close to its current location (in the Redlands Fashion Mall) as the result of a property trade with Redlands Hardware Company. Two years later the adjacent building, occupied by Smith Brothers Oriental Gifts, was purchased and space was more than doubled.

Meanwhile, the San Bernardino store had been enlarged in 1915 with the acquisition of the adjoining Pritchard's Dry Goods, and an additional expansion involving Rudolph Anker's Clothing brought the total square footage to 23,500 by 1919.

Just when both stores appeared to be in high gear, fire completely demolished the Redlands location in 1925. Miraculously, Harris' reopened the following day in temporary quarters and rebuilt a new, more elaborate structure, which was completed on the same property one year later.

During this period the company was also looking at the Third and E streets area as a future site for the San Bernardino store. In early 1927 construction was undertaken, to be completed in November, on what was recognized as one of the country's finest department stores. Though a highly acclaimed event, the move was made a scant two years before the Depression, and the business was faced with a major downturn.

Nonetheless, the Harris Company managed not only to keep itself afloat, but to maintain sufficient deposits to sustain the American National Bank, now BankCal. The department store similarly demonstrated its support of the community a few years later by paying for its advertising months in

The fine-jewelry department reflects the storewide remodeling, finished in the fall of 1982. Reprinted by permission of the San Bernardino Sun.

This elegant entrance court greets customers entering Harris' in San Bernardino. Reprinted by permission of the San Bernardino Sun.

advance after a fire destroyed the Sun Company newspaper offices and plant.

Likewise, the firm participated in nearly all civilian defense programs during World War II and has continued its involvement in community service projects. Most recently, sponsorship of Santa Claus, Inc., benefited 6,000 needy children through a presentation of professional entertainment and high-fashion modeling.

In earlier years the three sons of Philip—Leslie, Harold, and Melville—ran the stores, leading to a successive line of Harris family members and in-laws who have played leading roles throughout its corporate history.

In 1957 Harris' established its third store as anchor in the new Riverside Plaza, adding a third floor in 1963 and opening the basement in 1967.

Still on its Third Street site, the San Bernardino store expanded to 250,000 square feet in 1973, serving as the foundation for the new Central City Mall. The fourth and fifth Harris' stores were added in Indio during 1975 and at the Hemet Valley Mall late in 1980.

Even before the new locations, however, the Inland Empire had paid tribute to the Harris family. The applause of 6,200 persons literally shook the Swing Auditorium on the National Orange Show Grounds as Roger Wagner, Jim Backus, and John Raitt presented a musical history commemorating the department store's 60th anniversary in 1965.

Though by no means a bid farewell to its thousands of customers, Harris' Department Stores was purchased in 1981 by El Corte Inglés, the largest retailer in Spain with 15 stores, 22,000 employees, and $1.7 billion in annual sales.

Harris', now with a total staff of 1,200 persons, has made an indelible mark on the Inland Empire. The fourth generation of the family is now working in the stores, and Hap Harris, grandson of one of the founders, is still general manager at Riverside.

Jorge Pont, chief executive officer for the Harris Company, said in 1983, "As I look back on 78 years of Harris history, I'm struck by how much some things have changed—and how some things have not changed at all, and never will.

"From the start, the Harris Company built its business on an unswerving commitment to fashion, quality, value, and service—and these are the principles by which we operate today."

The Harris' Department Store in downtown San Bernardino in the mid-1950s.

VINEYARD NATIONAL BANK

Seven o'clock in the morning until six at night are hardly banking hours by any conventional standard. Nonetheless, that's the order of the day at Vineyard National Bank in Rancho Cucamonga—not to mention being open from 9 a.m. to 1 p.m. on Saturdays.

To the knowledge of anyone at the bank, 59 hours of operation per week is more service than is provided by any other financial institution ever known. And that's not the end of it! Even longer hours are planned as the young but expanding bank opens new branches throughout the area.

That, however, was the plan from the very beginning and a key reason why Vineyard National has become one of the fastest-growing banks not only in the Inland Empire, but probably anywhere in Southern California.

When Vineyard was just getting organized in 1980, president Steven R. Sensenbach and his nine colleagues on the board of directors were united in one basic objective and that was to create a bank to truly serve the needs of the local community—residents and businessmen alike.

They had several important facts in mind. San Bernardino County's west end was experiencing unprecedented increases in population—a trend all reliable projections indicated would continue throughout the decade.

Steven R. Sensenbach, president.

Many, if not most, of these new residents held jobs a substantial distance from their newly purchased homes, making long daily commutes a necessity. Thus, not only did a rapidly developing business community require additional financial services, but also local citizens needed an institution that could accommodate their demanding schedules. In short, if a close-to-home bank was not open early in the morning or after normal hours, local customers would simply take their business to the area where they work.

That theory proved correct. By December 1983 Vineyard's assets had grown to more than $22 million with deposits in excess of $18 million. Equally important, the bank had some 5,000 accounts and, at that time, was still adding at least 100 new customers per month. Loans totaled $16 million with a solid 90 percent of the indebtedness within the immediate community.

"We were strong from the start," says president Sensenbach. "The few problems we've had have resulted from simply growing too fast, not the usual struggle to survive for the first few years."

The true start was, however, not very impressive or even known to many. Sensenbach opened the bank's first organizational office in early 1980 at Sunrise Center on Baseline Street in Rancho Cucamonga.

Without a recognized name in the financial community, and with no so-called proven track record, the would-be bank's greatest asset was held in the reputation, determination, and dedication of its 10 founders.

Those initial participants included Steven R. Sensenbach, former vice-president of Valencia Bank; Bert C. Francis, owner of well-known Bear Gulch Realty; Lester Stroh, prominent physician associated with the Southern California Permanente Medical Group at Kaiser Foundation Hospital in Fontana; S. "Buster" Filpi, owner and manager of a 36-acre, 15-building industrial park in Rancho Cucamonga; Catherine J. Barnes, a 28-year employee of the Bank of America; Neil R. Zoller, a principal partner in Inland Valley Engineering, Inc.; Charles L. Keagle, founder of the Cask 'N Cleaver, Lord Charley's, and El Gato Gordo restaurant chains; Gilbert B. Rodriguez, owner of U.S. Properties Real Estate in Upland; Phillip Schlosser, former mayor of Rancho Cucamonga and the president of

The head office of Vineyard National Bank is located at Vineyard Avenue and Foothill Boulevard in Rancho Cucamonga. © Joe Friezer.

This was the teller staff of the bank in December 1983. © Joe Friezer.

Schlosser Forge Co.; and Frank Alvarez, certified public accountant and partner in the firm of Bowen, McBeth, and Co.

Joel Ravitz succeeded Zoller in 1983, bringing to the board vast experience and success in stock-brokerage. All board members have been active in both the community as well as their bank, bringing in literally hundreds of customers.

Late in 1980, the charter application was filed with the Controller of Currency in Washington, D.C., setting in motion the extensive review in which a proposed bank must demonstrate a need within the community and prove that it can satisfy that need.

The request was approved and, in September 1981, Vineyard National Bank opened its headquarters on the southwest corner of Foothill Boulevard and Vineyard Avenue. A long-remembered opening celebration drew more than 700 persons the first day as the bank began business in five modular trailers designed largely by Sensenbach.

Vineyard was initially capitalized at $2 million with its 10 directors owning a 56-percent interest, the balance being sold at public offering. More important, the stock, which was then being bought at $10 per share, had risen to $24 by 1984. There are more than 220 shareholders, nearly all local.

It is a full-service bank with all the usual amenities plus departments for real estate, payroll, and business loans, including those of the U.S. Small Business Administration.

The original location has been expanded to nine units encompassing 4,600 square feet, also providing drive-up lanes and a 24-hour automatic teller machine. Despite these facilities, Sensenbach notes that there are situations a customer must discuss in person and that extended hours are still a major feature.

Thus, this unusual service will continue—not only in Rancho Cucamonga, but also at the new Chino branch, which opened in early 1984 at 5425 Riverside Drive, and at the Diamond Bar office, scheduled to begin operation in 1985.

Remarkably, Vineyard will have fulfilled its original three-branch, five-year plan in only about three and one-half years with current plans for even further expansion. Directors are now looking at potential sites in both Claremont and Rialto for construction in the latter half of the decade.

Neither customers nor employees mind the long hours. The bank operates on three shifts with a number of part-time employees working the early and late duty.

The situation speaks for itself. Vineyard National Bank began with a staff of 12 and less than three years later had 40 employees. "We can't stop now," says Sensenbach, "the bank is just growing too fast."

A dollar-laden ribbon cut by Michelle Knight, "Miss Chino," and Mark Larson, vice-president/manager of Vineyard National Bank, marked the official opening of the Chino branch of the bank in February 1984. The money was contributed by the bank to Chino Community Hospital. © Joe Friezer.

GOLDIE LAW CORPORATION

Goldie Law Corporation, now highly respected for its expertise in civil litigation, began early in 1958 when Ray R. Goldie opened his office. A law-school friend came to San Bernardino to establish a partnership later that year.

Then known as Goldie and Kaufman, the new firm was first housed in leased quarters in the Katz Building at the intersection of Third and E streets.

Both Ray Goldie and Marcus Kaufman were top law students at the University of Southern California and, since graduation, had also acquired valuable professional experience.

As one of the top 10 percent in his class, Goldie was initially employed by the state attorney general and was a key figure in a still-famous case involving oil drilling rights off the Santa Barbara coast. Kaufman had worked on the staff of California Supreme Court Chief Justice Roger Traynor.

This reputation produced early prominence for the young lawyers, and in 1959 Ray Goldie constructed his own law building at 560 North Arrowhead Avenue, leasing a portion to other attorneys.

Because of his early success in several precedent-setting cases, Goldie first became known for his criminal work. Not, however, desiring this field on a career basis, he insisted on pursuing civil matters and emerged outstanding in this area as well.

Kaufman left the firm and eventually became a justice in the Fourth District Court of Appeal. Goldie continued on his own, but his practice grew rapidly and additional staff members became necessary.

The Goldie Law Corporation was formed in 1972 and, three years later, Goldie undertook yet another building—this time at 432 North Arrowhead Avenue where his offices remain today, occupying the entire facility.

Ray R. Goldie, principal member of the Goldie Law Corporation, is widely recognized as one of the Inland Empire's most accomplished attorneys.

The firm is now composed of five attorneys with a diversity of experience. Goldie's professional team handles all types of civil legal matters with emphasis on corporate, real estate, land development, general business, family law, and appellate matters.

Goldie, himself, carries much of his firm's general business, real estate, and land development clients. His son, Ron, serves the firm in an "of counsel" capacity, while conducting his own practice in Marina Del Rey. In addition to Ray Goldie, other members of the firm include Stephen Anderson, Keith D. Davis, Dennis J. Ponsor, and Vivian L. White.

Goldie is past president of the Inland Empire Chapter of the California Trial Lawyers' Association and has been active in several other professional organizations. To his credit, he is also mentioned in *Who's Who in American Law, Who's Who in Finance and Industry,* and *Who's Who in the West.* Additionally, he has published articles in professional journals and taught law courses at San Bernardino Valley Community College.

From his career beginning with the attorney general and later on E Street, Ray R. Goldie has developed a law corporation that has compiled a record envied by many and respected by all.

SEVEN W ENTERPRISES, INC.

Today owner of a 66-acre industrial park in Redlands, Seven W Enterprises, Inc., began as a cattle, horse, and buffalo ranch in Montana.

Erwin H. Weder—conservationist, salesman, and innovator, among numerous pursuits—had bought the Montana ranch in 1965 largely with the objective of preserving a herd of the then nearly extinct buffalo.

Having succeeded, in 1978 Weder recognized the potential for the development of an industrial park in Redlands and soon had purchased the complex previously owned by Lockheed Propulsion Co. Located near the intersection of Crafton and Madeira avenues, the complex is comprised of more than 20 structures in a variety of sizes ranging upward to 40,000 square feet.

Weder's own company, Highland Supply—the world's major producer of florist foil—was the first to move into the new park. Other major tenants currently include Bergsma, Baumac, General Telephone, Westel, and Orbit Machine.

General Telephone occupies three buildings, one of which was constructed by Seven W in 1981 to house the company's computerized customer inquiry referral service. In addition to the Lockheed facilities, Weder has added two new units to the park. Seven W offers both existing industrial space or will build to suit tenant specifications. Weder says there is "no project too large or too small" and believes he offers some of the most attractive rates in the area.

With the Seven W's representing Weder, his wife Louise, and their five children, the firm has always been a family-owned entity. Seven W is managed in Redlands by Wanda Weder, daughter of the founder. Erwin remains chairman of the board with his son, Donald, serving as president. Another daughter, Dona Abbott, handles advertising and promotional activities, while daughters Mary Kay Foley and Jan Weder are active members of the corporate board of directors. Management consultant John Creatura, who played a key role in Seven W's purchase of the Lockheed property is their local leasing agent.

Weder moved his Highland Supply Corporation to the Seven W Industrial Park from a small building on Congress Street in Colton where the firm had been located since the late 1950s.

From the new plant in Redlands, Highland Supply serves its West Coast market with a line of floral accessories. Although the company manufactures such items as corsage bags, Easter grass, and chicken wire, the bread-and-butter product has long been the decorative foil often used to wrap potted plants.

An aerial view of Seven W Enterprises Industrial Park in Redlands.

Erwin H. Weder, founder and chairman of the board of Seven W Enterprises and Highland Supply Corporation, circa 1930.

This use of the foil was conceived by Weder in the 1930s when he was a salesman for the Metal Goods Corporation in the Midwest. The young man carried a variety of pots, pans, and utensils, but also aluminum-backed Christmas paper, which he introduced to retail florists for plant decorating. In 1937 Erwin was joined by his brother, Herb, and a friend, Ralph Kamm, in founding Highland Supply to manufacture florist products. Their first production equipment was a bag machine made by Erwin and his father from a wringer washer and treadle sewing machine. Products were frequently manufactured on this equipment by Erwin's wife, Louise.

In time, Weder would become the guiding force not only behind Highland Supply, but also in his more recent and separate undertaking, Seven W Enterprises Industrial Park in Redlands.

BRUBAKER-MANN COMPANY, INC.

Brubaker-Mann Company, Inc., one of the nation's largest producers of specialty rock products, began operation in June 1950 when two innovative partners conceived a new product—colored rock, initially to be used as a roofing material.

This idea, which would quickly revolutionize the rock industry, was that of two cousins, Ronald W. Brubaker and William J. Mann, who had become interested in a site not far east of Barstow.

Today that location produces approximately 150 tons of rock per day for shipment throughout the continental United States, Hawaii, and Mexico. Equally important, the original product line has been expanded to include mineral supplements for cattle as well as landscaping material.

The business got started when Brubaker and Mann were introduced to Lee and Alma Haney by Mann's mother, who taught school with Mrs. Haney in Fontana. It seems the Haneys owned desert property and a mill suitable for crushing the naturally colored rock as envisioned by the young men.

Although the mill consisted only of an old crusher, a wooden screen, and a dilapidated bucket elevator, Brubaker and Mann added new equipment as they prepared to start production. So financially committed to the project were the men that they used literally their last dollar to post the $150 deposit required by the power company.

One of the first orders the new enterprise received was for the roof of a relative's house in Claremont. Brubaker-Mann delivered red rock to the job and had to match the price of white rock, which had been the only type available to that point. The new color attracted attention throughout the area and was in great demand almost immediately.

At the outset, the rock was broken with sledge hammers and loaded by hand onto a small truck—a procedure with a capacity of about 10 tons per day. As profits rose, however, the firm was able to afford new drilling, mining, and loading apparatus vastly increasing production.

In 1960 Brubaker-Mann was incorporated and has continued to buy better crushers and upgrade its total line of equipment ranging from trucks to blasting devices.

After 29 years in the business Ronald Brubaker retired in 1979, selling his share to William Mann. Two of Mann's five children joined the organization, with Jennifer Mann Henderson taking charge of production and Julie Mann Rohn heading distribution. Mann, himself, is now semiretired and spends his spare time traveling.

To the undisputed credit of the firm is the remarkable fact that more than 50 similar operations have been attempted and failed with only a few remaining. Despite serious fluctuations in the rock industry, Brubaker-Mann Company, Inc., has maintained an even keel—always taking advantage of strong economic conditions to help offset the impact of less favorable periods.

Ron Brubaker observes the installation of his firm's newly acquired jaw crusher in 1950. The machine, circa 1900, was purchased from a tin mine south of Valley Wells.

A truck from American Products, one of Brubaker-Mann's early customers, is loaded with rock for shipment to San Diego. The rock was transported in sugar sacks that were hand tied.

CLAYPOOL AND COMPANY

Claypool's, probably the most well-known commercial establishment in the Needles area, had its beginning in 1883 when two Irish immigrants with the Santa Fe Railroad arrived in the Colorado River town.

Frank Monaghan and Dan Murphy went into business as general merchants, using a boxcar as their first store, but moved quickly to a building on Main Street as both their trade and the community began to grow.

After 28 successful years, Monaghan and Murphy sold their store to W.M. Claypool, Sr., a mining engineer who wanted to settle in Needles. The Claypool family has owned and operated the business since 1911 with the present-day hardware and department store situated at 725 Broadway Street, only one block from the original boxcar and building.

By 1945 seven members of the family had served in two world wars and the store itself had survived the Depression.

In addition to the Needles location, a feed mill had been purchased in San Bernardino. The company was managed until 1948 by Claypool Sr. with his two sons, Bill Jr. and Jack, and a daughter, Frances Boom.

W.M. Claypool, Jr., took over in the late 1940s assisted by five members of the family's third generation—Bill III, John, and Jim Claypool—working together with Herb and Courtney Boom.

Rapid development of the Colorado River communities spurred the business onward, and at various times the family had both retail stores and/or beer franchises in Needles, Blythe, Parker, Bullhead City, Lake Havasu City, Mojave Valley, Twentynine Palms, Yucca Valley, and the Imperial Valley.

Claypool's one-stop shopping centers have included supermarkets, convenience stores, hardware and home accessories, dress shops, and variety outlets.

Early in the 1970s the Parker store was gutted by flames. Rebuilt in only 88 days, the structure was later sold to another firm and is still a credit to its founders.

In a move made before its time, the Claypools also converted their feed mill experience into the world's first large aluminum can recycling plant and operated it, for a time, as a cooperative in Highgrove.

Most important, though, it was the family's untiring efforts to provide better merchandise at lower prices that made the company a leader in the formation of a retail hardware buying group. This co-op later joined a 7,500-unit independent hardware chain now recognized under the True Value® name.

Needles and Claypool's, alike, have grown and matured with the family's third generation now approaching retirement. As a result, the business is being tailored, not only to meet the ever-changing needs of its customers, but also to assure that the abilities of the next generation are used to greatest advantage.

In the immediate future, Claypool's will concentrate primarily on hardware, clothing, and beverage distribution. The family, too, recognizes that it must continue to buy on a cooperative basis and that ongoing efficiency will be essential in order to compete with the discount stores that will inevitably arrive with the increasing population.

The Claypools are proud to be a part of the Colorado River area's history and development. Their goal is to serve visitors as well as local residents and to do so "at low, city prices, but with a friendly, small-town smile."

Claypool's is located at 725 Broadway Street in Needles, only a block from the site where the business began more than a century ago. The family-owned store now specializes in hardware, clothing, and beverage distribution.

EDWARDS MANSION

The Edwards Mansion (above), built in the 1890s, has been a restaurant since 1975. Specializing in continental cuisine, it has a Victorian decor accented with lace, crystal, and silver. Visitors may dine indoors (below) or on one of two outdoor patios.

J.S. Edwards never knew the mansion he built in the 1890s would become one of the area's finest restaurants, but 80 years later Don Wilcott would have different ideas.

Today, certainly unique and unquestionably one of the top-quality dining experiences in San Bernardino County, the Edwards Mansion provides the best flavor of yesteryear combined with the most lavish culinary delights of today.

Wilcott got a bargain on the aging house: one dollar to a well-known local retirement community called Plymouth Village. But it cost more than $60,000 to literally cut the mansion in two pieces and move it the five miles to its permanent location adjacent to the county museum in Redlands.

Site of the old Barton Ranch, the 33 acres included some of the most historic orange groves in the Redlands area. Citrus Investments, Inc., and Wilcott donated five acres and $100,000 to the county for development of the new museum.

The restaurant opened on December 31, 1975, with a spectacular New Year's Eve celebration. Since that time the Edwards Mansion has become a favorite of not only thousands of local customers, but also numerous movie stars and entertainers traveling from Hollywood to Palm Springs.

John Travolta, Roger Williams, and Raquel Welch are just a few who have dined here on more than one occasion. Betty Ford was among the guests at a wedding reception held in the late 1970s.

The wedding chapel itself is a reproduction of a 19th-century church. The stained-glass windows and pews incorporated into this structure were once part of the First Evangelical Church, built in Redlands in 1904. The chapel seats 110 persons and hosts about 400 weddings per year.

The Edwards Mansion, with its Victorian charm and continental cuisine, has also been the scene of many movies as well as several commercials: the *Howard Hughes Story* and advertisements for Inglenook Wine, to mention only two.

The restaurant is a romantic delight of alcoves and nooks accented with the finest in lace, crystal, and silver. Though many patronize the Edwards Mansion for its fine prime rib, the most renowned specialties of the house are homemade orange muffins and orange pie. Most think of it as a "special-occasion place" often enjoyed for engagements or anniversary parties. The Orangerie Patio, one of two outdoor dining areas, accommodates 200 persons and has witnessed the functions of numerous local politicians.

Although the kitchen is designed for maximum efficiency and the highest quality of food preparation, the restaurant is, nonetheless, the finest of antiques in every respect. Its 6,000 square feet and 14 original rooms are a tribute to both the original owner and the current proprietor.

From its formal parlor to the gazebo on the grounds, it is not easily duplicated, and from the flaming coffee to the Coquille St. Jacques the menu not quickly forgotten.

With 90 employees serving 100,000 persons per year, the Edwards Mansion lives in the hearts of the old and in the most discriminating appetites of generations to come.

OTTO'S INSTRUMENT SERVICE, INC.

Nearly every morning, Bill Otto makes his routine 18-minute commute from Big Bear City in the San Bernardino Mountains to his business in Ontario.

If that seems like good time for the nearly 70-mile trip, it's because Otto is a veteran, instrument-licensed pilot and travels in his 210 Centurian plane. William R. Otto is the founder and president of Otto's Instrument Service, which repairs and modifies aircraft instruments for customers based throughout the world.

Located on the south side of Ontario International Airport, the company turns out approximately 1,000 instruments per month ranging from basic altimeters to sophisticated auto-pilot systems. Like Otto, most of his customers arrive by plane at Ontario and taxi into the instrument repair shop.

The firm dates back to 1946, but Otto himself has been involved in aviation since 1936. He studied aircraft mechanics at the University of Denver and worked at night for Wilson Flying Service.

He moved to California in 1938 and, after a stint with Lockheed, accepted a position with the Department of War in charge of instruments and bombsights at March Field near Riverside. Following World War II Otto, by that time with considerable knowledge of instruments, began his one-man business in a 120-square-foot leased office at Rubidoux Airport. The young technician had laid out the runway, made the first landing at the new field, and was becoming a known name in aviation circles.

Several years later he added three employees to his operation and moved to larger quarters, a 50-foot Quonset hut adjacent to an airfield then located on the site of a current residential development near Kendall Drive north of San Bernardino. Otto bought the building in 1950 and moved it to Ontario Airport. He sold it three years later to Lockheed, which remains its owner to date.

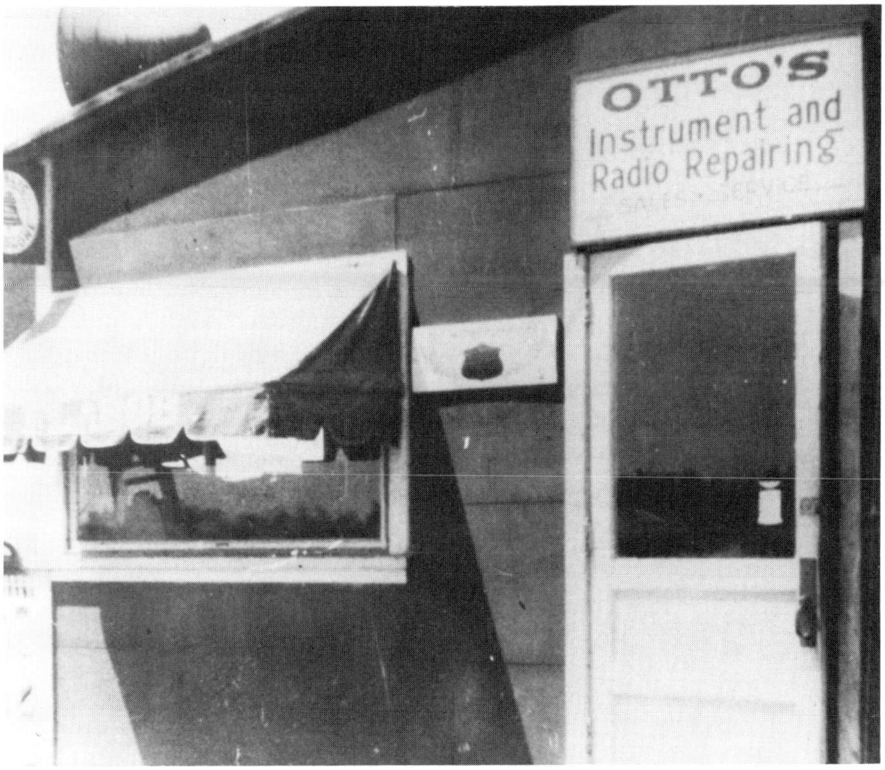

This small office at Rubidoux Airport was the first home of Otto's Instrument Service in 1946. The business is now located at Ontario International Airport, where it services aircraft instruments for customers throughout the world.

At that time, Otto undertook construction of his current 6,400-square-foot facility, originally situated on land in the northeastern portion of the airport. American Airlines, however, purchased the property in 1970 and built a new terminal which now provides a facility for commuter flights.

Otto remembers well the Saturday morning work crews that jacked up his shop on 50 sets of wheels for transportation to its permanent site on the opposite side of the airport. "They taxied her right down the main runway as if she could take off," says Otto with a grin.

While the building itself has never flown, the business has continued to gain velocity and currently has 20 employees. The plant is lined with manned repair benches, intricate testing equipment, and includes a stockroom overflowing with countless gauges.

Though still the active head of his firm, Otto looks forward to retirement in years ahead when he will spend more time at his mountain home and turn over the business to his only son, William Jr., who is now vice-president.

The father-and-son team notes with particular pride that their firm has not only the technology to repair the most modern devices, but also machinery capable of making parts to replace those so old they can no longer be ordered.

ALUMIN-ART PLATING COMPANY

He has no enemies and even his staunchest competitors are his friends. That's Sol Rudy, founder and owner of Alumin-Art Plating Company in Ontario, the oldest operation of its type in the area.

Rudy has an unusual business philosophy: "If I don't have the money, I don't buy it," he says. As a result, Rudy notes with pride that he has never written a bad check and was only in debt for $750 during his company's first month of operation.

Unusual or not, his cash-only approach seems to have paid off in a big way. Alumin-Art now operates 24 hours per day, has 65 employees, and reports annual sales of $1.75 million. It has more than 500 regular patrons, but of particular importance to Rudy is the fact that his first five customers are still placing orders with the firm.

He describes the process as "high-quality metal finishing," but also points out that a key factor in his success has been specializing in the rapid handling of large volumes of small parts, essentially for the aircraft industry. About 80 percent of Alumin-Art contracts are government related, while the remainder come from commercial businesses in the private sector.

Perhaps most recognizable among its work are the many projects Alumin-Art has done for Lockheed Corporation on well-known aircraft, including the Constellation, C5-A Transport, L1011 Tri Star, XF-71, and F-104.

Sol Rudy was born in St. Louis and grew up with a strong background in graphic arts. Once on the West Coast, however, his career took a sharp turn, and in 1940 he was hired by Technical Products as a mechanic—his first real exposure to plating.

After World War II he changed jobs and went to work for Modern Plating Company, located near Los Angeles International Airport, where he remained until 1955. At this point, Rudy was offered yet another position—this time with Anadite Inc., a new company in South Gate, with which he would become a supervisor in charge of warehousing and pricing.

Rudy's true ambition, nonetheless, was in metal plating and so, in 1950, he looked to the Pomona area for a place to start his own business. He knew this would be no easy task, but he also recognized that the predominance of Lockheed and Convair (now General Dynamics) in the area afforded an exceptional opportunity.

Rudy had married in 1939, and 21 years later he and his wife opened their first plating shop in a 500-square-foot building at 1492 East First Street in Pomona. Dorothy did the anodizing in the early days and Richard Montrose, still with Alumin-Art after 25 years, was their first employee.

Alumin-Art's first plating tank was only 24 inches long, 12 inches wide, and 18 inches deep, but despite this limitation the company somehow managed $800 in business during the first month.

With only a year behind it, the firm incorporated and undertook a move to facilities twice the size of the original plant on Second Street, also in Pomona.

A large part of Alumin-Art's work came initially from five major sources in the local area: Celco, Delbert-Blinn, Everett/Charles, Lockheed, and Orbit Company. These regular jobs, combined with a number of small accounts, required still another

Founder Sol Rudy (left) confers with son David Rudy and the plant's general manager, Russ Guthrie (seated).

Two Alumin-Art employees rack parts to be anodized.

expansion and, in 1963, the operation moved to its current location at 803 West State Street in Ontario.

This new plant totaled more than 10,000 square feet, including 6,500 square feet of plating factory and 4,000 square feet of warehouse and office space. Despite the fact that the firm was then the only anodizer in San Bernardino County, the building was far too big for Rudy's immediate needs and only about half could be used. Remarkably, however, within two years the business had continued to grow to a point where the entire structure was busy with activity.

Among the products that made this rapid progress possible was a new chemical film developed by Alumin-Art for the Minneapolis-based Honeywell Corporation. Another involved the plating of thousands of flashlights for Kel-Lite in Barstow.

As if all this was too good to be true, a massive blaze nearly destroyed the plant in 1978, causing $250,000 in damage and leaving literally only the accounts receivable as assets. As one would expect, Rudy rebuilt and was out of operation for only a brief period.

Shortly after reconstruction, Alumin-Art received one of its largest orders ever from Aerojet-General and ultimately was fully back in business, shipping as many as 150,000 projectiles per week to its customer.

Today Rudy's company draws contracts from all parts of the greater Los Angeles area and from points as distant as Oregon, Chicago, and San Diego. What's more, Alumin-Art is the only such operation east of Los Angeles County that has full government approval.

In all respects, it is a family business. Rudy's wife is a partner and their son and four daughters are all trustees. Son David is in charge of the plating department while daughters Barbara and Joyce are responsible for office management and accounts receivable. Darlene's husband, Russell Guthrie, is the plant's general manager, and Candy has worked in shipping and receiving. In addition, all of Rudy's other key employees have been with him 10 years or longer.

A worker removes a rack of parts from one of Alumin-Art's plating tanks.

LUCKEY LABORATORIES, INC.

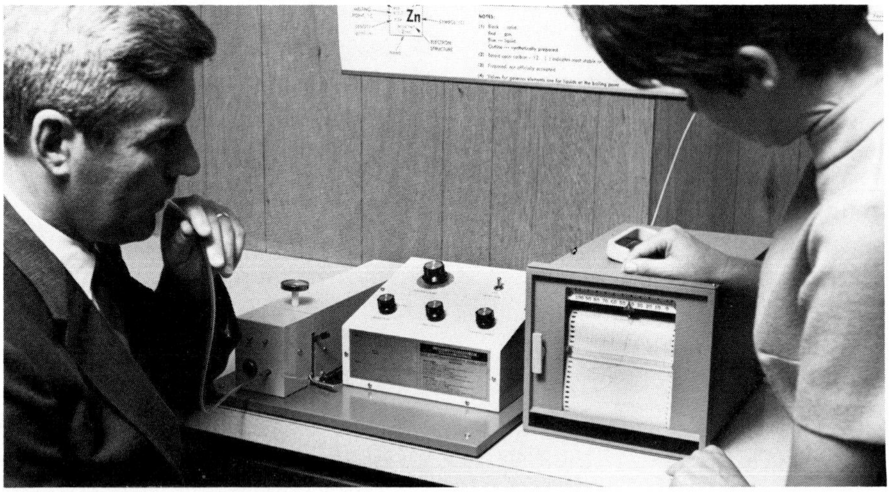

Technicians at Luckey Laboratories demonstrate a gas chromatograph, one of the most accurate devices used to measure blood alcohol. The firm developed the machine in 1970 and has since sold it to law enforcement agencies throughout the world.

Drinking drivers beware! Luckey Laboratories of San Bernardino may help put you behind bars.

This company designs and manufactures sobriety-testing devices ranging from the simplest balloon-type breathalyzer to the most sophisticated and foolproof gas chromatograph. In fact, Luckey Laboratories is one of the world's three largest producers of such equipment.

President and founder Manley Luckey says the objective of his company is to encourage more responsible drinking practices through both law enforcement and self-detection.

Interestingly, one of Luckey's newest products is a coin-operated "sober-meter" that can be used in bars, restaurants, clubs, resorts, or literally any place where alcohol is served. Resembling a video game, the test costs 50 cents and produces a digital blood-alcohol reading within a few seconds after the individual provides a breath sample by blowing into a straw. Meanwhile, a second test checks reflex time and alertness.

Although most often used voluntarily by persons who question their own condition, the machine is also valuable to bartenders who suspect that a customer is intoxicated.

Many police vehicles carry Luckey sobriety testers as standard equipment. The 15-second breath test involves yellow crystals which turn green to indicate intoxication.

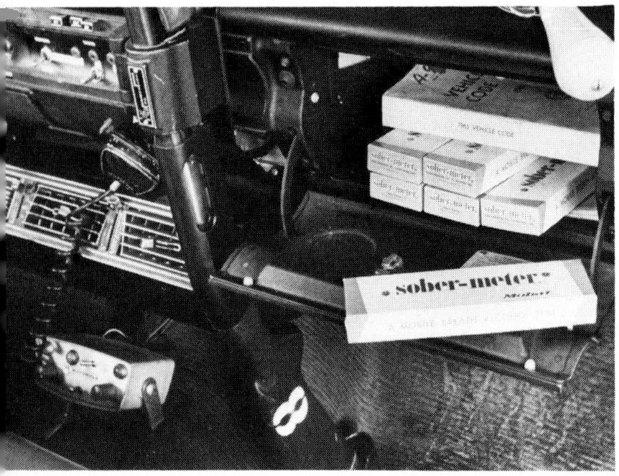

Now a nationally recognized expert in toxicology, Luckey began his career in 1950 as a biochemist at San Bernardino County Medical Center. Before long he had conceived improved alcohol testing methods that impressed both the district attorney as well as the highway patrol and were soon implemented by a total of 27 California counties.

In 1952 Luckey opened his own lab at the corner of E and 13th streets in San Bernardino. At the beginning, the business was almost entirely blood-alcohol analysis, but Luckey's reputation often made him a key witness in court cases and he was frequently called on to train aspiring technicians.

A professional building in the 1700 block of Waterman Avenue was to become the home of Luckey Laboratories in 1957, followed by a move in 1973 to the current location at 7252 Osbun Road. By this time, however, Luckey had made a transition from analysis to manufacturing and was producing the increasingly complex equipment used to determine blood-alcohol.

Perhaps as a highlight of his career, in 1970 Luckey developed the first gas chromatograph (GC), now extensively used by police throughout the world. The GC comes in several models and is the only completely self-contained system available. Another of Luckey's products is the Mobil Breath Alcohol Tester (MOBAT), a hand-held unit measuring only six inches high and four inches wide.

The firm's line is completed by a number of disposable testers varying from the balloon type to the newer tube of crystals which change color to indicate intoxication. These can be used in the field to provide a preliminary reading and, in some cases, will retain a breath sample for further testing.

Manley Luckey looks to the future with plans for a new two-story, 40,000-square-foot building and projects that his annual sales may reach $10 million in the next five years. He figures, "As long as people drink our business will grow."

WISSAHICKON INN

Pictured here is the main building of the Wissahickon Inn, a retirement home in Redlands. There are 10 other structures on the premises, some dating back to the 1880s. Courtesy of the Redlands Daily Facts.

Built in 1904 and once a resort hotel for wealthy eastern visitors, the Wissahickon Inn is now a retirement home for elderly residents who enjoy its serenity and Victorian charm.

In total, the inn is composed of 11 buildings spread over more than four acres at the corner of Center Street and Walnut Avenue in Redlands. Many of the 40 residents spend peaceful hours strolling the paths that meander throughout the property's lush landscaping and citrus trees.

The lobby of the light-blue, three-story main building is the inn's gathering place, featuring antique furniture, colorful oriental rugs, and a grand piano. Here friends converse or perhaps dwell over a game of chess. Others chat or just rest in the light breeze that caresses the porch.

A short distance away a bright and cheerful dining room awaits the next meal with gold tablecloths, greenery, and party decorations.

Wissahickon's oldest building, known as The Gables, was erected in the 1880s by the Tatnal family who had purchased the property after arriving from England. A second structure, The Highlands, is believed to have been built about 1890 for their daughter when she married.

It was Mr. Tatnal who brought from his homeland an English elm seedling, which now stands majestically and is thought to be about 100 years old.

Near the turn of the century the property was purchased by a Mrs. Johnson and her son, who had come from Philadelphia to build a resort hotel which they called the Wissahickon Inn. They so named it for a river that runs through their hometown; the word, itself, means "catfish" in the language of an old Indian tribe.

For many years the Wissahickon was an extremely popular and prestigious resort, with thousands of well-to-do guests journeying by train to escape their harsh climates and take advantage of the mild Redlands winter.

Two Pasadena women bought the inn during the 1920s and, while continuing the hotel operation, began what would become one of the community's most acclaimed dinner houses.

The late 1940s, however, marked the inception of an era in Wissahickon history characterized by many short-term owners, and the inn was converted to its current use in 1956 by Ed Haldy of Oregon. Three Beverly Hills investors completely restored the structures in 1959 and soon the facilities were fully occupied.

Changes in title continued through much of the '60s and '70s, but in 1980 current owners Samuel and Elizabeth Ramos purchased the inn from a group of doctors and have extended plans for its operation and improvement.

Throughout its history the Wissahickon has been the site of a number of noteworthy and interesting occurrences. A few years back two residents—both in their eighties—met, married, and spent the rest of their lives together at the inn. Another woman who retired there had, coincidentally, skated as a child on the Wissahickon River.

Whether as an elite resort hotel or as a distinguished retirement home, the Wissahickon Inn has a long and rich heritage which will continue to be a credit to the community for many years to come.

Residents relax during the evening in the old hotel's main lobby, which is frequently the center of social activity and conversation.

BONADIMAN-McCAIN, INC.

Currently one of the Inland Empire's leading builders of public works projects, Bonadiman-McCain, Inc., was established in 1942.

Although the company began principally with grading jobs, more recent contracts have included some of the most specialized types of concrete work.

The business was founded by Joseph E. Bonadiman and his partner, Bike McCain, combining Bonadiman's engineering experience with McCain's background in construction.

A graduate of the University of Southern California, Bonadiman had started an engineering firm in 1941 and wished to expand into the construction field.

Bonadiman-McCain opened its first office on Seventh Street in downtown Los Angeles and began developing a sound reputation at that location. Although McCain left the company in 1950, Bonadiman was widely recognized five years later when he successfully undertook a massive 250-foot fill for residential construction in Bel Air.

His family having homesteaded land on the high desert shortly after the turn of the century, Bonadiman moved his business to San Bernardino in 1958 and reopened at the intersection of Seventh and D streets. By that time Bonadiman's son, Bill, had become part of the organization, beginning the construction career that would ultimately lead him to the presidency of Bonadiman-McCain.

Another son, Joseph C. Bonadiman, would similarly assume responsibility for his father's original engineering company.

The founder maintains an active interest in both the construction and engineering operations, though they are now separate corporations.

Joseph E. Bonadiman, founder of Bonadiman-McCain, Inc., as he appeared in the early 1970s. Bonadiman developed the firm from a basic grading operation into a highly specialized builder of drainage structures.

With numerous well-known projects to his credit, the senior Bonadiman is perhaps most respected for the design of Ontario International Airport. In addition to a long list of professional involvements, it must be noted that he is a former chairman of the San Bernardino Valley Municipal Water District, served as a board member of the San Bernardino County Air Pollution Control District, and was city engineer for the cities of Victorville and Hawthorne.

In 1961 the firm moved again—this time to the Kendall Drive area later to become known as Shandin Hills. Here Bonadiman-McCain would remain until 1975, when it completed construction of its own new facilities at 280 South Lena Road.

Bonadiman-McCain, at this point, had become deeply involved in its specialty: bridges, box culverts, and drainage channels utilizing precast, prestressed, and reinforced concrete. Beyond this extensive drainage work, the firm has completed recreational facilities at Glen Helen County Regional Park as well as at Lake Silverwood, and is the builder of nearly all of the Pacific Drive-in Theaters in Southern California.

Like his father, Bill is active in the community. He is a member of the Park Commission in Redlands and has served as chairman of the local chapter of the Associated General Contractors. The County Board of Supervisors has appointed him to both the Business Consulting Council and the Solid Waste Task Force.

Bonadiman believes his corporation can both continue to prosper as well as serve the needs of the local area, and he is training a third generation—two of his sons, Jeff and Carlo—to assure that future.

PATRONS FOR *SAN BERNARDINO COUNTY*

The following individuals, companies, and organizations have made a valuable commitment to the quality of this publication. Windsor Publications and the San Bernardino County Museum Association gratefully acknowledge their participation in *San Bernardino County: Land of Contrasts.*

Alumin-Art Plating Company*
Wacy Armstrong,
Attorney At Law
Associated Engineers*
Ball O'Dougherty and Associates
Barstow Unified School District
The Beaver Medical Clinic*
Big Bear Valley Historical Society
Patricia Blackwell
Bomatic, Inc.*
Bonadiman-McCain, Inc.*
The Book Attic
Brubaker-Mann Company, Inc.*
Steve and Eva Caldwell
Hair Dimensions
California State University, San Bernardino Bookstore
C.H.J. Incorporated
Claypool and Company*
Colton Morning Kiwanis Club
Coops Stamp and Coin Galleries
Data-Design Laboratories*
East Highlands Area Historical Society
Edwards Mansion*
Everett/Charles*
First American Title Insurance Company*
Fontana Paving, Inc.*
Futurus, Inc.*
Virginia and Ed Gaustad
Goldie Law Corporation*
Graber Olive House*
Gresham, Varner, Savage, Nolan & Tilden*
Harris' Department Stores*
H.M.C. Architects, Inc.*
Donald C. Hubbs, Inc.
Kemper Manufacturing, Inc.*
The Learning Center
Wilfrid Cunningham Le Mann
Lockheed Aircraft Service Company*
Loran, Inc.*
Luckey Laboratories, Inc.*
McAnally Enterprises, Inc.*
Miller's Honey Company*
Morey Mansion Preservation and Tours
Morgan Meat Company
Novack's American Metal Reduction Company, Inc.*
Otto's Instrument Service, Inc.*
Redlands Area Historical Sociey
Fredric H. Rubel Jewelers*
Jack B. and Linda Ann Russell
Stephen and Rose Ryland
San Bernardino County Central Credit Union
San Bernardino County Library
Scheu Manufacturing Company*
Scotty's Muffler Inc.
Secure Savings and Loan Association*
Seven W Enterprises, Inc.*
Mark B. Shaw Mortuaries*
The Shoretts
Dr. Gerald and Dr. Maxine Smith
Sorenson Engineering Incorporated*
The Sun
Synatek
TRW*
Video Mart
Vineyard National Bank*
Fred G. Walter & Son*
Welch's Overall Inc.
Wilden Pump and Engineering Company*
Wilson, Borror, Dunn and Scott
Wissahickon Inn*
Yucaipa Valley Historical Society

*Partners in Progress of *San Bernardino County: Land of Contrasts.* The histories of these companies and organizations appear in Chapter 7, beginning on page 148.

Bibliography

Ahlborn, William O. "Santa Ana River Basin Flood Hazard." *Quarterly of the San Bernardino County Museum Assn.* 29: no. 2 (Winter 1982).

Allen, Helena, ed. *San Bernardino County Museum Commemorative Edition.* Redlands, CA: Allen-Greendale, 1974.

Archer, Morse G., ed. *Yucaipa Valley California.* Yucaipa, CA: Cobb's Printing, 1976.

Bailey, Paul. *Walkara, Hawk of the Mountains.* Los Angeles: Westernlore Press, 1954.

Beattie, George W., and Helen P. *Heritage of the Valley.* Oakland, CA: Biobooks, 1951.

Black, Esther Bolton. *Rancho Cucamonga and Dona Merced.* Redlands, CA: San Bernardino County Museum Assn., 1975.

Bolton, Herbert E. *Outpost of Empire.* New York: Alfred A. Knopf, 1939.

Brown, John, Jr., and Boyd, James. *History of San Bernardino and Riverside Counties.* Western Historical Assn., 1922.

Burgess, Larry E. *Redlands: Remembrance and Reflection.* Redlands, CA: Redlands Federal Savings and Loan Assn., 1981.

Caballeria, Juan. *History of San Bernardino Valley from the Padres to the Pioneers.* San Bernardino, CA: Times Index Press, 1902.

Caldwell, Ernest. *History of Fontana.* Redlands, CA: San Bernardino County Historical Society.

Casebier, Dennis G. *Carlton's Pah-Ute Campaign.* Norco, CA: Dennis Casebier, 1972.

Clarke, Anthony Orr. "Quaternary Evolution of the San Bernardino Valley." *Quarterly of the San Bernardino County Museum Assn.* 26: nos. 2 and 3 (Winter 1978/Spring 1979).

Cleland, Robert G. *From Wilderness to Empire.* New York: Alfred A. Knopf, 1944.

Coues, Elliott. *On the Trail of a Spanish Pioneer and the Diary and Itinerary of Francisco Garces.* New York: Francis P. Harper, 1900.

Davis, C. Alan, and Smith, Gerald A. *Newberry Cave.* Redlands, CA: San Bernardino County Museum Assn., 1981.

Elliott, Wallace W. *History of San Bernardino and San Diego Counties.* 1883. Reprint. Riverside, CA: Riverside Museum Press, 1965.

Engelhardt, Zephyrin. *The Missions and Missionaries of California.* Santa Barbara, CA: Santa Barbara Mission, 1930.

Fages, Pedro. *A Historical, Political, and Natural Description of California by Pedro Fages, Soldier of Spain.* Translated by Herbert Ingram Priestley. Berkeley: University of California Press, 1937.

Fehrenbach, Larry. "San Bernardino Valley and the Impact of Kaiser Steel in World War II." *City of San Bernardino Historical Society Annual "Heritage Tales"* 1982, 29-47.

Fisher, Pearl Comfort. *The Mountaineers.* Bloomington, CA: San Bernardino County Museum Assn., 1972.

Grenfell, Christopher G. *Development of Skiing in the San Bernardino Mountains.* Redlands, CA: San Bernardino County Museum Assn., 1981.

Guinn, James M. *A History of California.* Los Angeles: Historic Record Co., 1907.

Haenszel, Arda. "The San Bernardino Asistencia—The Mission Period." *Quarterly of the San Bernardino County Museum Assn.* 7: no. 3 (Spring 1960).

———. "Where was Politana?" *Odyssey* 5: no. 1 (Jan./March 1983).

———. "The Old Court Houses." *Odyssey* 1: no. 1 (Jan. 1979).

———. "The Base Line Road." *Odyssey* 1: no. 4 (July 1979).

Hafen, LeRoy R., and Ann W. *Old Spanish Trail.* Glendale, CA: Arthur H. Clark Co., 1954.

Hartman, David N. *California and Man.* Santa Ana, CA: Pierce Publishers, 1972.

Hein, Erwin. *History of Redlands and Prospect Park.* Redlands, CA: Friends of Prospect Park Assn.

Hixson, Maureen D. "San Bernardino and the San Bernardino Air Depot." *City of San Bernardino Historical Society Annual "Heritage Tales"* 1982, 1-28.

Holladay, Fred. "The Silver King." *Odyssey* 1: no. 2 (March 1979).

Howe, Charley. *A Prehistory of Black Canyon.* Redlands, CA: Archaeological Survey Association of Southern California, 1980.

Ingersoll, Luther A. *Century Annals of San Bernardino County.* Los Angeles: L.A. Ingersoll, 1904.

Jaeger, Edmund C. *The California Deserts.* Stanford: Stanford University Press, 1965.

Keeling, Patricia Kernigan, ed. *Once Upon a Desert.* Barstow, CA: Mojave River Valley Museum Assn., 1976.

LaFuze, Pauliena B. *Saga of the San Bernardinos.* vol. 1, Bloomington, CA: San Bernardino County Museum Assn., 1971.

Lantis, David W.; Steiner, Rodney; and Karinen, Arthur E. *California: Land of Contrast.* Belmont, CA: Wadsworth Publishing Co., 1963.

Lavender, David. *California: Land of New Beginnings.* New York: Harper & Row, 1972.

Leadabrand, Russ. *A Guidebook to the Mojave Desert of California.* Los Angeles: The Ward Ritchie Press, 1966.

———. *Guidebook to the San Bernardino Mountains of California.* Los Angeles: Anderson, Ritchie & Simon, 1973.

Lee, Stories W. *The Great California Deserts.* New York: G.P. Putnam's Sons, 1963.

Lerch, Michael K., and Haenszel, Arda M. "Life on Cottonwood Row." *City of San Bernardino Historical Society Annual "Heritage Tales"* 1981.

Maltsberger, Elma. *The Story of Colton, California.* Colton, CA: Humidial Co., 1974.

McWilliams, Carey. *Southern California Country.* New York: Duell, Sloan & Pearce, 1946.

Miles, Lillian E. "Early Days in San Bernardino Schools." *Odyssey* 1: no. 4 (July 1979).

Nadeau, Rene. *Ghost Towns and Mining Camps of California.* Los Angeles: The Ward Ritchie Press, 1965.

Norris, Frank, and Carrico, Richard L. *A History of Land Use in the California Desert Conservation Area.* San Diego, CA: Westec Services, 1978.

O'Dell, Scott. *Country of the Sun.* New York: Thomas Y. Crowell Co., 1957.

Peirson, Erma. *The Mojave River and Its Valley.* Glendale, CA: Arthur H. Clark Co., 1970.

Richards, Elizabeth. *Guideposts to History.* 2d ed., rev. San Bernardino, CA: Santa Fe Federal Savings and Loan Assn., 1977.

Robinson, W.W. *The Story of San Bernardino County.* San Bernardino: Pioneer Title Insurance Co., 1958.

Rolfe, H.C. "The Old Fort." *Odyssey* 5: no. 1

(Jan./Feb./March 1983).
Schuiling, Walter C. *From Jantzen to Jensen: San Bernardino Valley College's First Fifty Years.* San Bernardino, CA: San Bernardino Valley College, 1978.
———, ed. *Pleistocene Man at Calico.* Redlands, CA: San Bernardino County Museum Assn., 1979.
Skinner, Byron R. *Black Origins in the Inland Empire.* San Bernardino, CA: Book Attic Press, 1983.
Smith, Gerald A. *Early Man in the California Desert.* Westerners Brand Book, no. 11, Los Angeles: 1964.
———. *The Mojaves.* Redlands, CA: San Bernardino County Museum Assn., 1977.
———. *Prehistoric Man of the San Bernardino Valley.* Redlands, CA: San Bernardino County Historical Society, 1950.
———, and Turner, Wilson G. *Indian Rock Art of Southern California.* Redlands, CA: San Bernardino County Museum Assn., 1975.
Spencer, Robert F.; Jennings, Jesse D.; et. al. *The Native Americans.* New York: Harper & Row, 1965.
Steele, Laura. *The Thirty Year Search for Ancient Man.* Redlands, CA: Archaeological Survey Association of Southern California, 1982.
Stoebe, Martha G. *The History of Alta Loma, California.* Alta Loma, CA: B & S Publishing Co., 1981.
———. *A History of Rialto.* Rialto, CA: Rialto Unified School District, 1976.
Thompson, Richard D. "The Pavilion." *Odyssey* 1: no. 5 (Sept. 1979).
———. *Pioneers of the San Bernardino Valley.* San Bernardino, CA: San Bernardino Pageant, 1976.
Vickery, Joyce Carter. *Defending Eden.* Riverside: University of California, 1977.
Waitman, Leonard. "Horse Soldier Forts of the Mojave Desert." *Quarterly of the San Bernardino County Museum Assn.* 15: no. 3 (Spring 1968).
———. "The Knights of the Golden Circle." *Quarterly of the San Bernardino County Museum Assn.* 15: no. 4 (Summer 1969).
Wang, Peter Heywood. "The Mythical Confederate Plot in Southern California." *Quarterly of the San Bernardino County Museum Assn.* 16: no. 4 (Summer 1969).
Whitehead, Roy E. *Lugo: A Chronicle of Early California.* Redlands, CA: San Bernardino County Museum Assn., 1978.
Wormington, H.M. *Ancient Man in North America.* Denver:Denver Museum of Natural History, 1957.
Wright, Lauren A., et al. "Mines and Mineral Deposits of San Bernardino County, California." *California Journal of Mines and Geology* 49: nos. 1-2 (Jan.-April 1953).
Wynn, Marcia Rittenhouse. *Desert Bonanza.* Culver City, CA: M.W. Samuelson, 1949.

A dam built in the late 1960s created Lake Silverwood out of a mountain valley that had been occupied by the small settlement of Cedar Springs. Courtesy, John Elk

INDEX

San Bernardino Partners in Progress Index

General Index

Italicized numbers indicate illustrations.